Vachel Lindsay

FIELDWORKER FOR THE AMERICAN DREAM

Christmas 1925
Vachel Lindsay

VACHEL LINDSAY

Fieldworker
for the American Dream

Ann Massa

INDIANA UNIVERSITY PRESS

Bloomington   London

*Frontispiece from the Vachel Lindsay Collection in the
Clifton Waller Barrett Library of the University of Virginia
Library.*

CONTENTS

IV: ART FORMS AND SOCIETY

THE WRITINGS OF VACHEL LINDSAY take on their full meaning within the context of his contemporary society and of the American experience which generated his concern for that society. Occasionally Lindsay's search for elements which might revitalize the American Dream led him outside this context, to Buddhism and Confucianism, for example. Morris and Ruskin were acknowledged antecedents in his theory of the social function of art, and William Blake his forerunner in the realm of applied Swedenborgian mysticism. But non-American parallels are only introduced when, as in these instances, there is an explicit non-American association, or a primary American context is lacking. There is no elaboration of Ruskin on agriculture or Morris on socialism (though there are analogies between Lindsay and the Englishmen on these issues) because both subjects have an immediate, pregnant American context.

I would like to thank a number of people who, in one way or another, have helped by interest in Lindsay to take tangible form. For their guidance and encouragement: Professor Marcus Cunliffe (University of Sussex), Professor G. S. Shepperson (University of Edinburgh), Professor Dennis Welland (University of Manchester), and Mr. Nicholas C. Lindsay. For their perseverance and patience in helping me to refine the original manuscript: Mr. Bernard Perry, Mrs. Dorothy Wikelund, and Mrs. Natalie Wrubel, all at the Indiana University Press. For providing the right atmosphere and environment: my parents, Miss E. M. Knott, Dr. S. K. Guthrie. For creating immaculate typescript out of complicated drafts and redrafts: Mary Hodges, Marjorie McGlashan, Melita Massa.

Vachel Lindsay

FIELDWORKER FOR THE AMERICAN DREAM

Introduction

BACKGROUND

Nᴵᴄʜᴏʟᴀs Vᴀᴄʜᴇʟ Lɪɴᴅsᴀʏ's description of himself as "the 'Casey at-the-Bat' of American poetry"[1] sums up his reputation during his lifetime (1879–1931) as well as today. Perhaps only a half dozen of his poems—"General William Booth Enters into Heaven," "The Congo," "Bryan, Bryan, Bryan, Bryan," for example—are regularly read; while the rest of his diverse literary output, from 1913 to 1931—nine books of poetry (and an incomplete *Collected Poems* made in 1923), five prose works, numerous short stories, articles, and private periodical publications—remains virtually unknown.

Lindsay's contemporaries were impatient when his writings did not tally with his image as the flamboyant author and mesmeric performer of repetitive, syncopated chants. Critics argued that his talent was for this kind of poetry. Lindsay called it the "Higher Vaudeville," for it encompassed the swift changes of mood and the incantatory tones and rhythms of vaudeville, and it was poetry to be performed. Audiences clamored for his performances. Sometimes they had a curiosity value, when he donned fancy dress, for instance, or accompanied his poems with snatches of song and dance, and they always had the attraction of his inimitable delivery, a mixture of revivalist sermon and stump speech. To hear the records Lindsay made in 1931, even though he was then past his prime, is to understand the demand for the Higher Vaudeville; although, as Lindsay ruefully pointed out, the Higher Vaudeville only constituted ten percent of his output.

3

The fascination of Lindsay's colorful career and dramatic presence has led to a tendency to explain away the ninety percent of his writings which did not conform to his early genre of poetry. It has also led to an almost totally biographical approach to his work. Interest has centered on psychological interpretations of the background of a man commonly assumed to be a twentieth century minstrel, a protagonist of agrarian society, and a typical Midwesterner. As he had "traded his rhymes for bread"[2] on tramping expeditions before his career got underway, and later traveled a recitation circuit, he was classified as an itinerant entertainer; on the contrary, his aim was to edify and reform, "to build our young land right."[3] Because he was from Illinois, but not from Chicago, it was assumed that he was a hidebound product of the rural Midwest. In fact he came from Springfield, the state capital, a city of about 50,000 inhabitants, whose most pronounced physical feature, noted in a survey by the Russell Sage Foundation in 1915, was a pall of grey industrial smoke and coal dust.

Lindsay was neither a typical nor a prejudiced son of his region. Certainly when it came to personal affinity, he was more at one with the Midwest than with any other region: he was "only happy among people in some way related to the [Midwestern] civilization."[4] But his loyalties were national, not regional. In "My Fathers Came from Kentucky," he defined himself as a Northerner: "I have Northern words/And thoughts/And ways," and a Southerner: "No drop of my blood from north/Of Mason and Dixon's line," as well as a Midwesterner: "I faint with love/Till the prairies dip and reel."[5] It was not the Midwest, but the last frontier of the Far West, or a New South which he chose for the role of the regenerative and leavening American region. Similarly, he was inextricably involved in agrarian America through his deep affection for his grandparents, farmers from Kentucky and Indiana, and through his own cross-country tramping expeditions. But while he looked back nostalgically to a mythically simple, rural way of life, his blueprint for the future in *The Golden Book of Springfield*, 1920, was a city comprising all the benefits of the machine age.

The salient facts of Lindsay's origins need restating. He was born, in 1879, into a household whose antecedents were Midwestern as far back as they could be traced. His father was an unsophisticated doctor, more attuned to the country half of his practice in the environs of Springfield than to the work he did in the city. He was disappointed in a quiet, book-mad son, incapable of assembling a skeleton, or of earning a living until the age of thirty-four. This fairly normal lack of compatibility between father and son has been construed by Lindsay's biographers as a permanent antipathy between the two, which, on Lindsay's part, snowballed into an inferiority complex and a subsequent lack of stability as an individual, a careerist, and a husband. They cite Lindsay's characterization of Dr. Lindsay in "Dr. Mohawk" as one who "will burn you to ashes and turn you to clay." But this, as Lindsay pointed out in the same poem, was "my notion, as a Ferocious Small-Boy, of my Ancestral Protector"; and throughout the poem he was at pains to equate his father with the essence of his own paramount interest, America: "The blood of the U.S.A.—that is the Mohawk." [6]

Lindsay's mother is regularly depicted as the artistic, intellectual source in his background. She was one of the world's organizers; Lindsay remarked that she just escaped being a Mrs. Eddy, a Mrs. Besant, or a Mme. Blavatsky. She was ambitious "that each of my children take up the torch lighted by the prophets and Christ, carried by Grandfather Frazee and Grandmother Austen, [Lindsay's maternal grandparents] and run with it, *from mountain top to mountain top*." Rather as Lindsay managed to recite his frivolous "King Solomon and the Queen of Sheba" in college chapels, she succeeded in staging a colloquy, "Olympus," in the Disciples' Church, and wangled into the pulpit Lindsay's Sunday School teacher as Venus, clutching a golden apple in one hand, and holding Cupid Vachel by the other. [7]

Mrs. Lindsay's social and intellectual assertiveness were not unjustified. She graduated at the top of her class from Glendale Female College, Ohio, in 1869, and, in an early American assertion of female potential, subsequently taught mathematics there and went on to become assistant to the President of Hocker College, now part of the University of Kentucky. Both before her marriage and on her honeymoon she had traveled in Europe and Asia. But do Mrs. Lindsay's cumulative abilities and achievements mean that she successfully molded and restricted her son? Did she monopolize and spoil him? Did she make him hang on to his celibacy until he was forty-five, and was she thus indirectly responsible for the almost inevitable anticlimax of married life? There is plenty of evidence of her cultural legacy to Lindsay, of her proprietary influence on him, of close bonds between them, and of Lindsay's general failure to adjust to the demands of friendship, marriage, and solvency. But his problems were the results, not the causes of what to him was a larger failure—that of his attempt to ferment socio-civic activity. His was less a convinced personal inadequacy than the frustration of one who felt he had something to say, but who reached a negligible audience. An analysis of Lindsay's career shows that his maladjustments were vocational; and the mother-son relationship falls into perspective as a normal involvement of love, duty and difference. Lindsay was speaking for any number of former children when he likened home to the Vatican, the dominant parent—in his case his mother—to the Pope, and himself to a Protestant making tactful efforts to conceal his convictions.[8]

Just as Lindsay's relationships with his parents and with the Midwest have been misinterpreted, so has his affiliation with Campbellism. Campbellism originated with Alexander Campbell (1788–1866), an immigrant Presbyterian Scotch-Irish clergyman, who chafed against the confines of sectarianism and elder-burgher church government. He broke with Presbyterianism in 1813, and by 1830 had attracted enough "Campbellites," or "Reformers," active and strong in Pennsylvania and Virginia, to unite with another dissident Presbyterian sect, "Christians," who were centered in Ohio. They formed the Church of Christ, also known as the Disciples of Christ, Disciples, or Campbellites. The church gained adherents throughout the Midwest and was dominated and largely shaped by Alexander Campbell.

Campbell's distinguishing teaching was to urge a return to primitive Christianity as the basis for the reconstitution of a single

Christian denomination; but after his death in 1866, Campbellism quickly became yet another splinter Protestant nonconformist sect. Dr. and Mrs. Lindsay were ardent Campbellites of this evangelistic, Midwestern sort. Mrs. Lindsay, with characteristic thrust, contributed to Campbellite journals (*Missionary Tidings, The Christian Century, The Christian Evangelist*); and as a delegate to the Ecumenical Congress of the World in Edinburgh in 1910 she upheld the Campbellite sect. The Lindsay household was permeated with religious talk and activity, as Jessie B. Rittenhouse found when she stayed there in 1917. She joined in morning prayers and Bible readings, and felt "transported to another century, another life than ours." [9]

Lindsay and his two sisters (Olive, the eldest of the children, born in 1877, and Joy, the youngest, born in 1889), were thus thoroughly indoctrinated with their parents'—and their grandparents'—rigid brand of Campbellism. Olive Lindsay remembered Campbellite summers spent at their grandfather's farm in Rush County, Indiana, when "never a day passed that we did not hear references to important teachings of his [Campbell's] on this subject or that"; and in "A Rhymed Address to All Renegade Campbellites . . ." Lindsay recalled:

> *As I built cob-houses with small cousins on the floor:*
> *(The talk was not meant for me).*
> *Daguerreotypes shone. The back log sizzled*
> *And my grandmother traced the family tree.*
> *Then she swept to the proverbs of Campbell again.*
> *And we glanced at the portrait of that most benign of men*
> *Looking down in the evening gleam.*[10]

However, in his characteristic divergence from his background, Lindsay rejected bastard, narrowly sectarian Campbellism. He took to himself the original Campbellite teaching of Christian unity and transformed it into his own doctrine of an inclusive world religion, a supra-ecumenism embracing any creed or philosophy which was compatible with the goodwill, egalitarian spirit of religion.

Lindsay's life falls into three parts: 1879–1908, years of formation; 1908–1913, years of crystallization: 1913–1931, years of enact-ment. The formative years saw the tentative construction of the foundations of his career and philosophy. Partly because he was a sickly child, and partly because of his mother's confidence in her abilities, he was educated at home until he was eleven. From 1890 to 1897 he attended Springfield schools; from 1897 to 1900 he studied medicine unsuccessfully at Hiram College, Ohio (a Camp-bellite institution). He attended the Chicago Institute of Art, 1901 to 1903, and the New York School of Art, 1903 to 1908, but in both instances he failed to graduate.

These formative years were marked by a contradiction in func-tion and inclination. Studying at first to be a doctor, and then to be an illustrator or cartoonist, Lindsay spent most of his time writing poetry. One of his instructors in New York was Robert Henri (1865-1929), an influential figure in the American art world, and a sponsor of the 1913 New York Armory Show which sprang Fauvism, Cubism, and Expressionism on the American public. Henri, with his own breakaway tendencies, preferred Lindsay's unconventional verses to his drawings, and encouraged him to write. Lindsay not only followed this advice, but began to develop that determination to communicate his ideas which was to dominate his life. In New York, in 1905, he devoted evenings (unsuccessfully) to trying to give away illustrated broadsides of his poems. With somewhat more success, in 1906 and 1907 he guided Y.M.C.A. classes around the Metropolitan Museum, and, already on the way to hagiology, he lectured to them on "Dominat-ing Personalities."

His gallery of heroes in these years was given over to William Jennings Bryan, whom he had heard speak in Springfield in his famous election campaign of 1896; to John Peter Altgeld, Gover-nor of Illinois, 1892–6 (from his bedroom window Lindsay could see into Altgeld's courtyard); and to Lincoln, commemorated all over Springfield. Lindsay was later to celebrate the three men in "Bryan, Bryan, Bryan, Bryan," "The Eagle That Is Forgotten," and "Abraham Lincoln Walks at Midnight." His fields of study were ranging from the visual arts and American legend to Egyptology, interests he was to retain and develop. In 1906 he inaugurated another lifelong practice, itinerancy; that year he went on his first tramping expedition—to the Carolinas, Georgia, Florida, and Kentucky—offering recitations and broadsides of his poems in exchange for board and lodging.

By 1908 the notebooks and diaries he kept from the age of seven, his academic record, and his activities began to show recurring characteristics: a social conscience (should he be a Christian cartoonist?); a talent for intricate, spidery drawings, based on the Spencerian system of penmanship; a predilection for meditation and introspection to the point of claiming visionary experience; and, above all, an urge to declare himself, in thought and in art, to the American public. With this latter aim firmly in mind, in 1908 he returned to his parents' home in Springfield and settled down to write and to seek publishing outlets.

From 1908 to 1913 Lindsay's ideas gradually took literary shape; in that period he had his intensive experience of Springfield as an archetypal American city: full of potential, but currently mediocre. In 1909 his first (private) publication, *War Bulletin No. I* appeared. It was a monthly pamphlet which ran to five issues; in article, story, and poem it indicted what appeared to Lindsay to be American cancers: the almighty dollar, the jungle that awaited immigrants, and race prejudice. He distributed his *War Bulletins* and various illustrated broadsides on Springfield streets; he spoke to whatever group would hear him, whether Y.M.C.A. or Anti-Saloon League; he went on a second tramping expedition to New Jersey, Pennsylvania and Ohio, in 1908, and on a third to Missouri, Kansas, and Colorado in 1912 to preach his "gospel," evolved in the years 1908 to 1912, "at short notice, and without a collection in every chapel that will open its doors as he passes by." [11] A frequently cool and incredulous reception both in Springfield and on his expeditions battered his initially romantic concept of a folk culture and a deprived audience; but the concept of communication as a privilege and a service involving minimal financial return stayed with him.

A bombardment of periodicals and of leading American writers began to bring results in 1911, Lindsay's breakthrough year. In

March *Current Literature* devoted an editorial to *The Village Magazine* (1910), a privately published anthology of Lindsay's ideas, written, illustrated, and edited by himself; and in May Hamlin Garland invited Lindsay to address the literary hub of the Chicago renaissance, the Cliff-Dwellers' Club. Gradually more journals accepted his poems. In 1912 Harriet Monroe, having read a recent article in *The American* on his "quaint" publications, wrote asking to see his work with a view to including some in her forthcoming magazine, *Poetry*; and in January 1913, literary America was electrified by the publication in *Poetry* of "General William Booth Enters into Heaven."

From 1913–1920 Lindsay rode the crest of the wave. *Poetry* awarded him prizes for "General William Booth . . ." (1913), and "The Chinese Nightingale" (1915). He not only recited publicly throughout the length and breadth of America, but in 1915 performed for Woodrow Wilson's cabinet "The Wedding of the Rose and the Lotus," written to celebrate the opening that year of the Panama Canal. The climax of his career came in 1920: *The Golden Whales of California* was published in January; in August he visited England, where he converted a sceptical Oxford University to the Higher Vaudeville, and was lionized; *The Daniel Jazz* was published in England to coincide with his visit; and he returned to America in October, in time for the publication of *The Golden Book of Springfield*.

Yet, paradoxically, in that year the tide swung against him. For critics and public alike, *The Golden Book of Springfield,* a prose work in which Lindsay called to Americans to rethink their society, set the seal of disapproval on him as a renegade New Poet and a purveyor of sentiments irrelevant in the twenties. In terms of popularity, although not in terms of social conscience, Lindsay had picked the wrong moment to be seen to be preoccupied with what Americans ought to be. Hedonism was about to set in, and only Mencken's unique brand of criticism was to prove acceptable. The novelty of Lindsay's poetry and recitations also wore off and his reputation went into decline.

The decade not only saw the partial frustration of Lindsay's career; it became one of further personal hardship. In 1922 exhaustion led him to spend a year teaching a poetry class at Gulf Park Junior College, Gulfport, Mississippi; and in 1924 a conglomeration of symptoms was diagnosed as epilepsy, a condition apparently present from youth. The accompanying schizophrenia took the form of an increasingly acute persecution complex and produced the moody, unpredictable conduct, in public and in private, which was construed as the resentment of a fading writer. In 1925, aged forty-five, he married a twenty-three year old English and Latin teacher, Elizabeth Conner; a daughter, Susan Doniphan, and a son, Nicholas Cave, were born in 1926 and 1927. In 1931, suspecting his wife of infidelity, and his fellow writers of some indefinable menace, he committed suicide by drinking Lysol. He explained himself in unbearably classic persecution-manic terms: "They tried to get me; I got them instead." [12]

THE OLD IMAGE

The publication of "General William Booth . . ." in 1913 marked the beginning of Lindsay's meteoric rise to fame. He had based the poem on the cadences and tunes of "The Blood of the Lamb" and had inserted marginal directions for recitation. The poem compressed intensity into simplicity, and supplied the emotional inauguration of the New Poetry movement. Edwin Arlington Robinson had anticipated the casual idiom of the New Poetry in poems published as early as 1896, but he had not yet made any perceptible impact. Within the effective history of the movement Lindsay's poem was preceded only by the publication of Ezra Pound's *Canzoni and Ripostes,* 1912, and by *Poetry* itself, founded in September of that year.

General William Booth and Other Poems was published in 1913. Nineteen fourteen saw the pattern repeated; "The Congo," a more complex poem, but with the same characteristics of beat, color, and original material originally expressed, was followed by *The Congo and Other Poems.* The titles of these two books embody the limited estimate of Lindsay by his contemporaries: only those strikingly innovatory poems which seemed to declaim the advent of a New Poetry were acceptable.

Within this damningly confined framework, Lindsay's critics and fellow poets were generous. Eunice Tietjens enthused in *The Little Review,* November 1914: "It is not too much to say that many of us are watching Vachel Lindsay with the undisguised hope in our hearts that he may yet prove to be the 'Great American Poet.'" "The Congo" was "perilously near great poetry." [13] But what began as accolade ended in scorn. Early in 1915 Ezra Pound had judiciously observed: "I wish Lindsay all possible luck, but we're not really pulling the same way, though we both pull against entrenched senility"; but by the end of the year he was saying of Lindsay's work: "Believe me one can write it by the hour as fast as one scribbles." As for *Poetry* awarding him a prize— ". . . oh gawd!!!" [14]

For the most part Lindsay was assessed with less vitriolic condescension. The cumulative effect of a half dozen good declamatory poems was quickly to establish a stereotyped Lindsay figure. The occasional image-piled, pounding poem was regularly excavated from his work for approval. But expectations of Lindsay were never reformulated, and the sparse, erudite, introvert products of the New Poetry and New Poets came to invalidate even his initial style. Lindsay's dilemma lay in the unreceptiveness of an audience which, at both professional and lay levels, was conditioned to demand the Lindsay of 1913–14, the thundering extrovert who dominated Harriet Monroe's dinner parties even when William Butler Yeats was present. His audiences used Lindsay as a social entertainment and were indifferent to him as a social theorist. One of Lindsay's recital engagement cards for 1929 demonstrates his dilemma. Note the misspelling of his name, the capitalization of his subject matter, and the inability of his hostess to remember his most popular poem, "The Congo," whose title recurs often enough in the text of that poem. One suspects Mrs. Schwartz had only heard *of* the poem.

NAME: Mr. Vachell Lindsay
AUSPICES: Book and Play Club
HOUR: 7.00 p.m.
Dinner (Dress, Tuxedo)
AUDITORIUM
LOCATION: At the residence of Mrs. U. S. Schwartz
SUBJECT: Recital of his Poems
FEE: $250
REMARKS: Mrs. Schwartz asks that you include in
your program "The Chinese Nightingale,"
"The Virginians are Coming Again" and the
poem about Negroes whose name Mrs. Schwartz
does not recall.[15]

It made no difference that Lindsay had chosen another role than that arbitrarily assigned to him of New Poet, one which critics minimized as aesthetic maverick and which Lindsay maximized as literary social worker. All shifts away from his inescapable image were deplored, and an output ranging through the evaluation of a new art form (*The Art of the Moving Picture*, 1915), a prediction of the nature of American urban society in the year 2018 (*The Golden Book of Springfield*, 1920), socio-religious theory (*Adventures While Preaching the Gospel of Beauty*, 1914, and *A Handy Guide for Beggars*, 1916), historical comment and political speculation (*The Litany of Washington Street*, 1929), and lyrical and committed poetry (*Every Soul is a Circus*, 1929) fell on deaf ears. His motivations, themes, and modes of expression were neglected. He commented wryly,

You call me "a Troubadour,"
But I am an adventurer, in hieroglyphics, buildings and designs.[16]

To some extent this neglect was understandable. Something had to go under in the literary swell which extended on both sides of 1920 and Lindsay's rarely interrupted career of recital tours contributed to the fixity of his public image. His predicament consisted of a failure to fall in with a contemporary trend which came to meet the style it anachronistically continued to demand of him with parody.

> *Then Dan'l in his corner*
> *Softly crooned 'is 'ymn of 'Ate,*
> *And yelled in the receiver:*
> *"HI!!!!! Belschazzer*
> *YOU'RE SHORT WEIGHT!!*
> *The LORD has found you wantin'*
> *And the lions wantin' too.*
> *I will not stay a prophet*
> *Unless you raise my screw.*
> *KI wung bang buzzah*
> *Hi wobble oggle ZOO!!!!"* [17]

Such parodies were not even based on an unsympathetic comprehension of Lindsay. He was not, as the parody suggested, artificially colloquial. Nor, stylistically, was he on a wavelength with Kipling; Kipling's was the rigid rhythm of the metronome, Lindsay's the regular, but expanding and contracting line of a concertina.

The average reaction to Lindsay's prose works was that of his friend and fellow poet Edgar Lee Masters (1869–1950) who wrote the official critical biography, *Vachel Lindsay, a Poet in America* (1935). Lindsay might state that "What I am lies between the lines of *The Golden Book of Springfield*," "the effort of my life";[18] Masters, after a few dismissive paragraphs on the book, concluded: "Lindsay could not think straight in prose . . . A discussion of his poetry will prove vastly more fruitful." [19] There was a single criterion for Lindsay: those writings which did not fit the rhythmic and melodic mold of his early poems were dismissed as eccentricities, lamentable deviations.

The present dominant misconceptions of Lindsay have stemmed largely from Masters, who has been lackadaisically taken for authority, and more recently, from the other major biography by Eleanor Ruggles, *The West-going Heart, a Life of Vachel Lindsay* (1959). One merit of both biographies is that they quote extensively from diaries and correspondence of Lindsay's made available only to them. But apart from their valuable primary source material, they are books to be treated warily. Masters worked from a standpoint of bigoted opposition to much that Lindsay loved—to Christianity, Abraham Lincoln, and racial equality, for example—while Ruggles forms part of the sentimental pattern of apology for Lindsay's ventures outside poetry. In his first two chapters, however, Masters succeeded admirably in evoking the atmosphere of the Illinois in which he and Lindsay grew up; he was a neighbor of Lindsay's at New Salem. The most satisfactory work on Lindsay is Mark Harris' *City of Discontent,* 1952, an informed flight of fancy, a mixture of novel and biography. But only a specialized knowledge of Lindsay allows one to distinguish between fact and fiction, although Mr. Harris does convey Lindsay's interest in cities.

Critical and scholarly comment on Lindsay has been slight. Theses have discussed Lindsay's influence on Edith Sitwell's poetry, his technics of recitation, and his rating in the hierarchy of world literature. A recent critical study of Lindsay appeared in Michael Yatron, *The Literary Revolt in America,* 1959, in which Masters, Sandburg, and Lindsay were depicted as city-hating Midwestern Populists. But Mr. Yatron overlooked *Spoon River Anthology's* substantial indictment of rural ways, *Chicago Poems'* love-hate essence, and *The Golden Book of Springfield's* explicit subscription to an age of intelligently utilized technology, an age of skyscrapers, an age of cities.

THE NEW ASSESSMENT

Lindsay has been set against universal, regional, and agrarian backgrounds, amid prejudices and fixations, obstacles and complications which inhibited the natural flow of his literary talents into a hundred "Congos." This supposition of Lindsay's stunted creative growth can only be feasible if we assume that his bent was for poems of his early genre. The tenuous basis for this supposition slips away when we find in his *War Bulletins* of 1909 onwards an affirmation of a life to be spent contributing to the regeneration of American society; when we learn that each of his books was written in this social context; and when we discover that of the books he was planning when he died four were prose works on such themes as "(1) a complete new conception of music; (2) a complete new conception of Americanism; (3) a complete set of religious ideas; (4) a complete set of new ideas of design" and that his seven unpublished works included only one book of (children's) verse—*The Ting-a-ling Jingle of Wallpaper Walter*— and comprised *American Sketches, The American Dream, Aesthetics, Sketches and Essays, Literature and Personalities,* and *The greatest movies now running.*[20] It is no longer a question of deploring the circumstances which prevented Lindsay from expressing himself; rather, his creative faculty was continually active in self-determined, but unpopular channels. What is to be regretted is his inability to secure a hearing. It was partly due to his own fluctuatingly effective expression, and partly to a national mood and climate of opinion which clashed with his ideology. It was also a consequence of the generally dense reception of his work in literary and critical circles.

To move away from the image of Lindsay as a versifier and to assess him as a man of ideas, to look not only at his poetry but at his works in their entirety, is to find a body of consistently interesting and occasionally brilliant writing. His works form a coherent whole, bound together by an intellectual and artistic commitment to improving America, and by an awareness of America's historic past, critical present, and dubious future. They are propaganda. Lindsay's fresh image is of a writer to whom content, not style, came first, a field worker for the American democracy in its physical, artistic, and spiritual dimensions.

In his introduction to *Collected Poems* (1923) Lindsay wrote that he had paid the penalty

for having written a few loosely rhymed orations. All I write is assumed to be loose oratory, or even jazz. . . . I knew and loved in infancy the lines of Keats:

> "*Heard melodies are sweet, but those unheard*
> *Are sweeter; therefore, ye soft pipes, play on.*" [21]

It is with Lindsay's unheard melodies that this book is concerned, melodies which in toto are unlike anything that Lindsay's contemporaries and predecessors produced, but which contain phrases and reflect tones and patterns of thought from a wide range of social, political, religious, and literary compositions. There are vibrations in Lindsay's work struck by Jane Addams, Edward Bellamy, John Dewey, and Walter Rauschenbusch; by Herbert Croly, Henry George, F. C. Howe, and "Golden Rule" Jones; by Alexander Campbell, Joseph Smith, Confucius, and Buddha; by Walt Whitman and William Blake.

Since Lindsay saw himself as the guardian of the promise of American life, he was not in the habit of standing on his creative dignity. He did not pretend to have a single original idea. "When you think of a thought be sure that five of the master minds have thought it better before you," [22] he told himself. He was a modest man, as an "Editorial for the Art Student" in *The Village Magazine,* 1920, showed:

My lettering is rude, my drawing thin, my verse uneven . . . Oh game and joyous craftsmen, it is likely that I will enjoy whatever *you* attempt that comes under *my* eye. Whether you are making a picture or a book, a newspaper a tombstone or a statue, a park, a skating rink, or a world's fair, I will grant you your thesis, accept your intention, laugh at your joke, frown at your sermon, find light where your ecstacy [*sic*] is recorded.[23]

This was modesty indeed, for Lindsay looked to *The Village Magazine,* edited, illustrated, and written entirely by himself, to communicate the whole man, not the "parrot and ape." [24] He wanted to reveal a propagandist eager to spread other men's ideas and to praise other men's inventions. He was flattered to have his own ideas borrowed and adopted: "I want your whole town to use *The Golden Book* after adding every revision it cares to make," [25] he wrote in a circular letter to civic dignitaries. He returned the compliment, frankly giving credit for ideas: for his theory of hieroglyphic art to the poet James Oppenheim; for "General William Booth . . ." to the Salvation Army, Springfield Branch, in action; and for much of *The Golden Book of Springfield* to Louis Sullivan, Frank Lloyd Wright, Ralph Adams Cram, and Percy Mackaye. But the whole into which Lindsay welded these heterogeneous elements was his own. One can only exclaim at the scope and tolerance of his knowledge and the dedicated eagerness which led him to seek out and encourage anything which might contribute to the realization of the American Dream.

Lindsay's writings and library provide ample evidence of his conscious focus of contemporary thought. But while he was informed about, and involved in his society, while he could be frankly imitative and unconsciously eclectic, he had an independent reaction to the problems that his contemporaries in the socio-political-architectural-literary spheres were facing. Lindsay was neither typical nor representative. While he was related to many groups, while he was a one-man sorting house of ideas, he remained peripheral. He was quick to react, but slow to become partisan, too concerned with the possible implications of every incident and trend to subside into a particular school of thought. More tolerant in his outlook, more willing to concede points of value in other men's theories, he appeared less committed than his contemporaries; but it was because his degree of commitment to ultimate social ends was so great that he could not be arbitrary or exclusive in his philosophy. He had an endemic simplicity, typified by his ambition to be a Christian cartoonist, to point up as earnestly as William Holmes McGuffey, or *The Hoosier Schoolmaster,* and with something of their nineteenth century veneer, the necessity and merit of justice, right, beauty, and truth. His terminology, often sentimental to the point of apparent naivety, tended to make his naggingly valid comments seem old-fashioned, and at times gave *The Golden Book of Springfield* the air of a museum piece.

Lindsay was also open to misinterpretation in that he examined his environment with such anxious detachment that he seemed not to be part of it. His attempt to transcend his immediate surroundings made him appear anachronistic. Lacking confidence in the manifestness of America's destiny, he was driven into the ambiguous position of gauging the shakiness of the American promise more accurately than the contemporaries in whose company he was made to seem an anomaly. He mirrored twentieth century America, its leaders, its happenings, its atmosphere; he described them vividly, yet he remained aloof. He appreciated twentieth century phenomena—automobiles, advertising, airplanes, skyscrapers—yet he emphasized their potential benefits rather than their existing merits. He approved the social legislation of Theodore Roosevelt and Woodrow Wilson, but it neither lulled nor satisfied him. He could not define the short-term, or the expedient, or the pragmatically progressive as the American reformation. For he took the view that only when rulers and citizens based their calculations on the tempering priorities of Religion, Equality, and Beauty could the machine age and a booming America be reconciled with human development. It was this reconciliation he worked for, but which he expected to be the task of many generations to come.

Lindsay's facility for objectivity and long-term value judgments meant that in the pre-1920 period he was unable to align himself with the sanguine Progressives and New Republicans. He thought and wrote in unoptimistic terms, alien to men who might be muckrakers, agitators, or reformers, but whose advocacy of one-stroke remedies—a Single Tax, the municipal ownership of utilities, the right to strike, trust-busting, the initiative, referendum, and recall—sprang from fundamental confidence in a just-off-course, easily-righted America. Nor was Lindsay at one with the dominant literary mood of the second decade of the century. Poetry, he Whitmanesquely argued, was social, not artistic. Only loosely associated with the New Poetry movement, removed from the imagist controversy, he sought to evolve a poetry whose form and content, while retaining beauty, would make the medium meaningful and pleasurable to the mass of Americans habitually ignored by poets. It seemed to him that America could not be fully realized without such a folk culture.

Lindsay's brand of pessimistic realism made him an alien figure in the 1920s, too. He had too few expectations to be disillusioned by the 1914–18 war, or by the Peace of Versailles. He found it hard to condone or understand the frenetic relaxation of taboos, the cultivation of materialism for its own sake, the irresponsibility of isolationism, and the crudely political presidential criteria. To the extent that he was out of sympathy with subjective reactions, he was out of sympathy with literary trends. He did not allow for the dilemma of the average inner man or artist, bewildered by shifts in science and politics, moving shakily from a belief to a negation, or to stages in-between. Consequently, the practice of such writers as Hemingway and Scott Fitzgerald to project universal dilemmas in personal terms alienated him, and made him alien.

But what consistently set Lindsay apart from his contemporaries was his uncomfortable and anachronistically persistent critique of society. His ideas and actions were rooted in the determination to create a climate of opinion aware of the alarming tendencies of America: its unintelligent submission to mechanization; its unplanned, and therefore menacing cities; its diminishing morality; its undemocratic politics; and its monopolistic commerce. He wanted a reaffirmation of America's physical and ethical promise, and its rerouting through a designed environment; a subservient technological milieu; and a community of greater cultural and political equality. The Lincoln fixation he developed was indicative not only of reverence for Lincoln, but of Lindsay's conviction that America was moving from brink to brink, though less visibly than in Civil War days, and stood in perpetual need of Lincolns. Perhaps he exaggerated, but in the America of his concern, tradition, culture, and democracy were tenuous propositions.

It was to put this shaky society on firm foundations that he suggested freshly conceived bases of Religion, Equality, and Beauty; that he spun a cautionary tale of the American future; that he used, and to a certain extent mythologized, data from the American past to try to stimulate a conscious Americanism. Conscious Americanism, by his definition, sprang from no-nonsense egalitarianism, conventional individual morality, unconventional group morality, and transcendental international morality. It would show itself at home in clean politics, a townscaped America, and a national culture with every class both contributor and participator.

These intentions and ideals of Lindsay's gave rise to his touring career of recitation and lecture to mass audiences, and to his belief in the motion picture as the art form for Everyman. They produced

Lindsay's most cherished and most original piece of writing and planning, his novel-cum-fantasy-cum-tract, *The Golden Book of Springfield*. It was a book in which Lindsay envisaged an American city in the year 2018, a city architecturally advanced, and a potential nationwide civic unit on the lines of Frank Lloyd Wright's Broadacre City. But in human terms Springfield 2018 had not progressed. It was as full of racialism, political corruption, and anti-intellectualism as Springfield 1918, and as little characterized by sustained reform movements, community spirit, and citizens of integrity. Lindsay did not depict a dream society, but a sub-utopia: he gave an excitingly sane picture of the dual trend in America toward physical change and mental continuum.

Lindsay's Gospel

Orientation

L INDSAY CALLED his basic philosophy a "gospel."[1] Gospel was a popular contemporary term to describe individual and social philosophies, and by using the term Lindsay aptly associated himself with attempts to reason out an American way of life. Theodore Roosevelt preached the "gospel of work," Andrew Carnegie the "gospel of wealth" (which the less fortunate interpreted as "the gospel of greed"), E. V. Harrington, the rags-to-riches tycoon in Robert Herrick's *An American Citizen* (1905) based his actions on "the gospel of man against man." Lindsay's gospel had more religious and doctrinal content than these philosophies but it was not dogmatic. He neither accepted nor preached any rigid set of beliefs: "I do not believe in the infallibility of any book, teacher or church."[2]

He defined his gospel as one of

Religion, equality and *beauty*. By these America shall come into a glory that shall justify the yearning of the sages for her perfection, and the prophecies of the poets, when she was born in the throes of Valley Forge.[3]

Such statements have led to his classification as an emotional protagonist of Manifest Destiny: a "rhyming John the Baptist, singing to convert the heathen" (Louis Untermeyer), an exponent of "Mid-American evangelism" (T. K. Whipple), and the victim of a "Messianic delusion" (Fred B. Millett).[4] The millennarian overtones of these descriptions imply that Lindsay heralded a reformation or claimed a revelation, that he was a prophet. But in an imaginary journey on "The Comet of Prophecy," Lindsay found

> *I look ahead, I look above,*
> *I look on either hand.*
> *I cannot sight the fields I seek,*
> *The holy No-Man's-Land.*

He returned from his "journey" able to discount the inevitability of decay, and determined to preach the good news that reform was possible.

> *And yet my heart is full of faith.*
> *My comet splits the gloom,*
> *His red mane slaps across my face,*
> *His eyes like bonfires loom.*[5]

But he felt bound to conclude that "civilization is on the edge of a flowering that is far indeed from the millennium." [6]

Certainly Lindsay was an exhorter, and he exemplified the type of reformer described by Henry Demarest Lloyd in *Man the Social Creator* (1906) as

a poet, a creator. He sees visions and fills the people with their beauty; and by the contagion . . . his creative impulse spreads among the mass, and it begins to climb and build.[7]

In Lindsay's own words. "I am knocking at the door of the [American] world with a dream in my hand." [8] But it would be misleading to label him yet another sanguine American dreamer. When he described "visions" and made "predictions" it was to stimulate, to exhort, and not to define. He saw the highs and lows of American humanity too clearly for his expectations to be anything but tentative. His reform activities had a pessimistic premise.

This is what I have to work with, this humanity . . . and they shall never infect me with their sickness. Arm yourself against the worst so that disappointment in humanity is impossible. We shall teach these cripples to fight for our fancies, fight with their crutches.[9]

His pessimism was accompanied by almost excessive realism, and an almost intolerable compassion.

When we see our people as they are—
Our fathers—broken, dumb—
Our mothers—broken, dumb—
The weariest of women and of men;
Ah—then our eyes will lose their light—
Then we will never play again—
We, who are playing to-night.[10]

But since he was aware of his sensitivity, he fought against depression and the inclination to be irate with his society. His resulting determination to see hopeful signs in unlikely situations led him to attempt patience and tolerance with apparently recalcitrant material.

I want live things in their pride to remain.
I will not kill one grasshopper vain
Though he eats a hole in my shirt like a door.
I let him out, give him one chance more.
Perhaps, while he gnaws my hat in his whim,
Grasshopper lyrics occur to him.[11]

On a personal level this hypersensitivity made his existence a vicious circle of self- and other-perception. A poignant illustration is "The Perfect Marriage," with its appallingly cynical comments on the transitoriness of love in such lines as "Love? . . . we will scarcely love our babes full many a time/Knowing their souls and ours too well, and all our grime." Yet, trying not to succumb to negative attitudes, he could hope, in "Epilogue to Adventure While Preaching the Gospel of Beauty," that out of the combustion of young lovers seeking a brave new world, "Out of the fire my spirit-bread shall come/And my soul's gospel swirl from that red flame." [12] He viewed his own limitations with much the same paradoxical mixture of hope and despair with which he viewed America's. In a letter to his wife in 1929 he wrote:

We are on the edge of Bryan's power. I mean it seriously. We are on the edge of Bryan's power. They are coming to *us*, dearest, for personal leadership in *citizenship* and *ideas*.

But a few letters later he concluded

I have not done *one thing* to set my town permanently aflame for God
and Beauty and Democracy. I have merely babbled and written about
these things.[13]

Lindsay lacked protective armor and his thinnest of thin skins
made him an intense American, incapable, for example, of Menck-
en's acidulous lightness, or of Sandburg's generous affirmations.
It also made him a reacting agent for his times, times in which he
saw his function as "Flame-like to hover over moil and grime/Striv-
ing, aspiring till the shame is gone." [14] The intensity and totality
of his concern led him to avoid select and detailed criticisms of
the sort that characterized the reform impulse in early twentieth
century America. He drew up an oblique, blanket indictment
which, for all its contrast to the specific charges of other reformers,
was part of what was essentially all one criticism and all one cry:
Something is wrong with the American experience—what? His
outlook on the American scene, comprehensive and constructive,
had its place midway between the ostrich mentality of Manifest
Destiny described by Van Wyck Brooks in *America's Coming-of-
Age* (1915) as a

soft, undisciplined emotionality face to face with crowds, millionaires,
prairies and skyscrapers—an open sea with plenty of wind for the
great American balloon[15]

and the evasive, scapegoat philosophy of the twenties which Malcolm Cowley retrospectively characterized in *Exile's Return* (1934)
as

something [that] oppressed them. . . . They did not understand its
nature, but they tried to exorcise it by giving it names—it was hurry
and haste, it was Mass Production, Babbitry, Our Business Civilization . . . the Voice of the Machine, the Tyranny of the Mob.[16]

Anxiety about America provided the impetus for Lindsay's gospel, a gospel which was a call to America to heed the direction of
her growth and a guide to the better channeling of her energies.
He refused to make it definitive; he tolerated and sometimes
adopted what he considered other sane, serious attempts to plan

for America; and he looked eagerly for a better design than his own as a sign of a stirring social conscience. Through an intentional concentration on what he could find of good in social and religious theories he aimed to prove that there was a natural brotherhood of men, irrespective of racial or credal differences; that apparent differences, examined, were often found to be nonexistent; that genuine differences were in some degree expressions of uniqueness and valuable to civilization. He brought to bear on all he observed a compassion, an unwillingness to condemn where the slightest point of concurrence might exist, an inclusiveness which gave his gospel diverse, and sometimes almost incompatible components.

Within this flexible framework Lindsay had preferences and periodic shifts of emphasis, but he always envisaged some sort of community as the starting point for his design for the American future. His gospel, formulated in the years 1908–12, and proclaimed in *War Bulletins* I–V (1909), *The Village Magazine* (1910), *Adventures While Preaching the Gospel of Beauty* (1914), and *A Handy Guide for Beggars* (1916), emphasized the desirability of organizing America on the basis of a network of small, semirural communities. In *The Golden Book of Springfield* (1920) he was to call for a new America urban unit, 50,000 strong; and in the 1920s he advocated the conscious development of a complementary regional structure. All his plans, however, retained a village ethos.

VILLAGE

Lindsay lessened his chance of being taken seriously as a social theorist when he chose the word village to express his conception of a desirable unit of community life. In most people's minds the term must have conjured up a picture like that painted by George Ade in "The Fable of the Boston Biologist and The Native with the Blue Hardware."

The Boston Man looked across the Street at the dun-coloured Hotel propped up by a comatose Livery Stable. Near at Hand was a Pool of Green Water within which the Bacilli were croaking loudly. . . . A brackish odor of Moonshine Whiskey tingled in the warm Air, and over the whole dejected Landscape lay a Pall of the real Simon-Pure Malaria—the kind that can be put up in Tins, sent from Place to Place.[17]

Any number of evocative place-names—Gopher Prairie, Winesburg, Spoon River, Fairview—conveys the inherent prejudice Lindsay encountered when he wrote about the village, although he was using the term idiosyncratically to describe a community which was both city and village.

As early as 1910 he had written, with the style and typography of Ade's fables, "An Editorial For the Local Statesmen, When the Cross-Roads Becomes a Big City";[18] and in 1912 he hopefully maintained that "chants of hammer, forge and spade/Will move the prairie-village yet." The new prairie-village was to inaugurate a pattern of modernity, beautiful, not crass:

> Let Science and Machinery and Trade
> Be slaves of her, and make her all in all.[19]

His concept of a village-city began to come through in the purposeful reiteration of such terms as "civic gospel," "civic church," and "civic beauty" in *The Village Magazine*. But before the six years (1914-20) spent on *The Golden Book of Springfield*, he did admit to a certain amount of rural bias, exemplified by his insistent use of the word village for something unlike the traditional image created by that word. His community designs were always part urban, part rural, but up to 1914, and the publication of *Adventures While Preaching the Gospel of Beauty*, the rural element predominated, and his urbanization of the village was somewhat reluctant. (*A Handy Guide for Beggars*, which also preached a somewhat rural gospel, was published in 1916, but it was a collection of reminiscences of his 1908 and 1912 tramps.) By 1920 he had come to believe that the cohesive, unitary qualities of village life—where they existed, and were not merely part of the American rural myth—were matched, if not surpassed, by the exciting possibilities of unprecedented social solidarity in cities, cities whose size and impersonality made their potential, as well as their challenge, enormous. An active urban social conscience and a campaign against slums and loneliness could parallel and outstrip leisurely village philanthropy and imperceptible rural change.

The Village Magazine of 1910, reissued with slight variations in 1920, and twice in 1925, conveyed the pervasive atmosphere of "spirit-power," beauty, democracy, leisure, and uncomplicated amusements that characterized Lindsay's village—or "some city on the breast of Illinois" and "our little town" as he described it in "The Illinois Village." It was this composite village ethos, concretely expressed in such village institutions as a watchdog local press and a pervasive church and churchmen, as well as in an abstract sense, that Lindsay wanted to see perpetuated in cities. Abstractly and ideally the village ethos was a strong community feeling flourishing in an environment of "civic ecstasy . . . so splendid, so unutterably afire, continuing and increasing with such apocalyptic zeal that the whole visible fabric of the world can be changed." [20] Realistically and immediately Lindsay thought in terms of an already transitional village community, what it should retain, and what it should relinquish.

His attempt to coin a new meaning of village led him to try to dispel existing misconceptions in a *Village Magazine* "Editorial for the Wise Man in the Metropolis Concerning the Humble Agricultural Village in Central Illinois." The editorial began:

Scene I a desert place enter three witches. Thus many people would begin if they expressed their feelings about the village to which they have not returned for fifteen years. And so certain smoke smothered suburbs of the metropolis could be described but if any have the notion that the Illinois agricultural town is today a tobacco-soaked railway station surrounded by "general" stores, they are to be immediately surprised the blasted heath is no more.

He went on to comment favorably on aspects of city life which had invaded the village. James Whitcomb Riley-type general emporiums were being replaced by "shining little department stores." The telephone was providing women with a gossip circuit equivalent to the male preserve of the post office-store. Traveling salesmen, rural free delivery, *Collier's, McClure's, The American,* and *Everybody's* were creating national patterns of consumption and conversation.[21]

But while Lindsay was eager to give his village urban features he did not want it to be a reproduction of the known city. Its existence was not to be justified by its industries, nor its attraction based solely on its bustle and size. "The next generation will be that of the eminent village," Lindsay wrote deliberately, using the word "village" with the dual meaning of a community of simple, sterling values, and one of the stature and inner diversity of the old Athens. Its inhabitants were to be cosmopolitan, but "no longer dazzled by the fires of the metropolis." The sort of miscellaneous achievements for which Lindsay hoped his eminent village—or new American community—would be famous were "its pottery or its processions, its philosophy or its peacocks, its music or its swans, its golden roofs or its great union cathedral of all faiths." In culture and in commerce the village was more or less what "you find around the corner in Los Angeles, or San Francisco, Tampa or New York."[22] The process should work in reverse; Lindsay liked to think that if Chicago, for instance, acquired the village ethos, it might be called "a little overgrown country town."[23] This virtual equation of village and city gives some idea of how misleadingly the word "village" described the embryo of his new community. The polarization of the word and its meaning made it incapable of succinct redefinition and lessened its impact, though it was this polarization which made the word pregnant with meaning for Lindsay.

CITY

In *The Village Magazine* Lindsay reprinted three pages of clippings from small town and rural newspapers, noting "some of the clippings throw difficulties in the way of theories which I shall air afterwards, but, as Newman said, 'Ten thousand difficulties do not make one doubt.'" He quoted the views of a Southern Dakota farmer in "The Calhoun County Democrat":

Attractions of farm life are dreams, and nobody has them except city
folk. . . . It seems to me that it isn't possible to improve country life
by injecting city life into it. The two won't mix.[24]

These doubting sentiments were not Lindsay's. In 1897, rereading
an essay he had written at the age of eleven, he drew the conclusion that he had then, and still had "a sense that man is fundamentally educated by the phenomena of nature, and that man is
the divinely appointed ruler of nature throughout the universe." [25]
A country loyalty and an admiration for the way men had har-
nessed and utilized the forces of nature was an ambivalence he
never lost.

Lindsay might not doubt the ultimately successful outcome of
the search for a city-country equilibrium in the early decades of
the twentieth century but it remained a national difficulty. As
Arthur Schlesinger commented in *The Rise of the City*, the issue
was not simply:

the City had come, and it was clear to all that it had come to stay. Was
its mission to be that of a new Jerusalem or of ancient Babylon? [26]

but the horrid fascination of the city versus the seductive turpi-
tude of the country. The frightening growth of mechanical forms
of communication and transport, of industry and of megalopoli,
made the encroachment of the machine age in its ugliest and
dirtiest manifestations throughout America seem a mere matter of
time. It appeared as if there would be only one form of community,
the commercial community, at best suburban (Forest Hills), and
at worst slum (Packingtown). Rural life offered a potential association of human beings, town life a potential set of amenities.
Could the two successfully coalesce?

Lindsay answered this question in the affirmative: "The signs
in the street and the signs in the skies/Shall make a new Zodiac." [27]
He did not belong to the school which thought that cities necessarily came into being for the industrial changeover, and that then,
somehow, the evolutionary process would rise above the technological and move back into a state of primitive simplicity. On the
contrary, he was drawn to the energies, the emotions, and the new

arts of living which were generated in an urban environment: the sensation of modernity and progress, the intensification of isolation and sociability. His feeling for the personality of the city was almost mystical, and akin to that of the sociologist Joseph Hudnut (1886—). In *The Invisible City* Hudnut developed his theory that the city was a good place to be; that people were happy there, in spite of and because of its noise, glare, and press; that "beneath the visible city laid out in patterns of streets and houses there lies an invisible city laid out in patterns of idea and behavior." [28] His "Invisible City" was Lindsay's "Town of American Visions" which Lindsay invited his public to enter "and meet Tomorrow's Man." It was "Springfield Magical"

> *. . . No Hindu Town*
> *Is quite so strange. No Citadel of Brass*
> *By Sinbad found, held half such love and hate;*
> *No picture-palace in a picture-book*
> *Such webs of Friendship, Beauty, Greed and Fate!*

This was not only an emotional subscription to urban life on Lindsay's part; America's potential urban beauty took his breath away.

> *Is it for naught that where the tired crowds see*
> *Only a place for trade, a teeming square,*
> *Doors of high portent open unto me*
> *Carved with great eagles. . . .*[29]

If Lindsay fitted so neatly into a sociological aspect of the city-country complex, how did he fit into the artistic reaction to the dilemma? Lewis Mumford (1895—), the versatile architect, city planner, and social philosopher recognized somewhat grudgingly, that Lindsay, too, had a foot in more than one camp. In 1923 Mumford commented:

It is a sign of a terrific neurosis—and no mark at all of aesthetic aptitude—that our genuine art is so completely disoriented and so thoroughly out of touch with the community [that] we must turn to a man of such uneven parts as Mr. Nicholas Vachel Lindsay before we have anything like a recognition of the classic role of the artist.

Mumford went on to define what he meant by art.

Art in its social setting is neither a personal cathartic for the artist, nor a salve to quiet the itching vanity of the community: it is essentially a means by which people who have a strange diversity of experiences have their activities emotionally canalized into patterns and molds which they are able to share. . . .[30]

It was this equal commitment to art and the community which brought together Lindsay and Frank Lloyd Wright. Lindsay, "Rhymer and Designer," as he sometimes signed himself, tried in his own way to plan American society; his advocacy of Broadacre City stemmed not only from his aesthetic response to Wright's concept of a new beauty, but from his concurrence with Wright's belief in the architect-artist-writer as a field worker for democracy. Lindsay had his *War Bulletins* in which he raged against cities which were Gehennas, Wright his "angry prophecy and a preachment."

Is the great city the natural triumph of the herd instinct over such sanity as humanity may know? Or is it only a temporary hangover from the infancy of the race, to be outgrown as the performance of humanity grows—modern? [31]

Few literary reactions were as community-conscious as Lindsay's. Theodore Dreiser, for instance, barely bothered to stop and indict the countryside, though his writings were permeated with the conviction that America truly existed, should, and would exist, in monster cities like Chicago. Another partisan school of thought was embodied by Sherwood Anderson and Edgar Lee Masters, writers who inveighed against stagnant, narrow country ways, but whose diatribes were often the results of their involvement with rural America. Like *Spoon River Anthology*, Anderson's description of a Midwestern childhood in *Tar* was perhaps a condemnation of human weakness rather than of environment. Only Carl Sandburg matched Lindsay's love for the countryside. In "Cornhuskers" he championed the prairies as residual America.

> *I am here when the cities are gone*
> *I am here before the cities come,*

> *I nourished the lonely men on horses*
> *I will keep the laughing men who ride iron*
> *I am dust of men.*[32]

But unlike Lindsay's would-be reconciliation of city and country, Sandburg's lines contained the same basically hostile antithesis of the two as Bryan's "Cross of Gold" speech. Lindsay differed from Sandburg, too, in that his feeling was less for wide open spaces than for farm land and the human countryside.

> Wherever there is tillable land, there is a budding and blooming of old-fashioned Americanism, which the farmer is making splendid for us against the better day.[33]

Here there *were* undertones of Bryan's and Sandburg's antithesis. And undoubtedly, while Lindsay approved the "invisible city" and the potential American urban dimension, he was hostile to those cities which were solely industrial and commercial propositions, which ignored the human element and blasted the landscape; and to those whose citizens overindulged themselves in the typical prosperous "Oil City . . . an ugly, confused kind of place. There are thousands like it in the United States." [34] In an America which lacked the rural-industrial cohesion of Springfield 2018, and which provided oppressive conditioning, he felt bound to urge city dwellers

> to whom the universe has become a blast-furnace, a coke-oven, a cinder-strewn freight-yard . . . turn to the soil, turn to the earth, your mother, and she will comfort you.[35]

Behind this statement lay not only Lindsay's belief that rural life was preferable to badly planned cities, but a consideration of the remedial aspect of contact with nature, of Jeffersonian agrarianism. When he developed his urban blueprint he made provision for large areas of national parkland, and he never ceased to urge contact with nature. All men should have

> *A net to snare the moonlight,*
> *A sod spread to the sun,*
> *A place of toil by daytime,*
> *Of dreams when toil is done.*[36]

But he came to think that one of the important aspects of contact with nature had been the outlet it provided for squirearchal instincts, the need for one's own "single spot of earth"; and in 1925, in an introduction to a pamphlet[37] celebrating the naturalist John Burroughs (1831–1921), he coupled his support of the conservation movement, and the work done for that movement by Burroughs in the Catskills, with the announcement that he felt an urban "single spot of earth"—house and garage ownership and maintenance, presumably—were adequate approximations of the mythical agrarian virtues of self-mastery and cultivation.

THE NEW LOCALISM

Lindsay lost his rural bias, almost to the extent of acquiring an urban prejudice. Ultimately, however, he was dominated neither by the cities nor the countryside of Illinois, the Midwest, or America; he tried to amalgamate their functional and aesthetic merits, and he hoped for their eventual fusion. He suggested an approach to the important psychology of this amalgam through what, in 1912, he christened "The New Localism."

The New Localism argued for America's adjustment to the changing material world and for her reaffirmation of the unchanging spiritual world at the only level which would make these stances nationally operable: the local level, ranging from the individual home through the urban community. The political commentator Mary P. Follett (1868–1933) made the same approach to what she hoped would be *The New State* (1918). She took for her premise that "all those who are looking towards a real democracy . . . feel that the most imminent of our needs is the awakening and invigorating the educating and organising of the local unit." She opposed the social atomism of cities as they were, and argued along Springfield lines for cities as they might be— with the village ethos, which she defined as "the group-spirit that is the pillar of cloud by day and of fire by night." [38] John Dewey (1859–1962), also thought in terms of local development. He followed up his insistence as an educationalist on the importance of the primary groups of family and school with his contention as a social philosopher "that the local is the ultimate universal," a statement which might well be Lindsay justifying the New Localism in somewhat philosophical language.

Dewey's search for "the Great Community" took him to the point where he concluded that "democracy must begin at home, and its home is the neighbourly community";[39] Lindsay, traveling the same road, looking for "The Ideal American Community," decided

the things most worth while are one's own hearth and neighborhood. We should make our own home and neighborhood the most democratic, the most beautiful and the holiest in the world.

In such integrated communities subscribing to Religion, Equality, and Beauty, the functions of the church, the state, and the arts would intertwine. Politicians would give consideration to beautiful churches, crossroads fountains, and people's palaces; clergy and artists would concern themselves with tariffs and grain prices.

For the first time in the history of Democracy, art and the church shall be hand in hand and equally at our service. Neither craftsmanship nor prayer shall be purely aristocratic any more, nor at war with each other, nor at war with the State. The priest, the statesman and the singer shall discern one another's work more perfectly and give thanks to God.[40]

But even more important than community leaders were the people who would produce and follow such leaders and call them to account. Lindsay's hypothesis was that the cells of the New Localism would provide for growth into a mature and altruistic nation and would finally constitute the international organism. He was formulating this theory while tramping through Kansas in 1912, and was influenced by the views of William Allen White (1868–1944), the forthright editor of America's one nationally famous local paper, *The Emporia Gazette*. White spoke out proudly for Kansans as the kind of other-regarding, community-conscious individuals who were acting out America's promise. Lindsay, temporarily converted, rhapsodized about "Kansas, nearer than any other to the kind of a land our fathers took for granted." He acknowledged that "White was the soul back of the Kansas chapters of *Adventures While Preaching the Gospel of Beauty*," and obviously drew on White's palpably sincere belief that Kansans were "a people neighbourbound by ties of duty, by a sense of obligation, by a belief in the social compact" for his own hope that in the communities of the New Localism "our mobs shall become assemblies and our assemblies religious; devout in a subtle sense, equal in privilege and courtesy, delicate of spirit." [41]

Such statements showed Lindsay at a rare level of optimism which was partly a reflection of White and partly a result of the euphoria of that particular tramping expedition. Sheer physical exhilaration in the harvest fields led him to think in terms of social ripening and reaping. He had lost this momentary optimism by 1920 and *The Golden Book of Springfield* when he turned to leaders and environment to recondition Americans, and not vice versa. He was to look back to his tramping days when he preached his gospel as "his days of glory/Of faith in his fellow-men." [42] In those days he hoped for individuals of quality and diversity in the communities of the New Localism: religious men like St. Francis, John Wesley, General Booth, and Cardinal Newman, "many types, but supreme of their type"; statesmen like Washington, Jefferson, and Lincoln; versatile individuals, practical and intellectual, like William Morris and Leonardo da Vinci. Whatever the diversity of men, however, the lowest common denominators, Religion, Equality, and Beauty would remain, to the transforming effect that "we shall have Shelleys with a heart for religion, Ruskins with a comprehension of equality." [43]

Such a rounded Ruskin would be a welcome member of a community of the New Localism, but the original lacked the vital, integrating "comprehension of Equality." Lindsay believed that community planning could be oriented around the proposition that "all men are created equal in taste," [44] and that when the faculty of appreciation was allowed to realize itself, it would prove to be equally powered, though differently constructed and routed. By way of contrast Ruskin did not believe that Everyman's priorities could be substantially altered, though he did see the diffusion of culture as a counterweight to the imbalance of grossness in all classes of society. He made a qualified effort, however, to question the dominant social motif of materialism, and to stimulate those members of the community who were capable of a nonmaterial response to join with the enlightened, paternalistic establishment. Lindsay planned to express his approval of this emphasis on spiritual and aesthetic values in the community in a book to be called "Ruskin vs. Thoreau," an unrealized project which would also have shown Lindsay's disapproval of Thoreau's individualistic isolation from the community and its problems.

Like Ruskin, William Morris was both germane and alien to Lindsay. Lindsay's gospel envisaged beauty conditioning the whole political, social, and physical fabric of the American nation, its communities and its homes; Morris' attempt to make every part of the daily environment aesthetically satisfying was part of the same stream of activity. Both men sought to balance town and country. Morris hoped for an end to city squalor and country stupor; in *News From Nowhere* he depicted the town invading the country, yielding to the influences of rural surroundings and producing a new race of country people with city merits of briskness and eagerness. But there the parallel with the New Localism—and with *The Golden Book of Springfield*—ends. The halcyon communities of *News From Nowhere,* unlike the projected communities of twentieth and twenty-first century America, did not come to terms with the machine age. Morris' London was evasively "new." It was a reversion to a machineless, medieval time; it was a rejection of the benefits of the Industrial Revolution as well as its blights.

Morris' view that all labor which men found uncongenial should be abolished took Lindsay still further away from him, since Lindsay held the almost aggressively modern view that "the machine shop should be as much the fashion as the football field to keep our dainty darlings rugged and grimed." [45] He did not agree with Morris that the products of joyful labor must automatically be works of art, but put forward the saner concept of beauty in the dignity of honest labor. He expressed this idea in the phrase "Blacksmith

Aristocracy,"[46] an idea embodying both the notion that all men are created equal and a belief in the intrinsically equal worth of all labor well done. His notion of a functionally aesthetic correlation of creativity and everyday life was very much that which John Dewey had tried to show in his experimental school's industrial shop at the University of Chicago. For example, to explain the history and significance of the textile industry in human development, Dewey collected machinery and materials; literature contributed "in its idealized representation of the world-industries, as in Penelope in the Odyssey." He made sure that "music lends its share, from the Scotch song at the wheel to the spinning song of Marguerite. . . . The shop becomes a pictured museum."[47]

Dewey's advocacy of the oneness of Art, Nature, and Science sprang from the pragmatic logic of integration, Lindsay's from a belief in an immanent God. He expressed his belief in a poem written for his niece, Catherine Frazee Wakefield, the daughter of his sister Olive. She was not one year old when "Sunshine" was written, and perhaps for that reason the poem reads like a baptismal reaffirmation by Lindsay of his beliefs.

> *. . . Sunshine fashions all things*
> *That cut or burn or fly,*
> *And corn that seems upon the earth*
> *Is made in the hot sky.*
> *The gravel of the roadbed,*
> *The metal of the gun,*
> *The engine of the airship*
> *Trace somehow from the sun.*[48]

It was this sense of the unity of the abstract and the concrete which led Lindsay to the concept of a network of integrated communities of the New Localism, which would form "a sort of landscape gardening system in the memory, a panorama of civic democracy."[49]

Lindsay particularly admired a man who in practice tried to integrate things material and spiritual, "Golden Rule" Jones (Samuel M. Jones, 1840–1904), a Toledo oil magnate turned civic reformer, whom the people of Toledo elected mayor three times, in defiance of both party machines and all city bosses. Lindsay particularly liked the reflective, moralizing letters Jones included in the weekly wage envelopes of his workers at the Acme Sucker Rod Company, Toledo, Ohio. One of Jones' aides was Brand Whitlock (1869–1934) who later became a national figure in his own right as a liberal reform mayor of Toledo (1905–13) and American Ambassador to Belgium (1913–22). Lindsay and Whitlock corresponded about Jones and about Lindsay's poem in celebration of another humanitarian, John Peter Altgeld, "The Eagle That is Forgotten." It is more than possible that Lindsay was encouraged in his belief in the unitary potential of the city by Whitlock's description in his memoirs, *Forty Years of It* (1910), of his, and probably Jones's ideal community, a city

in which there were the living conceptions of justice, morals, consideration, toleration, beauty, art . . . a city which the citizen loved as a graduate loves his alma mater, a city with a communal spirit . . . wherein the people at last in good will were living the social life.[50]

SOCIETY

Darwinism and its adaptations were the source of much reform activity—and inactivity—in Lindsay's America; Lindsay's attitude to Darwinism clarifies his conception of the nature of society and the nature of reform. In 1909, in a *War Bulletin* skit on "Dah Win, Scientific Conspirator," he deplored the attitude which made science a new religion, and attacked the "terrible saying 'None but superior men are fit to live.'"[51] But in one sense he concurred with Herbert Spencer's corollary to the theory of evolution: he hoped that by accepting technological advances gladly, and at the same time refining their obtrusiveness, man would prove his superiority over machine; and that he would not

> . . . *rest in his pleasure and toil*
> *His clumsy contraptions of coil beyond coil*
> *Till the thing he invents, in its use and its range,*
> *Leads on to the marvellous CHANGE* . . .[52]

from progress which left discord and disruption in its wake to the real progress of ease, beauty, and harmony in the social and physical unit.

Lindsay's most pungent comment on Darwin appeared in "The Litany of Heroes" which invoked Darwin, along with such varied figures as Amenophis IV, St. Francis, and Woodrow Wilson. Through the medium of Darwin, Lindsay looked ahead to a brutal flowering of the machine age as a stage leading to some higher form of development in cities which would be exquisitely refined products of the machine age.

> *Would that the hot dry wind called Science came,*
> *Forerunner of a higher mystic day,*
> *Though vile machine-made commerce clear the way—*
> *Though nature losing shame should lose her veil,*
> *And ghosts of buried angel-warriors wail*
> *The fall of Heaven, and the relentless Sun*
> *Smile on, as Abraham's God forever dies—*
> *Lord, give us Darwin's eyes!* [53]

The splendid paradox in which Lindsay asked God to make all men Darwins dispenses with any notion of his fundamentalism. His interest in the Genesis versions of creation was irreverent, almost heretical; he wrote one poem about "Johnny Appleseed's wife from the Palace of Eve," the palace "where all the bright beautiful girls come from"! [54]

Social Darwinism was a phenomenon of the late nineteenth and early twentieth centuries, and was made up of heterogeneous applications of Darwinism to American society. Interpretations ranged from William Graham Sumner's unflinching acceptance of the survival-of-the-fittest and laissez-faire doctrines, with all their harsh consequences for less able individuals (most Social Darwinists believed that "fittest" and "best" were synonymous and so retained their social conscience), to Lester Frank Ward's belief that the human environment could be and needed to be modified by purposeful action.

It is typical that Lindsay could not share what was the common delimiting, almost determinist characteristic of the Social Darwinists, their fundamental optimism. Their discussions were based on the assumption that man was bound to move in the "right" direction, to adhere to "good" values, and to form the "splendid" society. When their suggestions and criticisms indicated impatience and willingness to give man and society a push in that right direction, Lindsay was attracted to Social Darwinism, for he shared the emphasis the movement's reform wing laid on the beneficial potential of environment. But his estimate of what the most enlightened individual, body, or state could achieve in the field of social improvement was insufficiently optimistic to carry him into their camp. In his eyes social justice could not be achieved solely by the correct understanding of biological, economic, or social laws. He did not share the nineteenth and early twentieth century version of the eighteenth century belief in the perfectibility of man, which is the foundation of democratic complacency, and of the belief in the evolution of self-evident and ultimately self-administering laws. He was not, on the other hand, a member of the sit-back-and-wait school. He hoped "My whisper engenders lions/Out of desert weeds";[55] he campaigned and cakewalked in the belief that he could stimulate the reform impulse. But he considered man's pretensions to possess complete solutions to be as false and as dangerous as apathy. Radical change would only come about if and when man's efforts won God's approval, and even then the nature of change was unpredictable. "It may not be/What we may plan," [56] Lindsay warned in "Johnny Appleseed Speaks of the Apple-Blossom Amaranth that Will Come to This City," a poem whose title summed up his belief in the ultimately divine nature of reform.

Lindsay's common ground with the turn of the century Social Gospel movement was similarly limited by his concept of change and by his opposition to partisan panaceas. The Social Gospel was at first a reluctant attempt by the American Protestant churches, traditional middle-class supporters of laissez-faire, to meet the gross inequalities brought by industrialization with some modification of individualism. Lindsay could accede to its emphasis on egalitarianism and Christian brotherhood and welcomed the movement as a shift away from harsh Spencerian individualism toward a strongly led and regulated socio-economic order. But its specifically urban and Protestant characteristics did not mix with his conception of interfaith unity; nor could he tolerate its frequent anti-industrial bias and condescension to the working man. There is a parallel, however, between Lindsay and one of the more liberal social gospelers, Walter Rauschenbusch (1861–1918), whose lack of class bias was reflected in his books *Christianizing the Social Order*, 1912, and *The Social Principles of Jesus*, 1915. Rauschenbusch, like Lindsay, believed in the dignity of labor, that "a man making a shoe or arguing a lawcase or planting potatoes or teaching school could feel that this was itself a contribution to the welfare of mankind, and indeed his main contribution to it." Both men belonged to a select school of realists. Rauschenbusch stated plainly that

in asking for faith in the possibility of a new social order, we ask for no Utopian delusion. We know well that there is no perfection for man in this life, there is only growth toward perfection.[57]

and Lindsay commented cynically:

many a worker sees his future America as a Utopia, in which his own profession, achieving dictatorship, alleviates the ills of men.[58]

There were other flashes of contact between Lindsay and social gospelers. George Herron's statement that "The Sermon of the Mount is the science of society" bears comparison with Lindsay's belief "in the Sermon on the Mount as the one test of society."[59] E. A. Ross's view that "we need an annual supplement to the Decalogue"[60] and Lindsay's idea of using the beatitudes as the basis of a new economic order were both expressions of a longing for ethical political and financial practices.

But although religion was one of Lindsay's few constants, his impressionable, undogmatic, and susceptible mind prevented him from saying a great deal more than that there was a God and an afterlife, there were commandments and they must be kept. With an awareness of his own frailty even in this comparative certainty—

> *My God, my God, this marvellous hour*
> *I am your son, I know.*
> *Once in a thousand days your voice*
> *Has laid temptation low*[61]

—he differed considerably from the general run of confident, and even brash ministrants of the Social Gospel and Reform Social Darwinism, who believed that they had hold of a panacea for a society just on the threshold of perfection. A similar diffidence was apparent in Lindsay's attitude toward political theory. Again his ideas reflected the man who sought equality but who was not convinced of the validity of any known or projected method of bringing about such a state of being. He applauded anyone who put forward heartfelt theories of governmental and social improvement: Robert La Follette, Brand Whitlock, F. C. Howe, Jane Addams, Tom Johnson, "Golden Rule" Jones, William Allen White, John P. Altgeld, and Henry George were his heroes. He admired Henry George tremendously, envisaging an annual Henry George dinner in Springfield 2018, but he said wistfully of the circle he frequented in twentieth century Springfield: *"They* [my italics] circulated *Progress and Poverty* like a new Bible,"[62] He alone could not accept it as definitive truth, though a new Bible would have been a tailor-made gospel for him.

Herbert Croly (1869–1930), who was editing *The New Republic* (1914–30) while Lindsay intermittently wrote its movie reviews, typified the school of thought with which Lindsay had so much in common, but which worked from an optimistic premise to which he could not subscribe. Croly was part of the stream of thought which accepted that America must automatically progress. Certainly changes were needed, and he felt that one of the reasons for progress in America was that men perceived the need for change when that need arose. In early twentieth century America a plethora of new creeds—New Nationalism, New Freedom, New Federalism, New Democracy (and New Localism)—added up to a demand to replace the imbalance of privileged individualism by a more even participation. Croly was flexible as to the means of change, for openmindedness was another condition of progress. In *The Promise of American Life,* 1909, he argued that the assertion of the power of the federal government over the states would pave the way to social reorganization; in *Progressive Democracy,* 1914, he began to wonder if it would be more efficient to put more power in the hands of the people in their localities.

Croly was flexible; but unlike Lindsay, he was flexible within a framework of some satisfaction, much optimism, and high expectations. He saw problems in soluble, institutional terms; Lindsay saw them as the formidable problems of the American mentality. Croly urged America to seek out a lay St. Michael with a flaming sword to cut a swathe through corrupt political practices, and to prepare for "the crowning work of some democratic St. Francis." The phrases might have been taken from "The Litany of Heroes" or *The Golden Book of Springfield,* but it was religious phraseology without the religious spirit. Croly went on to claim that "a profound sense of human brotherhood is not a substitute for specific efficiency"—brotherhood which Lindsay saw as the only basis of reforms which would bring America nearer a genuine democracy. Like Lindsay, Croly wanted "the reign of the good, the beautiful, the true" (a kind of Religion, Beauty, and Equality), but he joined himself with the American assumption of "absolute confidence in the power of the idea to create its object" to such an extent that he verged on the philistine:

Here, in America, some of us have more money than we need. . . . We will spend the money in order to establish the reign of the good, the beautiful, the true.[63]

Lindsay, with his belief in the inadequacy of institutional reform, went to the apolitical extreme:

> *Oh money, money—that never can think,*
> *Money, money, that never can rule,*
> *Always an anarchist, always an idiot,*
> *Always King Log—never King Stork,*
> *Always rotting, reeking: —always a fool.*[64]

Both men were overstating their case but they were nevertheless far apart. The crux of the divergence between Lindsay and Croly, and Lindsay and his fellow critics of America, was his inability to think in terms of minor social problems which could be dealt with by changes of personnel and machinery. He diagnosed a run-down, generally sick society, which could be cured only with difficulty, over a long period of time, and with maximum cooperation from society itself. He defined "our democratic dream" as "a middle-class aspiration built on a bog of toil-sodden minds." [65] His gospel tried to take away the national preoccupation with material goals—which confined efforts to extend human potential to getting and spending—and to replace it with a way of life based on the priorities of his versions of Religion, Equality, and Beauty.

CHAPTER TWO

Religion

THE THEMES of Lindsay's gospel—Religion, Equality, and Beauty —were almost interchangeable. None of the three fully existed for him without the presence, in some degree, of the other two: a mutual dependence which arose partly out of the strong emotional content of his gospel. It made him see religion in goodwill, a means to equality in anarchy, and beauty in character and action. His gospel was also unified by its basic theme, religion. He believed in equality not because he was impressed by manifestations of natural equality, but because it was a Christian teaching, and beauty existed for him less in externals than in the kind of conduct that should result from following religious precepts. Since he assumed that some kind of deity existed and some kind of religion was right and necessary, many of his comments were restatements of traditional religious positions. But characteristically, he tempered convention with the unexpected and the arresting, in this case by a church which tried to embrace all religions and religious philosophies, whether deistic creed or metaphysic concept, and which was intentionally undefinitive.

A church and a god: an effective dispensary and a supreme power for good—that was Lindsay's residual faith. H. L. Mencken, remarking that Lindsay was the only poet in *Who's Who* who was in the habit of giving a religious affiliation, painted the common picture of him as "a member of the Christian (Disciples) Church, a sect in the No-More-Scrub-Bulls Belt, with a private hell of its own, deep and hot." [1] The converse was also true: Lindsay was consciously and temperamentally unorthodox in religion. He

claimed "I am starting a new religious idea"—a faith of faiths—
and set out to be a leader, not a follower: "In the end I want you
to join my gang. *I do not want to join yours.*" [2]

Joining Lindsay's gang would not mean changing one sectarian
allegiance for another, but participating in a supra-ecumenical
movement. If pressed he would call himself a Christian and admit, as he did in *Who's Who,* that he had been baptized a Campbellite; but he also called himself "a Catholic with a few fads." [3]
Sometimes he thought of himself as an amalgam of the two. In
1909 he noted that he had

arbitrarily chosen the doctrine of tran-substantiation [sic] and the
doctrine of the Union of Christians. The first binds me to a deep
sympathy with the Mass. The second holds me in my hereditary
brotherhood.[4]

There were Humanist overtones to his emphasis on the spirit
rather than the dogma of religion, the spirit that Humanists like
John Dewey, George Santayana, and Charles H. Cooley tried to
isolate from its ecclesiastical context. An emotional and a theological distinction between the spiritual and the institutional church
was crucial for Lindsay's ecumenism. In spite of a belief in the
value of organized religion as a communal activity, and especially
in the value of interdenominational worship, he held to the primary
concept of the church as residing ultimately in the faithful themselves, however disconnected, and of whatever apparently different
affiliations. With a kind of theological Marxism he envisaged the
withering away of separate churches and the evolution of a new
religion of mankind, a world church. But even in the short term
he queried institutional religion, for it ran the danger of producing
sectarian rigidity rather than religious fellowship.

THE INFLUENCES OF CAMPBELL
AND SWEDENBORG

Lindsay was moving toward a redefinition of "church" and
"god" helped by Alexander Campbell's prior attempt to reduce
religion to its lowest common denominators. The Campbellite col-

lege Lindsay attended, Hiram College, Ohio (1897–1899), was an institution with a distinct ambience. Raymond B. Stevens, writing in 1929 of *The Social and Religious Influence of the Small Denominational College of the Middle West,* noted that these colleges were oriented around "responsibility to humanity," "service to society," and "the worthwhile things of life" rather than academic study.[5] For Lindsay there was no institution "as completely the flower of America as the co-educational religious western schools, which grow up out of the ground as naturally as the blue grass and the Indian corn. . . ."[6] But, true to paradoxical type, his affection for Hiram did not make him a strict Campbellite; it was the college's idealistic, community-conscious mood, not its separatism that he admired. Campbellites were "as limited as any class as ever existed," he wrote, and they were consequently not palatable to a man who thought in terms of ecumenism, who felt affinity with "the Unitarians . . . all the Evangelical Protestants, especially the Disciples of Christ . . . the Mass, the Eucharist, the Virgin Mary."[7]

Lindsay had more in common with Campbell himself than with the organized church which bore his name. Campbell, seeking to reconstitute primitive, indivisible Christianity, taught that the Bible must be interpreted literally. According to him no church organization had a right to impose on its members any ceremony, duty, or activity not specifically provided for in the Bible. He did not profess any radical opinion, or commit any doctrinal unorthodoxy as such; he merely argued that each man with his Bible could serve and obey God to perfection. Lindsay, too, valued individual spiritual life above obedience to intermediaries, and adhered more strictly to the logical tolerance of this theology than the generations of increasingly sectarian Campbellites who pared down Campbellism proper. He applauded Campbell's plea that all Christians "call themselves 'simply' Christians and unite on those symbols and ordinances which Christendom has in common."[8]

Lindsay also associated himself with Campbell's ideas about civil society: his emphasis on the unity of education through the local interaction of family, church, and school; and his belief in international government and the missionary role of American democracy in the political world. Lindsay saw him as a father of the republic rather than a priest, and as a progenitor of the American way of life Lindsay himself advocated. In a preface to three poems dedicated to Campbell—"My Fathers Came from Kentucky," "Written in a Year When Many of My People Died," and "A Rhymed Address to All Renegade Campbellites Exhorting Them to Return"—Lindsay quoted an essay of Campbell's in which he explained the perpetual change and built-in obsolescence which characterized the American scene in the only terms Lindsay could accept: as a recurringly inventive, ingenious exploitation of the material universe, whose "new tenantries, new employments, new pleasures, new joys, new ecstasies" [9] were made possible by the limitlessness and fullness of God's creation.

Campbell's debates about Christianity with the utopian Robert Owen in 1828 brought out the latitude of thinking which attracted Lindsay as much as Campbell's rationalization of the forever New World. In the debates Owen stated that there were twelve discernible laws of human nature and that to obey them meant the incorruptible society. Campbell argued that life had only one certain principle—love. He opposed definitive utopianism and the concept of a uniquely enlightened group of people or faith; he hoped that his own comparatively undoctrinal church would be the beginning of an international, interdenominational Church of Christ. Lindsay went one step further by advocating that belief in any form of supreme power or principle of good was sufficient basis for a move toward universal spiritual unity. He paid a backhanded compliment to Campbellism in making the main religious leader in Springfield 2018 a Catholic priest, the reincarnation of a 1918 Campbellite minister. This gesture summed up his attitude toward the Disciples of Christ. He could not dissociate himself from them, for emotional ties were too strong, but he could happily have seen them dissolved in some more universal faith, of which Catholicism, though Christian, was the most tangible example.

From adolescence onward Lindsay came to be influenced by the eighteenth century Swedish philosopher, theologian, and mystic, Emanuel Swedenborg (1688–1772). Swedenborg expounded his idiosyncratic approach to Christianity in more than twenty books, the most popular of which were *Heaven and Hell* (1758) and *The True Christian Religion* (1771). He did not found a church as such, but his writings inspired the setting up of Swedenborgian churches—known variously as the Churches of New Jerusalem and the New Churches—throughout the world. The first such church in America was founded in 1792, and pockets of Swedenborgianism appeared throughout America, most strongly in Boston, Philadelphia, and Baltimore.

Lindsay called this informal church "an almost invisible sect"; he joined with interest in the discussions of Springfield's "Swedenborgian [mystic] circle." But he said firmly that he was "never a literal Swedenborgian," and only some of its teachings rubbed off on him. Swedenborgianism has habitually been many things to many men, a faith plundered by individuals seizing upon some congenial theory and calling themselves Swedenborgians without examining the whole corpus of Swedenborg's doctrines. Henry James, Sr., for instance, was not recognized by the official sect as a Swedenborgian though he called himself one since he subscribed to Swedenborg's central designation of God as "the grand and infinite man," a teaching whose traces were apparent in Lindsay's attempt to write about biblical events in human, proximate terms. But there is no evidence in Lindsay's writings of Swedenborg's corollary of divine humanity—his justification of human weakness. Swedenborg argued that if Christ had been man and became perfect God, other men, who could only hope to approximate his virtues sketchily, could rightly, even arrogantly, assume their perfectibility. Were God to demand spotless conduct and perfect respect he would be committing (impossibly) the sin of pride. He intended human beings to behave toward him as toward a fellow human being; and to approach him with feelings of humility or guilt, in the context of a special relationship, would be to commit the sin of "selfhood." [10] Lindsay, on the contrary, felt that a lack of "selfhood" was one of America's problems; in his own relationship with God he was conscious of an almost insurmountable inequality.

Why should I feel the sobbing, the secrecy, the glory,
This comforter, this fitful wind divine?
I, the cautious Pharisee, the scribe, the whited sepulchre—
I have no right to God, he is not mine.[11]

In this central point of Swedenborgian doctrine Lindsay was certainly not a literal Swedenborgian. But the almost equally important and vastly more colorful Swedenborgian teaching on the nature of heaven and hell was strongly echoed in his writings. Swedenborg claimed to base this teaching on a divine revelation about "The Science of Correspondences." This body of "revealed knowledge" emphasized the likeness of heaven, hell, and earth, just as Swedenborg had earlier emphasized the likeness of God and man. Divine truths had specific physical expressions on earth. For instance, "gardens and groves signified wisdom and intelligence and every particular tree, something that had relation thereto; as the olive, the good of love; the vine, truth derived from that good; the cedar, good and truth rational; a mountain signified the highest heaven, a hill, the heaven beneath." [12] Similarly, in *The Golden Book of Springfield,* Lindsay attributed a "higher" significance to natural objects. In Springfield 2018 "he who eats of the Amaranth Apple is filled with a love of eternal beauty, and it is used as the City's understood symbol of beauty." "He who, after certain prayers, eats of certain acorns or walks under the oak saplings that come from them, accepts in some sense, divine promptings towards eternal goodness." [13] But again, Lindsay was not a literal Swedenborgian. He was modifying the Science of Correspondences, for the significance of natural objects in Springfield 2018 was a significance given to them by man, not stemming from spiritual prototypes. The symbolism was conscious, not inevitable.

As part of the revelation of the Science of Correspondences Swedenborg claimed to have been taken on a conducted tour of heaven and hell by God, a tour which showed him the total correspondence of the spiritual and natural worlds. All countries and nationalities were to be found in the spiritual world, and although America and the Americans did not appear in the reminiscences of his travels in *The True Christian Religion,* England and the English did.

In the spiritual World there are two great cities like London, which most of the English enter after death. I have been entitled to enter and explore the chief of the two. The centre of the city answers to the London Exchange, where the merchants meet, and this is where the rulers live.

Men and women continued their earthly lives in eternity, made love, felt hate. The really bad happily continued their earthly wicked ways in the state of hell, the rest in the state of heaven, with the mere difference of "more interior delight." [14]

This aspect of the Science of Correspondences demonstrably stimulated Lindsay's imagination. It has often seemed strange that in "Simon Legree," while Lindsay was on the side of Harriet Beecher Stowe, he made Legree's hell such a rollicking place. It was simply a Swedenborgian concept: Legrees would be at home in hell. There he and the devil contentedly

> . . . *sit and gnash their teeth,*
> *And each one wears a hop-vine wreath.*
> *They are matching pennies and shooting craps,*
> *They are playing poker and taking naps.*
> *And old Legree is fat and fine.*

Similarly, Lindsay came to think of heaven in Swedenborg's topographical terms; he wrote of "the gold-built cliffs of heaven" in terms of the Deep South, with the "streets knee-deep in moss/And the mansions heavy with trees." He could visualize heaven as a physical state, as a celestial circus where he and a girl

> . . . *Will ride in the joy of God*
> *On circus horses white.*
> *Your feet will be white lightning,*
> *Your spangles white and regal,*
> *We will leap from the horses' backs*
> *To the cliffs of day and night.*[15]

The "Map of the Universe," which Lindsay published in 1909, also sprang out of Swedenborgianism. Its importance for him was shown by the fact that he proudly reproduced a slightly different version of it as the frontispiece to *Collected Poems,* and explored

the same territory in twelve poems.[16] The Map and its detailed
key depicted an earthly heaven, a place of chaos and constant flux.
Lucifer was safely sealed in his tomb, but the scar of his fall remained in heaven in the form of the Gulfs of Silence; there were
still jungles there, untrimmed vines, rotted harps, swords of rusted
gold, and desolate, deserted halls. Angels had to shed their blood
for the redemption of the world; prophets had to bring it down
to earth in their boats to anoint men and to recruit forces for
Christianity. In its own way heaven was a work-a-day world, with
its reminders and consciousness of the perpetual conflict of values.
Lindsay's Map symbolized these as a spider (Mammon) and a
butterfly (Beauty).

Lindsay drew the "Map of the Universe" to emphasize that
heaven and hell were as integral and inescapable parts of the
world as earth. His use of physical imagery and symbolism was
intended to bring spiritual abstractions to life, and so was the
liberty he took with tradition. He replaced the mystical concept
of redemption through Christ on the cross and in the sacraments
with the more easily imagined picture of angels continually shed-
ding their blood in the battle with evil for man. But if anything,
Lindsay diminished imaginative interest in religion; heaven and
hell tend to lose their unfathomable fascination when reduced to
comprehensible worlds of fairy tale and nightmare. His Map was
a trial and an error of propaganda; it was a curiosity; but it was a
measure of his belief in the growing irrelevance of traditional
Christian imagery and concepts.

"In a time of critical reason and definite division, he was possessed by a fervour and a fury of belief. . . . He had a devil and its
name was Faith." [17] These words were written not, as might be
supposed, about Lindsay moving in an intellectual climate of Darwinism, Pragmatism, Humanism, and Fundamentalism, but about
William Blake, with whom as an artist, a poet, some species of
mystic, and a Swedenborgian, Lindsay had so much in common.
They were also both epileptics, a condition to which visions—or
hallucinations—are often attributed.

Lindsay had plundered Blake's illustrations of Dante's *Inferno*

One of several versions of "The Map of the Universe."

and *The Book of Job* for the structural outlines of his Map (Blake's diagram of the fall of Satan), for his boats of the prophets (Charon's boats), and for his style of drawing clouds and tree roots (Job's background). Blake's Druidical Temple of Moral Law became Lindsay's Palace of Eve; his truncated primeval giants sunk in the soil became Lindsay's Thrones of the Trinity. Lindsay admitted [18] that he tried to draw like Blake (though he did not mention the details of his plagiarism), and that he was also reflecting some of Blake's ideas. Blake, like Lindsay after him, had explored the topography of heaven and its relation to hell. In *The Marriage of Heaven and Hell* and *The Four Zoas* he had visited worlds different in space and time from his own, and, just as Lindsay in his Map (and later in *The Golden Book of Springfield*), found strife and warfare there on a vast scale. The contrast between the two men is equally telling. Blake used his considerable artistic talent and a complex mixture of paradox, satire, allegory, and inversion to point home a compelling moral of religious reformation, and to make more real the relationship between this world and the next. These aims were also Lindsay's, but by comparison, the structure of his ideas and their execution seem sketchy and slight. Yet the comparison gives Lindsay definition, and Blake in turn becomes more comprehensible after looking at the rudimentary terms of Lindsay's vision. For the "Map of the Universe" bore the Swedenborgian hallmark which was on Blake too. Both men were characterized by their derivation from Swedenborg of an intense perception of the reality of heaven and hell, and each might have described himself in Swedenborg's words as just an "enterprising traveller to a far country." [19]

It is almost impossible to draw the line between such super-realism and mysticism. For the mystic vision has the substance of reality, and can be seen with the mind's and the body's eye. Lindsay and Blake both claimed such vision. "You have only to work up imagination to the state of vision, and the thing is done," Blake wrote, and Lindsay described the state of vision as "a real dream." What for other men were mere vague allegories became for them hard facts. Blake explained himself by the phrase "For

All Things Exist in the Human Imagination"; Lindsay saw "pictures burning heart and conscience away." [20]

Lindsay did not delude himself that he was more than intermittently mystic. His visionary capacity was not of the sort that "I might in some ignorant stratum of society have built a better city than Salt Lake City or Zion City." [21] His visions were "inspired but by no means infallible. They were metaphors of the day, consolations of the hour." So he "determined to make them the servants, not the masters of my philosophy," and turned his visions to literary use. Their vividness enabled him to translate God, Christ, heaven, and religious incident almost casually into an effective twentieth century idiom. For example, he saw Old Testament Daniel as Darius the Mede's "chief hired man."

> *He whitewashed the cellar. He shovelled in the coal.*
> *And Daniel kept-a-praying:—"Lord save my soul."*

> *His sweetheart and his mother were Christian and meek,*
> *They washed and ironed for Darius every week.*
> *One Thursday he met them at the door:—*
> *Paid them as usual, but acted sore.*

> *He said—"Your Daniel is a dead little pigeon.*
> *He's a good hard worker, but he talks religion."*
> *And he showed them Daniel in the lion's cage.*[22]

Nevertheless Lindsay's occasional "visions" sprang from an intensity of imagination which he felt was tantamount to experiencing the past. "I tell you I was Solomon, the son of David, king in Jerusalem; and the Queen of Sheba came walking to me upon the crystal floor . . . I was Mohamet . . . I was Confucius . . . ," [23] he wrote after a visit to Europe in 1905, when he was soaked in religious art and history to the extent of claiming such mystical identification. Blake underwent a similar projection: "I am Socrates —Moses—Isaiah." [24] For Lindsay such emotional identification was certainly temporary. In the cool of rationality he pared down his vision to the unspecific perception that "hidden behind many veils of sense, lies the future, lies the infinite." [25] But his continuous sense of the infinite interacted with his attempt to show America the awful and glorious implications of infinity, and it sustained and reinforced him in keeping ultimate goals in mind, however modest the immediate destination.

CHRISTIANITY

Each notebook and diary that Lindsay kept in the first thirty years of his life began with the dedication "This book belongs to Christ." At one time he tried to make the chronology of his development parallel Christ's, planning to reach manhood and maturity as the Jewish Christ did at the age of thirty, and it was in 1909, when he was thirty, that he began to theorize publicly in his *War Bulletins*. As an eighteen-year-old, grandiose missionary fever had taken hold of him. "I have a world to save, and must prepare, prepare," he wrote in 1897. This aim never entirely left him, though growing maturity and lack of success diminished his self-confidence. He never lost, however, his conviction of the intrinsic worth of the simple religious beliefs of childhood.

I say one may ascend terrace after terrace in this scale of illuminated doubt and the last shall be nothing but the dogmatic unquestioning faith we left so far below us in childhood.

This was a description of "that tolerably right dogmatism," [26] faith in the reality of a good, omnipotent deity that was the only form of religious dogmatism that Lindsay permitted himself: childlike, and unspeculative. The reconciliation of specific dogmas of different faiths presented an unknown, potentially negative, and possibly interminable challenge, and Lindsay chose instead to try to get to the core of the instinct of faith, the instinct which could subscribe to his residual concepts of a church and a god.

He moved away from the traditional picture of the Holy Ghost as the carrier of Christianity to depict a nondoctrinal spirit of goodwill, fellowship, and unselfishness, a spirit which could easily be preempted for ecumenism. This spirit became a recurrent theme in his writing on Christianity, and he used a suitably pervasive image, that of incense, to represent it. His drawings and poems abounded with censer images: the illustrations to the *Village Mag-*

azines, "Incense and Splendor," and "Johnny Appleseed Speaks of Great Cities in the Future," for example. In "The Soul of the City Receives the Gift of the Holy Spirit" verbal and pictorial censers swung over all denominations of Springfield's churches, its public buildings, and every place in Springfield associated with Lincoln. Censers and the incense they emitted had a composite symbolism: they were at once the source of reformation

> *Censers are swinging*
> *Over the town,*
> *Censers gigantic!*
> *Look overhead!*
> *Hear the winds singing:—*
> *Heaven comes down,*

the need for reformation ("City, dead city/Awake from the dead"), and the augury of religious resurgence:

> *My friends, the incense-time has but begun.*
> *Creed upon creed, cult upon cult shall bloom,*
> *Shrine after shrine grow gray beneath the sun.*

Without doctrinal trappings, "religious," not "Christian," became the definitive adjective for the incense spirit. It would be the common element in a cult to include worshippers from the Chinese hills and the Ganges; it prefigured "one shining, universal church/ Where all Faiths kneel, as brothers, in one place." [27] Lindsay described this envisaged mingling of creeds most lucidly in "The Wedding of the Rose and the Lotus." He illustrated the poem with a drawing of a kind of amalgamated flower, "a visible symbol of good-will between all the races of mankind. It can be painted on the wall of every temple, shrine, tomb, state-house, court-house and hut of the world." Amalgamation could ultimately be achieved "without destroying or interfering with any government, race integrity, religious prejudice or philosophic dogma of Buddha or Swedenborg or any saint between." For just as each form of Christianity (Catholicism's authoritarianism, Christian Science's belief in the miraculous, for instance) was justified by human diversity and the variety of human needs, so, in a faith of faiths, each creed made its special contribution: Buddhism, the cool lotus, an emphasis on meditation; Christianity, the burgeoning rose, an active social conscience. The relationship of non-Christian faiths and Christianity was complementary:

> *The genius of the lotus*
> *Shall heal earth's too-much fret.*
> *The rose, in blinding glory,*
> *Shall waken Asia yet.*[28]

Lindsay's belief in the viability of interdenominational cooperation was not merely wishful thinking; it was based on experience. In his circle at Springfield, he had the pleasure of seeing "Catholic, and Protestant, Jew and Greek . . . all brought to fine speaking terms . . ." In visiting churches, cathedrals, meetinghouses, and synagogues he was often struck by the sheer holy atmosphere of a building, for example,

In the great synagogue of Amsterdam I felt tempted, I was even eager to bow and kiss the law after the Jewish manner, and to do it honor, as the host in an R.C. church.[29]

But what of the elements in which faiths and philosophies differed from each other? Lindsay ignored (and probably intended to abandon) controversial tenets which would negate ecumenism; ecumenism had become his personal new religion. He tried not to be didactic while remaining honest, and not to be exclusive while remaining principled. He was forced back on generalities, which *he* found acceptable. Exegesis was not likely to secure wide audiences for Lindsay's gospel, and it might have prevented the theory of his ecumenism from getting off the ground. But for many more conventional and analytical believers there had to be minute doctrinal comparisons before it could be seen if such a variety of beliefs had enough in common even to talk of unity or reconciliation. Lindsay's technic of maximizing unifying factors in a faith of faiths was perhaps the only possible starting point, but he paid the penalty of a tolerance which was at once the virtue and the vice of his ecumenism. It enabled him to think in terms of a world church, but it led him to underestimate sectarian integrity and individual tenacity of belief. He arrived at a concept which was only realistic in terms of his own inclusiveness. He did avoid another pitfall of tolerance, the excuse for a passive acceptance of the status quo which a belief in some good in all manifestations of humanity provides, for he believed that individual and social salvation were contingent on a Christ-like involvement in the full range of human activities.

Christ's humanity, like the spirit of the Holy Ghost, was an aspect of Christianity Lindsay thought universally sympathetic and comprehensible. All people—workers, politicians, teachers, and criminals, for example—could identify with some part of Christ's diverse experience of what it meant to be a human being, and each individual could have his image of Christ. General William Booth and the Salvation Army imagined a tactile Christ, the miracle worker and savior.

> *Jesus came from out the court-house door,*
> *Stretched his hands above the passing poor.*
> *Booth saw not, but led his queer ones there*
> *Round and round the mighty court-house square.*
> *Then, in an instant all that blear review*
> *Marched on spotless, clad in raiment new.*
> *The lame were straightened, withered limbs uncurled*
> *And blind eyes opened on a new, sweet world.*[30]

Lindsay's Christ was physical, too, but in terms of Christ's human, not his divine nature.

> *He was ruddy like a shepherd.*
> *His bold young face, how fair.*
> *Apollo of the silver bow*
> *Had not such flowing hair.*[31]

In the mystical aftermath of his trip to Europe in 1905 Lindsay felt his hands on the fringes of Christ's Angelico-red robe; he heard Christ's song of peaceful happiness: "how can I write the gray memory of that song?"[32] Here was another dimension of the god-like man, supremely beautiful and supremely artistic.

Lindsay came nearer to the spirituality of Christ in a pantheistic sensing of

> *Christ the dew in the clod,*
> *Christ the sap of the trees,*
> *Christ the light of the waterfall,*
> *Christ the soul of the sun.*[33]

But Christ's relationship with his divine father, his mystical dimension, eluded Lindsay, who puzzled:

Was Christ's experience based on real facing of the facts of his life, the God he actually knew, or the God he dreamed he knew? Was it a spiritual short-circuit in the head, the flash of fuse, like Paul's vision; or was it a true hand to hand contract? [34]

The metaphysics of divinity bewildered him, for he was unable to approach theology intellectually. Ironically, while he was trying to make the abstract real to others, he himself could not come to grips with the abstraction of God (nor with the concept of the trinity). He was too conscious of human predicaments and injustices to think in terms of a benevolent father figure or a temperate arbiter; and for all his ingenuity in adapting biblical history, he could not find an alternative propaganda image. His continuing profession of belief in God stemmed from an idiosyncratic act of faith: faith in a deity of which the Christian God was probably only one valid aspect, faith held as much in aversion as in adoration of the revelation of divinity. For to accept a world of chaotic and tragic incident as God-given, or God-permitted went against the grain of his emotional logic; he could only rationalize his dilemma through an acceptance of the Old Testament God.

In " 'The Scissors Grinder' (An Unconscious Prophecy, written in 1913)" Lindsay described this jealous, punitive God who habitually used the moon as an emery wheel to whet his sword of righteous wrath.

> *The ditches must flow red, the plague*
> *Go stark and screaming by.*
> *Each time that sword of God takes edge*
> *Within the midnight sky.*[35]

Blake had shied at the old God in "Tiger, Tiger": "Did he who made the lamb make thee?"; and on the American scene, some years before Lindsay, the utopian Edward Bellamy (1850–98) had found God an obstacle when he sketched out his "Religion of Solidarity," in which he too sought for an international spiritual brotherhood "to call men out of the narrow paradise of selfish loves and interests, and make them realise the larger ties and greater duties . . . as sons, not of men, but of man, as brothers, not of this man or that man, but of all men." He could not associate God with the loving and giving of ecumenism, or with Christ, for

to suppose Christ God would be to detract from his glory, would be to hold him responsible for the woes of humanity, which, far from being responsible for, he tried to cure.[36]

Bellamy turned sometimes to humanism, sometimes to pantheism to resolve his dilemma; Lindsay, in spite of his emotional inability to comprehend God, continued to believe in him. The term "mystery of faith" could hardly be more appropriate than in his case; he believed in a truth above and seemingly contrary to his reason. But he did exercise an independent judgment in demanding an explanation of God which made religious sense in the twentieth century, a new God.

> *Oh Lord my God, awaken from the dead!*
>
> . . . .
>
> *I see you there, half-buried in the sand.*
> *I see you there, your white bones glistening bare*
> The carrion-birds a-wheeling round your head.[37]

"I Went Down into the Desert," in which Lindsay wrote of God as dead, implied that even Christ, and ultimately the Holy Ghost, would die with God the Father, as his resurrection was vital to Christianity. And since his God was as much an emblem of deity as a Christian God, Lindsay was suggesting the peril of all concepts of spirituality and "otherness." He could not find a new image for the old God, or bring new life to the concept of deity any more than the current protagonists of the "God is Dead" controversy have so far succeeded in doing, but he pinpointed what may well prove to be the crucial theological debate of the second half of the twentieth century.

Lindsay ran the gamut of Christian attitudes. The old God might be dead but the old devil was very much alive, and as a member of the Church Militant, Lindsay rejoiced in the Salvation Army. "Every time the General hits the drum he hits the Devil in the eye for me."[38] God might be dead but Lindsay remained heavily conscious of sin, praying, "Give us no other joy but our repentance." And yet, he noted in "General William Booth . . . ," God could pardon

> *Lurching bravos from the ditches dank,*
> *Drabs from the alleyways, and drug fiends pale—*
> *Minds still passion-ridden, soul-powers frail.*

The God of "Daniel" would answer simple faith:

> *And Daniel did not frown,*
> *Daniel did not cry,*
> *He kept on looking at the sky.*
> *And the Lord said to Gabriel:—*
> *"Go chain the lions down."*[39]

Retribution and compassion, the Church Militant and a dead God: so much of the complex fabric of Christianity was mirrored in Lindsay's writings that his attachment to Christianity cannot be dismissed. It would seem that ecumenism was an effort, even for him, and was all the more remarkable because of the effort involved. Lindsay did, in fact, admit that if religious unity had to come through the assertion of one faith, and not through the amalgamation of many, he had to favor Christianity. In the context of this hypothesis, in "Foreign Missions in Battle Array," he wondered "will Christ outlive Mohammed?/Will Kali's altar go?" and acknowledged:

> *This is our faith tremendous,—*
> *Our wild hope, who shall scorn,—*
> *That in the name of Jesus*
> *The world will be reborn!*[40]

Yet even if Christianity were to prevail, Lindsay warned, a new spirit of religious tolerance would be required in the West. There would be "a Christ with an elephant's head carved in India . . . a Christ guarded by gilded dragons in China"[41] that would seem alien, disrespectful, even heretical to Western eyes, though he found nothing strange about radically different expressions of a universal truth. It was this acceptance of the unconventional, even when he was at his most conventional, that set Lindsay apart from the contemporary American religious reform movement to which he was closest: Christian Socialism (which was virtually synonymous with Walter Rauschenbusch's wing of the Social Gospel movement). To make the point that Christianity was meant for and needed by the whole of society, Christian Socialists, like Lindsay preached an immanent rather than a transcendent God, worked for social rather than individual salvation, and subscribed to the good-will ethic as the only means of ensuring lasting reforms. But unlike Lindsay, they confined such precepts to reaffirming the relevance of Christianity; and while he noted, approvingly, that Alexander Campbell had been something of a Christian Socialist,[42] Christian Socialism, Campbellism, and Christianity itself could only contribute to his faith of faiths; they could not constitute that faith itself.

HEROES OF ECUMENISM

An emotionally religious man like Lindsay found spiritual ideas most comprehensible in terms of personalities, and to try to get men to admit the truths of common origins and interests, common bodies and souls, he decided to emphasize the likeness of religious leaders and philosophers. He chose as ecumenical heroes the reasonably uncontroversial figures of St. Francis, Confucius, and Buddha, all of whom already had a minimal intellectual acceptance in America. (Not so Mohammed, who was therefore limited to a brief but ecumenical reference in "The Litany of Heroes" in which Lindsay looked forward to the time when "New America, ancient Mizraim/Cry: 'Allah is the God of Abraham.'"[43]) The three men were Lindsay's heroes for formulating principled ways of life which were standing the test of time, and they had genuine relevance to his gospel: St. Francis for his teaching of anti-affluence, Confucius for his attempt to recruit for government on the egalitarian basis of merit, and Buddha for his indictment of covetousness. Lindsay was also attracted to them for personal reasons: to St. Francis in his capacity as an itinerant poet, "God's Troubadour," [44] to Confucius for his conception of the ideal man, and to Buddha for his teaching of sexual continence.

St. Francis' prime importance for Lindsay's gospel was to show what the world might be—a huge, peaceful brotherhood—and what it was not. The mere hypothesis of his presence in twentieth century San Francisco was incongruous and ironic. While he wanted to hear the prayers of young Christians

> *White-souled like young aspens*
> *With whimsies and fancies untold:—*
> The opposite of gold.

he heard the gross inquisition of "The Golden Whales of California," wallowing in materialism.

> What *is the color of the cup and plate*
> *And knife and fork of the chief of state?*
> Gold, gold, gold.
> What *is the flavor of the Bartlett pear?*
> What *is the savor of the salt sea air?*
> Gold, gold, gold.[45]

The simplicity and minimal wants of the Franciscan way of life provided the strongest contrast that Lindsay could supply to this America. He wanted to see a sense of spiritual priorities and an other-regarding philosophy, and wrote that had he the power to make every man see a revivalist vision; that vision would be of St. Francis.

I wish that, going out of the church door at noon, every worshipper in America could spiritually discern the Good St. Francis come down to our earth and singing of the Sun. I wish that saint would return.[46]

Confucianism too had morals for America. Confucius had believed in co-operation as the natural state of society, and had seen the feudalism and aristocracy of his China as social perversions. To critics who pointed out obvious inequalities of ability and responsibility he replied that people were naturally reasonable and moral, and they could be educated to make decisions and value-judgments: Lindsay's contentions for Americans. But although Confucius believed in a meritocracy, he thought that it would be a new elite, governing the people rather than reflecting its wishes; he did not subscribe to Lindsay's profound egalitarianism of capacity. Yet in spite of their differences, Confucius was important to Lindsay as a reformer like himself, who gave a serious diagnosis of social ills, and who prescribed no overnight remedy. Recovery was distant, and as Lindsay looked to "the far future," he celebrated Confucius as "the world's most patient gentleman."[47] In "Shantung" he meaningfully compared Confucius with the impatient reform mentality of Trotsky and Nietzsche, and the quickly spent, easily satisfied reform impulse of Roosevelt and Wilson.

Confucianism was not a religion in the deistic, Western sense of the word, nor was Confucius a conventional religious leader. Viewing heaven as an impersonal ethical force which human beings could not hope to fathom, he urged concentration on this life. But for Lindsay, Confucius' appeal lay in this effective secularization of ideals which seemed to confirm the viability of the Christian code in Western political society. And in celebrating through Confucius the vaunted Chinese qualities of dignity, humility, patience, and a measured way of life, Lindsay also managed to imply that they could be profitably imitated by Americans. The ramifications of ecumenism extended to political society and national character, as he was to make clear in his definitions of Equality and Beauty.

The element of Lindsay's personal interest in Confucianism sprang from the Confucian concept of "gentleman." Lindsay was familiar with James Legge's translation of Confucius' *Analects,* and "gentleman" was Legge's rendering of *Shih. Shih* was later better rendered by Arthur Waley's "knight," and this Chaucerian and Tennysonian concept was close to the chivalric, contemplative species which Lindsay thought the masculine ideal. Lindsay made the point that this was as yet an un-American type in a brutal contrast: holding up as an example of *Shih* in "The Chinese Nightingale" Chang, a Chinese laundryman, a racial type traditionally regarded by Americans as inferior. Chang maintained his equilibrium and courtesy amid the "license, lust and play" of San Francisco; he burnt his joss sticks with precise religious observance; he knew his source of contentment to be his subscription to non-material standards:

> *"I will tell you a secret," Chang replied,*
> *"My breast with vision is satisfied."* [48]

Jefferson and Emerson had been influenced by the Confucian concept of a meritocracy, and in the mid- and late nineteenth century there was considerable interest among American intellectuals in Buddhism. Much as Lindsay reacted against the limits of Midwestern Campbellism, Emerson, Thoreau, and Alcott, in their Transcendentalist reaction against New England Calvinism, read extensively in and around world religions. In his book *Ten Great Religions,* 1888, their neighbor and collaborator James Freeman Clarke, a Unitarian minister in Boston, came to subscribe to a single spirituality, like Lindsay after him. Clarke tried to popularize among a less elite public than the Transcendentalists the idea that "if one worships a being as supreme and . . . most merciful, most wise, . . . is he not worshipping the true God? Does it matter what name he gives him—Jehovah, Jove, Brahma or Buddha?" [49]

His conviction, and Lindsay's, that it did not matter is surely arguable. If Confucianism is hardly a religion, Buddhism is oddly Christian. Christian joy in creation, and the total involvement of Christ in society is not obviously paralleled by the central Buddhist aim of self-immolation from any kind of social contact in an effort to purify oneself, and to shorten the number of expiatory rebirths into a tedious and painful world. Nevertheless, Buddhism has traditionally and validly been seen as a teaching of a species of compassion for the human state, and building on that base Lindsay felt able to write of Buddha and his followers in terms equally applicable to St. Francis and the Franciscans (though the setting was different):

> *Would that by Hindu magic we became*
> *Dark monks of jewelled India long ago,*
> *Sitting at Prince Siddartha's feet to know*
> *The foolishness of gold and love and station,*
> *The gospel of the Great Renunciation,*
> *The ragged cloak, the staff, the rain and sun,*
> *The beggar's life. . . .*[50]

With a similar identification, in "Above the Battle's Front" he imagined Buddha and St. Francis hovering in spirit over the battlefields of the 1914–18 war, anguished and compassionate.

But it was for its negation of physical desire that Lindsay personally turned to Buddhism. Buddha had stated categorically

do not make anyone or anything beloved, since separation from the beloved is bad; then there is neither fondness nor the absence of fondness.

He warned especially against relations between the sexes, against "the longing for sons and wives that is the strong one." [51] Lindsay developed this theme in his three "Poems speaking of Buddha, Prince Siddartha." In "The Fireman's Ball" he described a band seducing and intoxicating the dancers, until

> *Their eyes flash power,*
> *Their lips are dumb.*
> *Faster and faster*
> *Their pulses come,*
> *Though softer now*
> *The drum-beats fall.*
> *Honey and wine,*
> *Honey and wine.*

The result of this stimulation was the death of true love (not asexual love, but not solely sexual or temporary love). "I die,"

> *Cries true-love,*
> *There laid low.*

"When the fire-dreams come,
The wise dreams go."

The poem's moral was the evil of any consuming desire. In a prologue to the poem Lindsay had quoted Buddha.

Everything, mendicants, is burning. With what fire is it burning? I declare unto you it is burning with the fire of passion, with the fire of anger, with the fire of ignorance. It is burning with the anxieties of birth, decay and death, grief, lamentation, suffering and despair.

Lindsay translated this diagnosis as the words of "a teacher/Who turned from desire" and who warned "wine is a fire," "gold is a flame," "hate is a fire," "power is a flame." Certainly Lindsay opposed gold when it meant materialism at the expense of spiritual values, power when politically abused, hate as an irreligious sentiment, and wine when it mocked natural dignity. But to him the prologue was not solely a diagnosis of self-indulgence as the root of social evils; it was also an elaborate rationalization of his attraction to Buddhism. As one of the great religions, and as one viewed not unsympathetically in some quarters in America, Buddhism was an essential component of his inter-religious ecumenism. But he drew on it heavily for religious reinforcement and comfort during a long, uncomfortable period of premarital celibacy. In guarding against the sexual desires which he construed as a positive spiritual danger, Lindsay called on Buddhism to

> *Clear the streets,*
> *BOOM, BOOM,*
> *GIVE THE ENGINES ROOM,*
> *GIVE THE ENGINES ROOM,*
> *LEST SOULS BE TRAPPED*
> *IN A TERRIBLE TOMB.*[52]

St. Francis, Confucius, and Buddha and the faiths they represented were indispensable to ecumenism, not merely because they existed, and had to be assimilated, but because they made unique contributions to a potential world faith and to spiritual reform. Lindsay regarded all the components of his faith as positive assets, not grudging inclusions or tempered compromises. Yet could such a commitment hold good for anyone except Lindsay and his like? How many people could go straight to the essence of spirituality, morality, and brotherhood, discarding ceremony, institutions, man-made and revealed doctrines, and still feel that they retained a meaningful, principled creed? The irony of Lindsay's ecumenism was that it was only possible for those, like himself, capable of commitment to humanity and ruthlessness with personal preference. And it was possible. Unlikely as it may seem in a world in which faiths are institutionally disparate and dogmatically hostile within themselves, Lindsay embraced with conviction the spirituality of all men in one divine creation, the same conviction which underlay his belief in the secular brotherhood of equality:

> *Hail to their loves, ye peoples!*
> *Behold, a world-wind blows,*
> *That aids the ivory lotus*
> *To wed the red, red rose!* [53]

CHAPTER THREE

Equality

EQUALITY AND DEMOCRACY are overworked terms in America; and Lindsay did little to clarify their infrastructure. He did not analyze electoral procedures, constitutional checks and balances, party conventions, or any of the components of the American democratic machinery. He did, of course, celebrate as democrats William Jennings Bryan in "Bryan, Bryan, Bryan, Bryan," John Peter Altgeld in "The Eagle That Is Forgotten," and Theodore Roosevelt in "Roosevelt," but in the primary contexts of American history and a potential American entity. He thought of Equality in general terms of the actual and possible effects of democracy rather than in tangible terms of political machinery, individual politicians, or substantial economic equality. Working from his religious assumption of a natural instinct for brotherhood which had been submerged in an artificial society, he based his theory of Equality on the belief "that the only social tie, and the only motive between citizen and citizen is to be respected."[1] He believed such a motive to be vital to that functional equality which could only exist when each American admitted and demanded every American's human and civil rights. He also believed that the discipline and sacrifice involved in the attempt to be a nation of real egalitarians would raise the quality of life and thought; and while he indicted current practice as mediocre, if not moronic, he stood firm behind theory. It was this duality which gave his writing on equality its merits: a keen awareness of the menace of crude egalitarianism, and a memorable expression of the bathos of democracy in America.

DEMOCRACY

The American Democracy; American democracy; America the home, the hope, the protagonist of democracy; America the lineal descendent of Athens: this was the national currency of democratic terminology. Lindsay did not use the terminology, nor did he subscribe to its complacency. To him life in so-called democratic America resembled "a jail where men have common lot/Gaunt the one who has, and who has not." [2] Masses and rulers alike comprised "the poor damned human race, still unimpressed/With its damnation." But he was ambiguous toward the citizens who comprised the American approximation of a democracy, an ambiguity which stemmed from his polarized feeling for a humanity pitiable yet with potentialities. Even within the poem in which he saw his poor, damned society, "The Raft," dedicated to Mark Twain, there was compensation; America, like Huckleberry Finn, was

> . . . *still lovely in disgrace,*
> *New childhood of the world, that blunders on*
> *And wonders at the darkness and the dawn.*[3]

Practical manifestations of democracy evoked derision and admiration in him. In "John L. Sullivan, The Strong Boy of Boston," he celebrated 1889 as a legendary time when America, united as a kind of democratic leviathan, followed fascinated, the last bare-fisted boxing match in which

> *John L. Sullivan*
> *The strong boy*
> *Of Boston*
> *Fought seventy-five red rounds with Jake Kilrain.*

But on the whole he could not sanction the average man's priorities in that year. He deplored the fact that Barnum's bears and tigers were rapturously greeted while

> *Ingersoll was called a most vile hound,*
>
> . . . .
>
> *Robert Elsmere riled the pious brain.*
> [*and*] *Phillips Brooks for heresy was fried.*

Thirty years later America still had topsy-turvy values; local news, like the 1889 flood in Johnstown, Pa., hit the headlines, and a determinedly introspective America, about to wash its hands of international responsibility,

> *Heard not of Louvain or of Lorraine,*
> *Or a million heroes for their freedom slain;*
> *Of Armageddon and the world's birth pain—*
> *The League of Nations.*[4]

Lindsay's ultimate subscription to the theory of democracy had especial force since it was made not only in the face of crude mass criteria (while he theoretically equated democracy with mass excellence), but because it went against his personal grain. He mocked his urge to be exclusive.

Sooner or later I am going to step up into the rarefied civilized air once too often and stay there in spite of myself. I shall get a little too fond of china and old silver, and forget the fields. Books and teacups and high-brow conversations are awfully stimulating things, if you give them time to be.

He tried to convince himself that

there is a baffling sense of futility in the restful upper air. . . . The feeling that the upper world is all tissue paper, that the only choice a real man can make is to stay below with the great forces of life forever . . . the feeling that, to be a little civilized, we sacrifice enormous powers and joys.[5]

If democracy was inextricable from mediocrity, then mediocrity must have undiscovered merits—the merits of compromise, perhaps—though he could not help feeling "the great forces of life" were uncommonly like a subculture, and that to join with them involved going back down the scale of human progress. The same image of descent to democracy, and the same conflict of theory and practice emerged in "The Would-Be Merman," a poem in which Lindsay described an intellectual and political elite sailing on the social ocean while the masses lived under water. Although Lindsay determinedly "grinned at all the roaring" and dived in,

"defying death," he lost his breath, and came up for air. But he
rebuked himself for his lack of endurance; he had to develop the
technics of survival. He *would* be a merman,

> *Not in desperation*
> *A momentary diver*
> *Blue for lack of air.*
> *But with gills deep-breathing*
> *Swim amid the nation.*

The beauties of the water nation, he maintained, were in the sea
depths and its occupants, not in its skimming rulers, "conceited
folk at ease." Virtue and delight alike were found under water:

> *Wisdom waits the diver*
> *In the social ocean—*
> *Rainbow shells of wonder.*

What to other people were "crude, ill-smelling voters" in "draggled
clothes" were sea horses and dragons to him, democratic noble
savages in "scales of gold and red." [6]

Elsewhere, in a different use of the clothing image, Lindsay
felt he had to accept that democracy was expressed by "the mood
of high-class ready-made-clothing" as accurately as the pyramids
expressed a once prevalent tyranny, and that no conscientious
democrat could prefer the products of a tyranny to those of a
democracy. Or could he? This was Lindsay's dilemma as he
looked at Americans, and he argued himself into the ground. In
spite of his attempt at identification with the kind of society that
appealed to the American people, he could not suppress his disappointment with the way democracy was expressing itself, or his
disillusionment with a depressingly average man, who, in his
ubiquitous Hart Schaffner and Marx suit seemed

from the standpoint of culture, to be a mechanical toy, amused by
clockwork. He is clipped to a terrible uniformity by the sharp edges of
life. He knows who won the last baseball game and who may be the
next president. He knows the names of the grand opera singers he has
heard on the phonograph. He turns over luxuriously in his subcon-

cious soul the tunes he has heard on the self playing piano in front of the vaudeville theatre. He will read a poem if it is telegraphed across the country, with a good newspaper story to start it. All of his thinking is done by telegraph and fancies that are too delicate to be expressed by the comic supplement seldom reach him. Dominated by a switchboard civilization, he moves in grooves from one clockwork splendor to another.[7]

Lindsay was not enough of a psychologist or a political analyst to understand why democracy was making for conformity and mediocrity. He was discussing what political parlance had long before summed up as the tyranny of the majority; but the phrase did not suit his purposes; its overtones of condemnation were too strong. It was not the fact of conformity that he was knocking, but the crude outlets and the materialistic trimmings of this age-old tendency to think and act en masse, not the absence of an elite of excellence, but the lack of national standards of excellence in all but the material sphere.

Where did the blame lie? In Lindsay's view it lay not so much in the institutions as in the people who ran them or who submitted to the status quo. His call for a new type of leader in the communities of the New Localism had indirectly indicted the politicians who surrounded Americans with unidealistic politics, pandered to their materialistic tendencies and their local prejudices and who did not admit (or realize) the politician's responsibility for the total environment. He also hit out with aversion against the profit ethic, though he had no specific association with the muckrakers' dramatic exposure of graft in local politics and sharp practices in industry. He was, however, a friend of Upton Sinclair (who included five of Lindsay's poems in his anthology of five hundred years of international social protest, *The Cry for Justice,* 1925) and with a vehemence worthy of *The Jungle* Lindsay inveighed against Babbitts who crippled the democratic process with their networks of graft and patronage, small-town and big-time. Babbitts were those "sons of ward-heelers" and "sons of bartenders" who

> *Kicked out the old pests in a virtuous way.*
> *The new tribe sold kerosene, gasoline, parrafine,*
> *Babbitt sold Judas, Babbitt sold Christ.*
> *Babbitt sold everything under the sun.*[8]

Incensed, Lindsay clamored for a purge of the "commerce-made manners and fat prosperity of America"; for an end to the dollar worship which was as much a characteristic of socialism as capitalism. He saw all too well that he was pulling against a national, not a class tide. He wrote, explicitly to a man-in-the-street audience:

You hate the kings in oil and grain and cattle and the like. Behind clean bodies, quick and nerved with wire, their souls squat like giant spiders ready to spring. . . . And you sirs, are tiny spiders of the same breed. . . . Your little souls are full of the venom of covetousness. You are subscribing to the business axioms that make this a Land of Death.[9]

"A Land of Death": death of the American Dream, which was falling into desuetude, and perhaps dying. For Lindsay the problem of the American Democracy was not simply the problem of the bathetic nature of democracy, or of America's particular democratic machinery: it was a problem of the acquisitive, competitive, individualistic American outlook, the outlook which made an individual only want equality of opportunity until he had left his former equals behind. Such a mentality bred aggression, and in the context of the conformity which appeared to accompany democracy, aggression was likely to be channeled into an antisocial act or a primitive self-expression. Mass pleasures, tastes, and sounds sanctified desire, Lindsay pointed out; they were animal.

> *Listen to the lion roar,*
> *Listen to the lion R-O-A-R!*
> *Hear the leopard cry for gore,*
> *Willy, willy willy wah HOO!*
> *Hail the bloody Indian band,*
> *Hail, all hail the popcorn stand,*

Hail to Barnum's picture there,
People's idol everywhere,
Whoop, whoop, whoop, WHOOP!

Primitivism threatened to dominate: "Popcorn crowds shall rule the town."

This characterization of the democratic menace occurred in "The Kallyope Yell," 1913, an ironically popular poem in which Lindsay likened America to a circus of apparent glamor, but real sawdust and tinsel. The moods of democracy seemed to him as contrary as the "sizz-fizz" and the "hoot-toot" of the circus calliope, and as intractable. And yet, Lindsay argued with himself, this could not be finalized democracy; it must be a halfway house. The Kallyope was "tooting hope"; it was "but the pioneer/Voice of the Democracy"; now "the gutter dream," then "the golden dream." The democratic process in America *would* breed equality; "Steam shall work melodiously/Brotherhood increase." The Kallyope was surely not Democracy's complete composition, but its overture. One day, it was singing,

> *Prophet-singers will arise,*
> *Prophets coming after me,*
> *Sing my song in softer guise*
> *With more delicate surprise.*[10]

In "Every Soul is a Circus,"[11] written in 1929, near the end of his life, Lindsay was still trying to see the circus audience as an embryonic affirmation of the nation's spiritual and intellectual dimensions, and as a pointer to the fullness and unity of democracy that would have been made possible by the leaven of the constitution. He believed that throughout American history the supposedly egalitarian, enlightened, and moral essence of the constitution had staved off the death of the American Dream; he looked to it once more to lead "the whole nation in search of the secret of democratic beauty with their hearts at the same time filled to overflowing with the righteousness of God"[12] (Equality: Beauty: Religion). Lindsay subscribed to the constitutional mystique: the most unadulteratedly American characteristic of his gospel.

He had shown a precocious awareness of the significance of constitutional symbols. When he was nine years old he went with his
father to Trinidad, Colorado, and kept a detailed diary of the
journey. Getting out of the train one morning

what a sight met our eyes . . . upon one hand the sublime sight of a
jet black porter picturesquely banging upon a piece of dazzlingly bright
tin pan with a clothes pin that had seen cleaner days, and upon the
other peer where I may see nothing but white Glorious white! Yes
. . . Oh what emotion filled my breast as my eyes beheld piercing the
gloom beheld [*sic*] the star spangled Banner.[13]

The rhetoric of the mainstream American political heritage mesmerized him. Stephen Graham recalled that when tramping with
him in the Rockies in 1921, Lindsay used to make the mountains
echo by declaiming Webster's sonorous "Lib-er-ty *and* Un-ion—
One and ins-sep-ar-able—Now and for-everrr," and Andrew Jackson's toast "The Federal Union! It must be preserved."[14]

By constitution Lindsay meant not only that document but the
Declaration of Independence and the Union itself, as exemplified
in the Gettysburg Address and the Emancipation Proclamation: a
collection of principles which amounted to the secular religion of
democracy. But while he himself put a strictly egalitarian construction on the constitution, he felt keenly that different reactions
to the constitution formed part of the democratic dilemma. This
feeling was apparent in the *The Litany of Washington Street*
where he juxtaposed the original Gettysburg address with a not
improbable misinterpretation.

Our fathers brought forth on this continent an old nation, conceived
in tyranny, and dedicated to the proposition that all men are created
unequal. Now we are engaged in a great Civil War testing whether
that nation or any nation so misconceived and so misdedicated can long
endure. We are met on a great battlefield of that war.[15]

Harriet Beecher Stowe had similarly satirized partisan interpretations of the constitution. In *Uncle Tom's Cabin* Augustine St. Clare
facetiously justified slavery in a free adaptation of the preamble
to the Declaration of Independence:

When, in the course of human events, it becomes necessary for a fellow to hold two or three dozen of his fellow worms in captivity, a decent regard to the opinion of society requires. . . .[16]

Like the abolitionists, but with a wider issue in mind, Lindsay felt the need for Americans to stop using the constitution to perpetuate individual affluence and privilege (though the founding fathers may have intended it as just such a defense mechanism!). Unless the nation codified the constitution, unless it redefined its bases and its aims, it ran the risk of serious internal dissension, and laid itself open to a charge of hypocrisy. And indeed, without a humanitarian interpretation of the constitution, without a national subscription to Lindsay's basic belief in respect between citizen and citizen, America has on occasion approached a negation of the fundamental human and civil rights she claims to stand for. The America of the fifties and sixties has shown the divisive effects of a variously, often selfishly interpreted constitution. The assertion of states rights holds up integration and prevents the federal government from bringing criminals to justice; the assertion of the archaic right to bear arms encourages a terrible violence. And in Lindsay's lifetime the fine essence of democracy was subject to an increasing number of violations. Springfield, Illinois, like many American cities at the time, had its race riot in 1909. Chicago had its deluge of violence in the 1920s, in which police and people were sometimes implicated by their (indirect) participation, their indifference or their vicarious thrill, by their phony, exclusive sense of brotherhood. Chicago in the 1920s showed how a democracy might revert to the law of the jungle, and it is surprising that more of Lindsay's contemporaries were not shocked into joining him to seek an effective restatement of American ideals. He thought this restatement might come from socialism.

SOCIALISM

The Christian content of Lindsay's gospel made him want to see a reasonable equality of existence in America to parallel the equality he visualized God wanting, and ultimately providing, for humanity.

> *God has great estates just past the line,*
> *Green farms for all, and meat and corn and wine.*[17]

His brand of socialism was also part of an emotionally induced sympathy for the underprivileged and the victims of any kind of tyranny. Typically, it was socialism as humanitarianism rather than the American Socialist Party that attracted Lindsay; he was a compassionate rather than a doctrinal socialist. His poem "Why I Voted the Socialist Ticket" was written in 1909, and represented a declaration of principle tantamount to the *War Bulletins* of that year, not a hard-line party commitment. His vote, cast in 1908, does not seem to have been an anti-Taft or an anti-Republican vote (he accepted Theodore Roosevelt's record—questioned nowadays—as a trustbuster and a philanthropic friend of labor and capital alike). His attitude was one of dissatisfaction with himself as well as with other Americans whose consciences were assuaged by partial reforms, and who overlooked the spoils system and the pork-barrel measures which went with the old parties and the machine politicians. He noted in *War Bulletin No. III* that he tended to abandon his standards in order to please or placate the people around him; and in "Why I Voted the Socialist Ticket" he wrote of the symbolic importance for him, as an inconsistent humanitarian, of casting his vote for Eugene Debs for President.

> *I am unjust, but I can strive for justice.*
> *My life's unkind, but I can vote for kindness.*
> *I, the unloving, say life should be lovely.*
> *I, that am blind, cry out against my blindness.*

His support of socialism, like his support of democracy in general, often went against the grain of comfort, and was more poignant for that reason. Stripping down doctrines of laissez-faire, trusteeship, and survival-of-the-fittest to their core, he tried to make himself "vote against our human nature." [18] It was the mentality which perpetuated capitalism, and not capitalism itself which he saw as the root of all evil. He admonished the utopian socialist: "Oh soap-box friend, it is not the alleged 'capitalistic system' that is doomed. There is no such system. But the office supply system is doomed." In the long run only practical, humanitarian affirmations of brotherhood would improve the quality of existence of every man, irrespective of increased or reduced material wealth. He drew a moral from the folk culture of the early American Dream.

What has an orchard of Johnny Appleseed to do with either capitalism or socialism? When men of the Western Reserve found an unexpected splendid appletree blooming at the end of a field hedge, where no one was known to plant it, they said to one another that Johnny Appleseed had been there twenty years before. And he did not return to collect the debt or trade with them, on capitalistic or socialistic terms.[19]

Just as he saw socialism in a humanitarian context, and voted the Socialist ticket on broader grounds than the industrial inequalities and grievances that drew most voters to that party, so Lindsay tended to attribute a wide significance to pockets of industrial unrest. He could not see them as isolated occurrences, but as symptoms of weakness in American society. Since industrial and technological America was the new America, its failure to solve disputes peaceably boded ill for the nation. In "Factory Windows Are Always Broken" he argued that such apparently minor acts of belligerence meant that "Something or other is going wrong/Something is rotten"[20] in the whole American fabric; they meant that the American Democracy and the American Dream were not automatically realizable.

Lindsay's warning had a moving urgency, but it was not as effective as it might have been had he written about specific strikes or labor problems. If he could write sympathetically in letters about Eugene Debs' imprisonment by Woodrow Wilson for "seditious" pacificism,[21] if he could vote for Debs for President, why could he not comment on Debs' leadership of the American Railway Union, particularly during Chicago's memorable Pullman strike of 1894, when the A.R.U. nearly won out against the employers. (His favorable comment on Altgeld, who virtually supported the strikers, was a very indirect species of comment on the A.R.U.) If he could celebrate Theodore Roosevelt in general terms as a curb on big business, in "Roosevelt," why not write an anti-trust poem?

His lack of specific comment may have tantalized and annoyed his readers, but his vagueness was intentional. It was characteristic of Lindsay's gospel to avoid a plethora of detail which would impede the momentum of his overall indictment and exhortation. He did not want topicality, with its inevitable controversy, to cloud the general points he made about democracy; he did not want to give his readers a chance to digress, or to sink back into their prejudices. And certainly a man whose only stretches of conventional employment consisted of three months in 1901 as a sorter in the Toy Department at Marshall Field's, Chicago, and three months in 1905 as a porter in a gas-tubing factory in New York City was unlikely to come up with concrete solutions for a new deal between employers and employees.

But in whatever way Lindsay wanted to approach the subject, he had to write in the context of widespread American antipathy to socialism. Socialist theory seemed un-American. It presupposed the existence of classes; it suggested that the American social and political structure was comparable with that of feudal, decayed Europe. Moreover, there was the difficulty of separating the precepts of socialism from acts of violence in the industrial sector, which were laid at socialism's door (though they were more often the acts of unaffiliated individuals or the avowedly anarchical Industrial Workers of the World). In such a climate of opinion Lindsay was up against the fact that socialism was an American scapegoat; and he could probably have done no better than he did in pitching socialism in his usual broad ideological terms, this time in terms of Marxism. In a comparison of Marxian socialism and American capitalistic democracy Lindsay could rate the theory of an international workingmen's alliance above the recurrent American philosophy of isolationism; the unfavorableness of the comparison might at least shock Americans into self-examination.

Lindsay also believed that Marxism had genuine relevance for America as an essentially humanitarian ideology. His wholehearted subscription to the egalitarian constitutional mystique led him to take the radical view that Marxism was merely an extreme version of the social and political theories of *The Federalist Papers* and Jefferson's letters. Logically followed, the pronouncements of the founding fathers, their "American system" as Lindsay called it (contrasting it with "capitalist," "socialist," and "office supply" systems) "would eliminate classes, and we would have no class war, nor anything that could be misdescribed. . . . All America would be upper middle world." But in order to fulfill this logic, the dormant spirit of the constitution needed an injection of socialism, a tinge of active Marxism humanitarianism. It was, after all, Lindsay's own contact with the theory of Marxism that brought him nearest to putting his concept of equality in concrete terms; when he wrote that the possibility of fulfilling the dream of leveling out upwards, of an "upper middle world," would be contingent on the hope that "the total of our private citizens used the pick and the shovel as the drafted men do in camp, and used the ballot in the same way." [22]

Lindsay thought in terms of an international, nondoctrinal spirit of socialism to match his undogmatic ecumenism. He found Hamiltonianism, Jeffersonianism, and Marxism compatible, and was quick to attribute universal characteristics to the first Russian Revolution of 1917.

> *The Russian Revolution is the world revolution—*
>
> . . . .
>
> *. . . by freedom's alchemy*
> *Beauty is born.*

Except for Russian political activists, few people realized that Kerensky was a new despot, not a revolutionary, and in common with world socialists Lindsay saluted Kerensky, though with a hint of accurate incredulity, as the "prophet of the world-wide intolerable hope." Lindsay's feelings about the October Revolution are not known, but at a guess he was probably more approving than most people. It must have encouraged him to see in his lifetime an enormous and effective revolution, which, in spite of its atrocities, was basically humanitarian. He never ceased to celebrate the soap-box; however ranting and partisan it might be, he saw it as the ultimate guarantee of free speech, the safeguard against tyranny, and the necessary impetus of any movement toward social justice:

> *The Pericles, Socrates, Diogenes soap-box,*
> *The old Elijah, Jeremiah, John-the-Baptist soap-box,*
> *The Rousseau, Mirabeau, Danton, soap-box,*
> *The Karl Marx, Henry George, Woodrow Wilson soap-box.*
>
> . . . .
>
> *Platform of liberty:—Magna Charta liberty,*
> *Andrew Jackson liberty, bleeding Kansas liberty,*
> *New-born Russian liberty.*[23]

Lindsay showed considerable interest in anarchic, revolutionary tendencies. He was a radical, and a worried radical, whose interest was a measure of his near despair, as well of his own theoretical barrenness. As early as 1909 the original version of "The Litany of Heroes" had hailed Oliver Cromwell in "God Send the Regicide," and in 1917 Lindsay had written "Here's to the Mice" "with the hope that the socialists might yet dethrone Kaiser and Czar."

> *Here's to the hidden tunneling thing*
> *That brings the mountain's groans.*
> *Here's to the midnight scamps that gnaw,*
> *Gnawing away the thrones.*[24]

But these reflections were for Europe. In America, informed public opinion and the rousing leaders of open debate could pressure government to an extent that equaled revolution. The once quicksilver and increasingly ponderous William Jennings Bryan was, in this sense, the archetypal American revolutionary.

> *When Bryan speaks the wigwam shakes.*
> *The corporation magnate quakes.*
> *The pre-convention plot is smashed.*
> *The valiant pleb full armed awakes.*
>
> *When Bryan speaks, then I rejoice.*
> *His is the strange composite voice*
> *Of many million singing souls*
> *Who make world-brotherhood their choice.*[25]

Yet those in authority might willfully ignore vox populi; the establishment might find it comfortable to minimize problems, to perpetuate their own kind of society, to ignore the needs of a changing world. In such a contingency, Lindsay asked (and in such a likelihood, he implied),

> *Who will ride against all grown-up foes of Democracy?*
> *"To-morrow, to-morrow," their marvelous tune—*
> *"To-morrow," their marvelous cry of desire.*[26]

Where, he was asking, were the grassroots of democracy? Who would reject a society built on affluence and privilege, prejudice and hostility, and irrelevant habit? He remembered how he and his school friends had mobilized behind Bryan in 1896.

> *Oh, Tom Dines, and Art Fitzgerald,*
> *And the gangs that they could get!*
> *I can hear them yelling yet.*
> *Helping the incantation,*
> *Defying the aristocracy,*
> *With every bridle gone,*[27]

and answered himself:

> *"Youth will be served," now let us cry.*
> *Hurl the referendum.*

Perhaps youth, with its incoherent but idealistic dissatisfaction with the political mores and the "false gods" of his fathers, could reaffirm America's egalitarian promise, and pave the way for international goodwill. Lindsay looked, Marxianly, for a world-wide youth movement.

> *Great wave of youth, ere you be spent,*
> *Sweep over every monument*
> *Of caste, smash every high imperial wall*
> *That stands against the new World State,*
> *And overwhelm each ravening hate,*
> *And heal, and make blood-brothers of us all.*
> *Nor let your clamor cease*
> *Till ballots conquer guns.*[28]

His answer struck few chords in his lifetime; but it rings familiar today. It is an answer with validity in the context of a worldwide restlessness of youth, which, in the instance of the international student body occasionally transcends national self-interest, and in the title of Lindsay's poem of appeal to youth, momentarily seeks to "Sew the Flags Together." But his appeal was also made in the wider context of his belief that idealism and the will to improve should not be the prerogative of youth, just as his talk of revolution was part of the argument that progress toward an egalitarian society would entail radical self-examination and change. In these senses Lindsay himself was purposefully young in outlook and revolutionary in technic.

Yet in spite of his forceful perception and expression of some of the problems and trends of American democracy, Lindsay's thought had signal weaknesses. He made no attempt to justify equality on utilitarian or empirical grounds, which was an unrealistic approach to human nature and the rational man, but which was the idealistic point of his theory. He failed to reconcile the kind of deep rooted egalitarianism he apparently envisaged with the widespread contention that the citizens of a democracy must be free to differ and discriminate. He nominally affiliated himself with the American socialist movement, but he did not make it clear whether he regularly voted the Socialist ticket, or did so just once, in 1908; for the most part he omitted the socialist dialectic.

These omissions and the generally unspecific tone of his theory sprang from the fact that while he wanted the egalitarian ends of American socialism, he was antipathetic to its means: equality through consistent federal regulation of wages, profits, and prices; brotherhood through greater federal control of production, distribution, and consumption; charity through Acts of Congress; and utopia through the eventual elimination of capitalism. He was rarely able to work up enthusiasm for institutional reform, which in his lifetime he tended to equate with basic faith in the status quo; and though it is a questionable generalization, it was surely true of the mild American socialist movement, which envisaged the gradual evolution of a socialist society through regularly increased cooperation between workers and employers. Lindsay preferred Marxism to American socialism because of its ultimate belief in a natural union of people, transcending any governmental structure. He would not define the democratic decision-making process in the usual terms of majority rule or consensus compromise because his emotional egalitarianism was based on a belief in the natural harmony of men, and the ultimate, irrepressible evolution—or revival—of brotherhood. One is brought up against the paradox that in spite of his indictment of so many democratic phenomena, Lindsay continued to believe in a benevolent, mutual love of man for man.

It was an ever-present paradox. In 1909, in *War Bulletin No. I,* he castigated Americans for their stupidity, bigotry, conservatism, cheapness, and impatience; in 1910, in *The Village Magazine,* he marveled at their zest, resilience, and perseverance; they could be

stepped on by a fire-engine horse, shot through by currents from an electric chair, run through a rolling mill, pushed off a tower or baked in a pie, and come out still singing.[29]

At the end of his life he was depressed by the fact that he was only known, respected, and listened to for the Higher Vaudeville, a depression which his schizophrenia worsened into a feeling that the world—wife, family, fellow poets, America—was against him, and whose intensity led to his suicide. Yet he was still affirming in 1931, "whoever makes a cynic of me is mistaken. I *believe* in the human race." [30] Mass crassness might be more deeply rooted than he cared for, mass intellectual and spiritual potential so deeply buried that it caused him anxiety, but he never ceased to believe that if America so chose she could eventually blight that crassness and cultivate that potential.

It might be argued that Lindsay's was a paradox of bewilderment rather than intention, but not when one recalls his characterization of Andrew Jackson's election to the Presidency as "The old, old story/Democracy's shame/And democracy's glory," [31] nor when one has looked at the deliberate paradox of "Billboards and Galleons." In that poem he cast his image of the American democracy he knew in the substance of billboards:

> *America's glories flaming high,*
> *Festooned cartoons, an amazing mixture,*
> *Shabby, shoddy, perverse and twistical,*
> *Shamefully boastful,*
> *Slyly mystical.*

He juxtaposed the dream of Columbus and the glamor of the Spanish galleons with

> *Exaggerated Sunday papers,*
> *Comic sheets like scrambled eggs,*
> *And Andy Gump's first-reader capers.*

"Arrow-collar heroes proud" marked his "soul-road map of the U.S.A." The same mixture of repulsion and attraction which drew him to the average American committed him to the total bathos of American society, which could be marvelously exciting and appallingly mundane. For Lindsay, America and her citizens, like billboards, were

> *The valentine, filagree towers of mystery,*
> *The snow-white skyscrapers of new history.*[32]

But the fascination of the products of democracy did not lessen Lindsay's belief that the instinct for equality must be nurtured and directed. He believed in the divine institution of American Democracy and the Constitution, but divine institution was no guarantee of divine maintenance. Americans had to work at their democracy, and Lindsay might well have quoted them "Golden Rule" Jones's dictum that "it is the truth of Equality, of Brotherhood, that alone can bring the better days." [33] It was in an attempt to interpret this truth as a real concept of good citizenship that Lindsay rounded off his gospel with a definition of beauty not as artistic or aesthetic, but as "democracy's beauty-sense";[34] the human beauty of egalitarian, moral conduct.

Beauty

LINDSAY GROUPED three poems together under the title "A Gospel of Beauty." He included the trilogy in *Collected Poems,* 1923, with the prefatory comment: "I recited these three poems more than any others in my mendicant preaching tour through the West. Taken as a triad, they hold in solution my theory of American civilization." [1] The poems were written in 1909, and while their setting was thus largely rural, their theme was national. "The Proud Farmer" was a statement of an ideal American citizenship, an anti-Babbittry; "The Illinois Village" dealt with the village ethos; and "On the Building of Springfield" with the future American city. The trilogy encapsulated the people, the spirit, and the shape of America: Beauty, Religion, Equality.

Lindsay gave his gospel the short title "Gospel of Beauty" because it was the experience of America's natural beauty which confirmed his belief in a divine creation, and therefore in human dignity and potential. *Adventures While Preaching the Gospel of Beauty* testified to his subscription to the remedial impact of visual beauty, and his own response to it. But in the context of his gospel he did not attempt to detail the beauty of the American environment or beautiful phenomena, for he intended the gospel as a theoretical basis for such specific and personal conceptions of beauty as his own *Golden Book of Springfield.* Instead he tried to capitalize on the urge to enjoy, preserve, and create beauty, an urge which he attributed to the kind of individual and community concern for the immediate and the total environment which was inextricable from an egalitarian concern for the fulfillment of every man. The beauty he delineated and wished to see emulated was beauty of character and conduct, beauty which was "inner" by comparison with the external world, but which amounted to an externalization of the spiritual beauty of brotherhood.

HUMAN BEAUTY

"We must have many Lincoln-hearted men" was Lindsay's prerequisite for the gospel of beauty. In his trilogy he called for men who, like Lincoln, were determined that nothing should stand in the way of their American Dream, men who traditionally governed the country, and who could, if they chose, shape it, men who cared for the conditions in which their families lived and the kind of society their children inherited. The beauty of thoughtfulness, planning, and cooperation was within their scope. In this sense in "The Illinois Village" and "On the Building of Springfield," Lindsay described the congregations of the village church "rich towards God,"[2] the teachers and classes of the district school, and the minuscule attempts of countless individuals and generations to improve some aspect of their home town as beautiful. With such examples he successfully drove home his point that the all important atmosphere of reform, as well as specific reforms, could be generated in small local units, whose activities would have cumulative repercussions. Good citizens, everyday humanitarians, were, by definition, beautiful people.

"The Proud Farmer," the key poem in the trilogy, gave in condensed form Lindsay's belief in inner beauty. Dignity, integrity, citizenship, and a sense of nonmaterial values were embodied for him in the life of his maternal grandfather, Ephraim Samuel Frazee, who died when Lindsay was eighteen. To E. L. Masters, who heard about the family's reputation at first hand, Frazee was "this enterprising and in many ways typical American,"[3] and he does seem to have been a successful and conscientious member of society. The organizer of the first livestock association in America, he was also the first farmer in Rush County, Indiana, to go in for such devices as a reaper, a double plough, and a wheat binder. He had studied under Alexander Campbell himself, at Campbell's foundation, Bethany College in West Virginia. Lindsay's description of Frazee as "a democrat well-nigh a king" captured the essence of the man, who had a fine sense of human worth:

> *His plowmen-neighbors were as lords to him.*
> *His was an ironside, democratic pride*

and who led a full life, as a lay preacher, in his daily work,

> *Watching the wide world's life from sun to sun,*
> *Lining his walls with books from everywhere.*[4]

In setting up Frazee as a model citizen Lindsay endowed him with a more comprehensive range of attributes and functions than was likely to characterize any one man, but he was purposely giving him both individual and communal stature. In *The Village Magazine* he wrote of Frazee as a farmer who had "gradually developed from the man who farms with his feet to the man who farms with his brain" and an exemplary exponent of the New Localism, a product of the mooted community spirit of the crossroads church, who "found a means of development in his mere citizenship in state and church." He functioned (busily, but not impossibly so) as a teacher of the farmers' bible class, as chairman of the prayer meeting committee of the trustees of the village church, as the designer of neat homes, and as the financial backer behind school building projects, chautauqua grounds, and electric light plants. To his family he was not merely a good provider, with "house painted and fields in order"; he found time to "gather . . . his children by the fireside to carve something lovely . . . to look into some wonderful new doctrine or old tradition; to tell an antique story or sing a home song." [5]

Lindsay managed to create in Frazee a figure who was not only a model American, but an ordinary American; he made beauty seem to be within everyone's grasp. But he detracted from his creation by choosing a farmer for his model citizen; he would have done better to transfer the character of Frazee to another setting. For at the time that he wrote, "farmer," like "village," was an overloaded word. The American agrarian myth of the farmer as the ideal citizen, the craftsman with a precapitalistic outlook, living the communal, altruistic life, seemed less and less plausible. Farmers were coming to have a reputation not associated with love of land and its capable exploitation, but with scrambling onto the wagon of urban prosperity and trying to reproduce *urbs in rure*. Yet the myth retained shreds of validity. The country crossroads church and the little red schoolhouse *were* community centers, and the mileage between neighbor and neighbor gave such bonds an importance which lapsed in tenements and terraces. Statistically, it was not until 1920 that America's urban population equaled her rural population. But although Lindsay's subscription to the agrarian myth might have some justification,[6] in articulating it he showed himself to be out of step with agrarian and anti-agrarian thinking. While Frazee was a model American citizen and farmer-citizen, he was not the average American farmer, or his current image. That individual, politically conservative, in the avant-garde of materialism, was bound to come between Frazee and Lindsay's American audience.

The effectiveness of the whole of the "Gospel of Beauty" trilogy was weakened by the fact that it was written in the midst of Lindsay's shift from distaste with the urban take-over to fascination with it. In "The Illinois Village" the sight of trains tearing through the countryside made him "sigh for the sweet life wrenched and torn/By thundering commerce, fierce and bare," and sigh for people to whom "the railroad is a thing disowned/ The city but a field of weeds." But in "On the Building of Springfield" he urged the construction of "some city on the breast of Illinois," utilizing "Science, Machinery and Trade." [7] His powerful, nostalgic evocation of the old order overbore his profession of belief in the new one, but he was obviously concerned to show that he accepted the physical and psychological impact of urbanization and the machine age. He rationalized his belief more cogently in "The Santa-Fé Trail," a later poem (1913), but based on the experiences of the same 1912 tramping expedition during which he recited his sometimes ambiguous trilogy. Walking along the old Santa Fe trail, the caravan route from Santa Fe to Independence,

Missouri, trying to listen to bird songs against the background of passing cars, he began to write "The Santa-Fé Trail" in the indignant conviction that "the auto at its worst made the most obscene and unclean sound on the earth." [8] But in the course of writing the poem he succumbed to the speed, power, exhilaration, and go-ahead symbolism that amounted to a new beauty. The auto honk became

> . . . *the music of the morning:—*
> *First, from the far East comes but a crooning.*
> *The crooning turns to a sunrise singing.*
> *Hark to the* calm-*horn,* balm-*horn,* psalm-*horn.*
> *Hark to the* faint-*horn,* quaint-*horn,* saint-*horn.*

It complemented the song of the Rachel-Jane:

> *Love and life,*
> *Eternal youth—*
> *Sweet, sweet, sweet, sweet*
> *Dew and glory,*
> *Love and truth,*
> *Sweet, sweet, sweet, sweet.* [9]

Lindsay eventually went so far as to say that "without the horns for a background, the Rachel wouldn't be much." [10] He made it clear in "The Santa-Fé Trail" that he was convinced that landscape and townscape, city values and country virtues would interact, and that realists like Frazee, who were already exploiting agricultural possibilities to their fullest, would adapt and not retrench. But in the less digested poems of the "Gospel of Beauty" trilogy, his choice of images and contexts disguised the fact that he was advocating change, and that to be as community-conscious as Frazee would mean radical reorientation for most Americans.

But neither the cars and horns of "The Santa-Fé Trail," nor the incipient urbanization of "On the Building of Springfield" were acceptable to Lindsay if they merely enslaved man to the material world, if they equated beauty with modernity at the expense of spiritual values. By setting his good citizen against a traditional background he hoped to emphasize that there was nothing novel about the beauty of conduct and character he described; they were immemorial virtues which were valid in any time or any milieu. Perhaps, too, there were the elements of perverseness and shock treatment in Lindsay's setting up of Frazee as a model of citizenship, as there had been in his choice of a Chinese laundryman as an exemplar of everyday spirituality, and in his use of the word village to describe a primarily urban community. But "The Proud Farmer" was also a compliment to an admirable man who made an indelible impression on his grandson.

When Lindsay wrote about women it was in such terms as "ladyhood," "queen-woman," "madonna," "seraph," and "maiden-queen." [11] He viewed them sentimentally and respectfully, as pure beings who might inspire national probity. In a poem dedicated "To all Crusaders against the International and Interstate Traffic in Young Girls"—a giveaway title—he wrote reverently: "Ah! they are priceless, the pale and the ivory and red!/Breathless we gaze on the curls of each glorious head," and asked Galahad, Tennysonianly pure-hearted, to "teach us to fight for immaculate ways among men." [12] "The Faces that Pass," one of his few free verse ventures, began in Whitmanesque style and apparent Whitmanesque mood:

> *I am on my knees to woman, because she is mysterious,*
> *carved of living flesh; the race life beating within*
> *her the treasure of the world.*
>
> *O woman to you I build myriad unseen altars.*

But he shied away from Whitman's voluptuous descriptions to celebrate women because they were "potent in childhood and virginity," [13] using childhood less in the sense of motherhood than to attribute endemic innocence to women of all ages.

However, while Lindsay accorded women unqualified respect in his published verse, he "unleashed the beast in him," as he described it, in his notebooks.

If you were a pebble I could crush you and drink you
If you were a fire I would burn like dead leaves.
If we were two lion cubs I would devour you
If you were a gleaner, my bones were your sheaves . . .

These words, written at age thirty, were a fine, forceful expression of his feelings. But while he continued to do no more than hold girls' hands and to believe that "When the red dreams come/The good dreams go," his desires increased, not abated; and so, aged forty, he self-consciously used slang to match what he considered correspondingly vulgar thoughts.

I want a little sweetey,
To talk baby-slang to me,
A regular Orleans molasses honeybunch,
Real easy on the eyes
Not so Goddam wise . . .

. . . a dam little canary . . .
Face tilted like a fairy,
Light of thigh and airy,
Round-breasted, quick and wary! [14]

Such verses were kept away from the public, for he felt that extra-marital impulses—let alone relations—defiled the female sex.

Desire complicated Lindsay's theory of beauty. He once said, ironically, that there was no danger of the moon falling into disuse as an adjunct of desire as it rhymed so conveniently with spoon. In 1896, planning twelve sonnets, the first three were: "1. To womankind. 2. To children. 3. To beauty beginning with the moon and ending with the voice of woman." [15] He elaborated the connection in a group of nearly one hundred moon poems. The various creatures he had look at the moon—a snail, a gambler, a miner in the desert, for example—saw reflected there the images of their own desire. The sluggish snail wished he "had a yellow crown/ As glistering . . . as . . . the moon"; the gambler visualized a sack of gold dust, and the thirsty miner saw "a brass-hoop'd water-keg/ A wondrous water-feast." [16] Lindsay's own image was of the moon sitting in the branches of a spice tree which sang

Hunger and fire,
Hunger and fire
Sky-born Beauty—
Spice of desire.

The roots and branches whispered "Love tomorrow" and "Love today." In Lindsay's imagination the moon was transformed into the nest of two doves:

And one is the kiss I took from you,
And one is the kiss you gave to me.[17]

So sometimes Lindsay gave his desire expression, but more often, in stern Galahad style, he tried to repress it. His long celibacy magnified an innate respect for women out of all proportion. E. L. Masters' description of his behavior with women may be taken with a grain of salt since Masters was as promiscuous as Lindsay was not. But in the light of Lindsay's creed of extra-marital continence one can accept Masters' claim that "any visiting poetess of amatory designs might play around him [Lindsay] as much as possible, he remained the Red Cross Knight, paying court to her as he would to the Virgin Mary."[18]

Female beauty equals female purity was the equation Lindsay intended for his gospel. His conflict of beauty and desire complicated the equation by suggesting that his etherealized adulation was the product of diverted sexual fulfillment rather than of rationality. But the association of beauty and desire had conceptual importance for his gospel, for beauty-consciousness did not merely increase sensibility; it was a spur to action. A beautiful woman could arouse sexual instincts and the wish to surround her with beauty; contact with an upright man could lead to self-improvement; solicitude for youth could lead to a critical assessment of what society had to offer future generations.

Lindsay considered children and adolescents as essentially beautiful, good, and pure as women. He interchanged childish and womanly characteristics. A future Springfield was embodied in a young woman, Avanel, and a future Tennessee "in the shining form of a child." He wrote of Elizabeth Wills, a girl of nineteen whom he taught at Gulf Park and whom he loved: "My child is like a bird's wing, a bird's wing, a bird's wing." [19] He had committed himself to young people as "colts of democracy," [20] and in terms of beauty they were his acknowledged symbols of human renewal and hope. When he became disillusioned about the quality of the audience he attracted and the audience response he evoked, it was only his contact with young people in schools and universities that provided him with an incentive for carrying on. He enthused about them: "I have met and addressed hundreds and thousands of dazzlingly beautiful boys and girls . . . and I am not ashamed to say the experience was profoundly intoxicating." He preferred reciting to them, for

Everywhere there was beauty and glory and the blazing heart of Young America. Everywhere there was love and kindness, and not one word of . . . literary spite or silly rivalry, of technical chatter, or social snobbery or cheap race-hate. They were all young! [21]

He wanted to identify himself with them and with their ambitions, and "in some sense to represent these honest, clean, devout young Americans." [22] The young were the America of the immediate future, and for Lindsay these were synonymous objects of concern. His concern was not alleviated by America's tradition of care for young people, for he feared it was a tradition of materialistic over-care, blunting sensibilities, a fear to which he gave moving expression in "The Leaden-Eyed."

> Let not young souls be smothered out before
> They do quaint deeds and fully flaunt their pride.
> It is the worlds one crime its babes grow dull,
> Its poor are ox-like, limp and leaden-eyed.
> Not that they starve, but starve so dreamlessly,
> Not that they sow, but that they seldom reap,
> Not that they serve, but have no gods to serve,
> Not that they die but that they die like sheep.[23]

The origin of Lindsay's poem (1911) was probably to be found in the words of Jane Addams of Hull House (1860-1935), in *The*

Spirit of Youth and the City Streets (1909). Reflecting on her experiences with young people in settlement work in Chicago she wrote:

Youth is so vivid an element in life that unless it is cherished, all the rest is spoiled. The most praiseworthy journey grows dull and leaden unless accompanied by youth's irridescent dreams . . . dreams that fairly buffet our faces as we walk the city streets.[24]

Jane Addams and Lindsay, who were friends, shared a belief in youth as the uncontaminated human element, without original sin, and Lindsay sought its protection through home and school. He constructed the New Localism on the primary unit of a stable home; and in "The Hearth Eternal," through the symbol of an ever-burning fire, identified the central virtues of a good home as permanence and solace. But he was afraid that the child-parent relationship was often—and perhaps inevitably—a slave-tyrant one, which suppressed children's instincts of independence and criticism; and he accordingly joined himself with such attempts to ensure an enlightened American educational system as Floyd Dell's *Were You Ever a Child?* (1919).[25] Dell argued that the authoritarian structure of the average school and its curriculum bias towards rote learning in traditional disciplines were in danger of cutting off a current of open-mindedness and challenge and of forcing the individual into the mold of national conformity; in "The Master of the Dance" and "The Lame Boy and the Fairy" Lindsay supported this doctrine of self-expression with a Rousseau-esque assumption of a special, innocent beauty of youth.

But sometimes his concern to protect youth from the corrupting prejudices and preconceptions of adult society turned into its own form of inverted corruption. In "For All Who Ever Sent Lace Valentines" he described how a small boy and girl met at a friend's birthday party, and how

> *The lion of loving,*
> *The terrible lion,*
> *Woke in the two.*

He seemed to regard this juvenile passion as something sacred rather than something premature, as something he wished to preserve, for he declaimed

> *If the wide state were mine*
> *It should live for such darlings,*
> *And hedge with all shelter*
> *The child-wedded heart.*[26]

The same theme was more explicitly developed in "Genesis" when a "half-grown boy" and a "girl-child slight" in some wild, Eden-like place, watched over by a benevolent cobra—

> *Beautiful friend he was,*
> *Sage, not a tempter grim.*
> *Many a year should pass*
> *Ere Satan should enter him*

—made love:

> *O Eve with the fire-lit breast*
> *And child-face red and white!*
> *I heaped the great logs high!*
> *That was our bridal night.*[27]

Perhaps in these poems Lindsay was subconsciously wishing for others a liberation from sexual inhibitions that he could not achieve. He was certainly indulging the youth in "These Are the Young" whom he declared to be the "darlings of his heart," even if, for example, they were not girls "Olympian white," but "painted to the eyes." In their case he apparently put gratification before Christian virtue. It would have been more in keeping with his usual train of thought to argue that "true" happiness, in his hands essentially a moral and religious concept, was inseparable from virtue. Sentimentality and indulgence had clouded his logic, probably because he wanted to believe in the instinctive rightness of young people's acts of protest and these acts could hardly be separated from their acts of affirmation. As small children they were "innocently wise," as adolescents "innocently wicked," [28] justified in almost any course of action by their idealistic ends and by previous poor trusteeship of their inheritance. To Lindsay theirs was the acceptable arrogance of beautiful people

> *. . . with faces*
> *Like books out of Heaven,*
> *With messages there*
> *The harsh world should read,*
> *The lions and roses and lilies of love,*
> *Its tender, mystic, tyrannical need.*[29]

Such tyranny would lead to "GLORY UNTOLD/WHEN THE TOWN LIKE A GREAT/BUDDING ROSE SHALL UNFOLD!" And so, in "Epilogue to Adventures While Preaching the Gospel of Beauty," Lindsay pleaded with young Americans about to give rise to a new, beautiful, and potentially beauty-conscious generation: "O, lovers, be my partisans."[30]

A series of drawings Lindsay made in 1910, "The Village Improvement Parade," clearly showed the thorough application of his belief in human beauty. The marchers in the parade carried banners with such slogans as "A BAD DESIGNER IS, TO THAT EXTENT, A BAD CITIZEN" and "UGLINESS IS A KIND OF MISGOVERNMENT."[31] If this broad—or far-fetched—interpretation of beauty meant that there was such a thing as political beauty, one of its followers was, Lindsay suggested, Robert Love Taylor, governor of Tennessee (1887–1891). Taylor was a master of the expertise of paternal politics, whose folksy regime thrived on "domestic art"—barn dances and candy pullings—and encouraged drama, music, and storytelling, the artistic arm of the New Localism. He did not confine himself to the rigidly political in his election campaigns and governorship, but with "democratic genius and initiative" he set about welding each crowd into "one beautiful school" and "teaching his state to flower"—or so Lindsay thought in "Bob Taylor's Birthday." In Lindsay's view, such enlightened government, permeating the whole social fabric, could mark the metamorphosis of Tennesseans into "artists, poets, musicians, architects"; and from being lovers and creators of beauty they would move on to become "statesmen, prophets, saints and sibyls."[32]

Like Taylor, all politicians "should believe in every possible application to art-theory of the thoughts of the Declaration of Independence and Lincoln's Gettysburg Address";[33] and then democracy and beauty would be convertible currency.

BEAUTY AND RELIGION

Lindsay's association of beauty and religion was as close as that of beauty and democracy. "That joy in beauty which no wound can take away and that joy in the love of God which no crucifixion can end" were two sides of the same coin. Churches had set themselves up as guardians of the divinely created world and the souls who inhabited it, and the clergyman incurred "responsibility as the custodian of a ripening civilization as well as the watchdog of its morals."[34] But the churches had sanctioned good conduct to the point where it had become ineffectively platitudinous, and Lindsay thought they might try his novel, emotive approach to the upright life through the concept of beauty. In his tramp across Missouri and Kansas in 1912 to preach his gospel, he urged "let the denomination to which you now belong be called in your heart 'the church of beauty'. . . . The church of beauty has two sides: the love of beauty and the love of God."[35] His talk of a church and a gospel of beauty did not mean that he was suggesting beauty as a new religion. All beauty, inner and outer, was religious (ultimately God-given, though often man-made), but religion did not consist solely of beauty. By itself, Lindsay affirmed, "beauty is *not* truth, for I *know* beauty already." It was an underestimated component of religion, a new path to religion's spirit.[36]

He could think of no better way "to worship the Lord than with glorious works of art," and turned to the Bible to settle American puritanical scruples about spending time to enjoy or seek beauty. He also had to counteract the taboos of revivalist preachers. Springfield was Peter Cartwright country and bore the imprint of stump diatribes against the sinfulness of cultivating beauty. In Lindsay's eyes such arguments showed only ignorance of the rainbow color, the dignity, the sculptural line of *the book*. The Gospels begin with the heavenly hosts singing of glory, with the

Magnificat of Mary with the gold frankincense and myrrh of the wise, and end with a blaze of resurrection light. There is hardly a parable but is passionate with that adoration of nature which is the beginning of art.

He saw music, sculpture, and all uses of color, light, and line as extensions of nature; the arts were under biblical patronage. Like Henry Adams he looked back to the time when the arts were an exact expression of life, but he derived more hope than Adams from his retrospection. "Why should not the Bible make your village of heavenly aspect, as it has many an old-world town? Remember the Romanesque and the Gothic architect and repent." [37]

Lindsay considered the combination of beauty and holiness valid for the total religious experience. Moses was "the Angelo of statesmanship, the inspirer of the laws"; the ten commandments intended "that all lovable things shall be nurtured to delight our eyes"; "the Sabbath is not a period of deadly inertia, but of artistic incubation." [38] Human beauty was naturally religious; in "The Springfield of the Far Future" Lindsay imagined a breed of city dwellers whose way of life expressed

> . . . *beauty's tradition sublime.*
> *Proud and gay and gray*
> *Like Hannah with Samuel blest.*
> *Humble and girlish and white*
> *Like Mary, the manger-guest.*

The quintessence of beauty was the religious imagination and the religious experience: the "strangely carved celestial gem/Eternal in its beauty light/The Artist's town of Bethlehem!" [39]

Lindsay's perception of spirituality and egalitarianism in beauty and of beauty in spirituality and egalitarianism gave the measure of the intellectual and emotional coherence of his gospel. "Consider Leviticus and Numbers champion a ministry, a peculiar priesthood, in which public health, national ritual and cleanliness are all bound together, to secure for the nation both holiness and splendor," [40] he wrote in justification and explanation of the gospel of beauty; and in his sense the adjectives religious, beautiful, and egalitarian were equally applicable to "public health," "national ritual," and "cleanliness." This unified set of attitudes was memorably described by Theodore Roethke in "Supper with Lindsay," when he had Lindsay say:

> *Who called me poet of the college yell?*
> *We need a breed that mixes Blake and me,*
> *Heroes and bears, and old philosophers—*
> *John Ransom should be here, and Rene Char;*
> *Paul Bunyan is part Russian, did you know?* [41]

This was Lindsay's gospel: a vigorous, idiosyncratic application of primary concepts which underpinned his determination to write for Everyman, which impelled his attempt to codify history, myth, and regional self-consciousness in a national entity, which provided the basis for the superstructure of *The Golden Book of Springfield* in year 2018 of the embryonic world state.

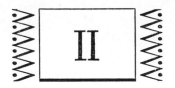

II

The Golden Book of Springfield

1918

Lᴵɴᴅsᴀʏ sᴇᴛ his picture of a future America in *The Golden Book of Springfield* in 2018, a hundred speculative years after 1918. Nineteen eighteen was important to him not only as the year which saw the end of the first world war, but because he felt that the ensuing discussion of international cooperation, even in the tentative, noncommittal form of the League of Nations, constituted a move toward establishing "in the name of God/The United States of Europe, Asia and the World." [1] He did not expect such a Union overnight: "Federation is going to be as hard for the world as it was for America," [2] he wrote to Katharine Lee Bates, and it was this juxtaposition of possible hopes and probable failures that made 1918 a base date peculiarly suited to speculation. It was a year whose achievement at one instant seemed positive and concrete, but which came to stand for flux and uncertainty; it was a time of transition from war to peace, and yet from optimism to pessimism; it was a time when some people looked nostalgically backwards, and others despondently forward: it summed up human contrariness and the human predicament on a grand scale. "When the lads returned from the war with Germany, and the girls returned from Red Cross work, and the like" [3] America's international empathy, which might have entered a period of gestation, was aborted into isolationism.

Pressures from his publisher and his own wish to make the book topical made Lindsay set the two Springfields in 1920 (the year of publication) and 2018, not in 1918 and 2018. The alteration detracted from the international moral he was drawing from 1918

for America 2018 and from the significance of 1918 for Springfield
itself. It was the centenary of Illinois' admission to the Union and,
even more importantly, it was the year that the Russell Sage Foundation of New York City completed a social survey of Springfield,
the first survey of its kind in America. The fact that it was taking
place encouraged Lindsay to see hopeful auguries in Springfield
for America's urban dimension, and many of the survey's findings
were reflected in *The Golden Book of Springfield*.

THE SPRINGFIELD SURVEY

Lindsay had chosen Springfield, Illinois, as the setting for his
main work because it was his favorite and most familiar town,
and because it had a national—Lincolnian—significance. His home-
town syndrome had been evident in the articles of *The Village
Magazine* (1910) and the poems of *The Tramp's Excuse* (1909),
well before the Springfield Survey was begun in 1914; but had he
scoured America to discover a representative city, and one capable
of substantial self-improvement, he could hardly have made a better choice, or so the Russell Sage team concluded. Springfield
emerged from the survey as "a city of many averages." [4] Lindsay
had always maintained that "Mason and Dixon's line runs straight
through our house in Springfield," [5] and the survey's statistics
showed Springfield to be just such an amalgam. Midway between
the Northern and Southern states, it was near the population
center of the whole country. With northern Illinois settled predominantly by Easterners and a preponderance of Southerners in
the southern part of the state, mid-state Springfield was a generic
and ideological melting pot. Of every 100 inhabitants 81 were
native-born whites, 13 foreign-born whites, and 6 Negroes, a sta-
tistic in between the 1910 regional (83:15:2) and national (75:
15:10) figures. In other senses, too, it was an average rather than
an exceptional city. Capital city status was offset by standing fourth
in Illinois' urban populations, eleventh in the number of factory
workers in the State's cities, and fourteenth in the value of its
products. As well as being one of forty-eight state capitals, Springfield, with 58,000 inhabitants was one of fourteen American cities

in the 50,000–60,000 population range. Located in the heart of a rich agricultural region, a center for mining, manufacturing, commerce, and public administration, it had much in common with many other American cities which functioned on the basis of two or more of these occupations.

Nine reports on various aspects of Springfield, including its public schools, recreational facilities, housing conditions, correctional system, and industrial structure were issued during the survey, and the director of the Russell Sage Foundation, Shelby M. Harrison, correlated the findings in a summary volume *Social Conditions in an American City* (1920). Harrison was swift to see the possibilities of what he called "this unusually American city" as a reform prototype.

Why not put the imagination and resources of the commonwealth into making the capital city of each state its standard municipality in health, housing, education, charity, correction, recreation, industrial relations and governmental efficiency? [6]

For Springfield seemed to the survey team to bulge with unexplored potentialities: It was economically and socially diverse, it was expanding, and it was not without healthy elements of introspection. In 1911, as part of the nationwide Progressive movement for more direct political participation by the electorate, Springfield had adopted the commission form of local government which provided for election by the total voting population and not by delegates; election of commissioners to oversee experts, not to substitute for them; and the initiative, referendum, and recall. The changeover indicated a desire, however temporary, for civic involvement. Above all, Springfield had produced a group of people with enough public conscience and with a sufficiently long-term view of reform to invite the surveyors to the city, a group with a feeling that "more than the improvement of local conditions might hang on their enterprise," looking for "the leaven of civic renewal" [7] throughout America. They were fictionalized in a twenty-first century Springfield, which was "as National and Federal as the District of Columbia," as "The Prognosticators Club." [8]

Harrison's hopes and conclusions about the national significance of a reformed Springfield were so much Lindsay's that the latter urged people who read his own book "to read, in conjunction with it, a book issued the same day, prepared through the same years, and based on the same Springfield Survey reports: SOCIAL CONDITIONS IN AN AMERICAN CITY."[9] Lindsay commented on the exhibition which the Foundation mounted to show its findings and its recommendations:

The picture of this survey exhibit will remain in the minds of the citizens as the general concept toward which they are all going. . . . We have the serious expectation that henceforth Springfield's graver rank and file and leading citizens of whatever party are enlisted for steady lifetime tasks, each in his own chosen place.[10]

The exhibition intensified Lindsay's existing concern for America and confirmed his instinctive fears, for it was a series of pictures of stagnation. The educational system on which he placed so much reliance[11] was one community failing. The teaching staff was entirely inbred: all the teachers were graduates of Springfield High and Springfield Teaching College. Of 224 teachers in the public schools only five were allotted to drawing, music, and domestic science, and only two to crafts and manual training; the national educational trend toward vocational training and instruction in subjects related to everyday life was ignored. The proportion of illiteracy was on the increase; at five percent it was greater than that in any other city over 30,000 in Illinois.

Children certainly came off badly in this Springfield. One-tenth of them died before reaching the age of one. There was no adequate provision for the care and treatment of those who indulged in juvenile crime: young offenders were kept in cells with alcoholics and prostitutes, and formed a large proportion of the fifty-eight percent of annual false arrests. Many children younger than the legal age worked a ninety-hour seven-day week (illegal for adults), and the authorities connived at this shortened schooling by employing only one attendance officer. Growing up, youth found regular employment hard to obtain; the staple mining industry virtually closed down in winter. Good health was equally scarce in the face of insufficient medical attention, a high death rate from tuberculosis and pneumonia, the suffocating smoke nuisance, and the increasing number of unhygienic privies and open wells. Springfield provided grim conditioning for its young people; it was on the way to producing generations of "The Leaden-Eyed."

The city's major environmental asset was its generous ratio of parkland: one acre to every 131 inhabitants, while Chicago, noted for its parks, only averaged 1:193. Clarence Arthur Perry, recreation surveyor, suggested that this open air dimension lent itself to pageantry—"a drama in which the place is the hero and the development of the community is the plot." [12] Lindsay's admired Percy Mackaye (1875–1956), collector and creator of American legends and organizer of communal dramatics, was putting forward much the same view at the same time. In *The New Citizenship,* 1915, he contended that external historical consciousness—wearing costume, observing anniversaries with precise ritual, recalling the past in plays and ceremonials—would make for better patriots and more conscientious citizens. [13] Lindsay tried out the theory in the green expanses of Springfield 2018; and while he found even the fictional practice artificial and occasionally ludicrous, he maintained his belief that it was as important to look comprehendingly backwards as it was to look intelligently ahead, and that an appreciation of the national and local heritage would breed responsibility.

The deficiencies and resources uncovered by the Springfield Survey were of national importance, the Russell Sage Foundation argued, because of the increasing significance for America of her urban patterns. Shelby Harrison pointed out that

each year . . . the population of the United States becomes increasingly a city population [the 1920 census showed that for the first time as many people lived in the city as the country]. When the cities were few and small we could be relatively less concerned for the fate for their people. . . . But now the nation goes as the city goes. [14]

"The nation goes as the city goes" was the contemporary nature of Lindsay's concern, which led him to draw his community of 2018 from the actualities and possibilities of 1918, though he added some personal flourishes. The fundamental correspondence of twentieth and twenty-first century America was nowhere more apparent than in the architectural and environmental concepts which Springfield 2018 was trying to put into operation.

THE THEORY OF THE
ARCHITECTURAL ENVIRONMENT

At the end of the nineteenth century architects and planners were coming to rethink their crafts not only in terms of the implications of new technics and new materials but in terms of their function. They were moving away from the idea of designing for an elite privileged in wealth and/or taste and toward a belief in America's national architectural necessity. For they had begun to put a Darwinistic interpretation on environment: it became the cause of evil, ugliness, attrition, and failure; a necessary condition of goodness, beauty, health, and success; and a factor which could make or mar the individual and the nation. Lindsay reflected this belief in the total social significance of architecture by seeing it as yet another means to gospel ends—and perhaps an insidiously effective one.

The great material projects are often easier to realize than the little moral reforms. Beautiful architectural undertakings, while appearing to be material, and succeeding by the laws of American enterprise, bring with them the healing hand of beauty. Beauty is not directly pious, but does more civilizing in its proper hour than any sermons or laws.[15]

Concomitantly he argued that America could not call herself a civilization until she had buildings which were as American as the Taj Mahal was Indian; and in the imprecise but enthusiastic terminology of *The Village Magazine* he wrote:

Friend, let us toil that this our raw and rasping western nation may be redeemed, and wear such white robes of marvel, such minarets of quiet snow. Through our great missionaries we send the East the gospel of brotherhood. Let us not be too full of spiritual self-sufficiency. Let us receive in return from them the silent gospel of beauty. It is not that we are to imitate these special forms, or carry on the Arabesque tradition. We are rather to interpret our own land in that rare hour when it is serene. Let it remain the free young West, yet become a land where sacred rivers have place.[16]

He called in more specific terms in *The Golden Book of Springfield* (and *The Litany of Washington Street,* 1929) for a nationally uniform and uniquely American architecture of serenity and modernity. (But can the two ever be compatible in an America whose perpetual change is the essence of her attraction?) He wanted a style embodying the best of the Machine Age—its precision, its cleanliness, its hard illuminations, its unflinchingly functional logic—and which would assimilate these qualities into a perspective of individual adjustment, social progress, and total beauty. This style, he considered, would be a mature American architecture, and he believed it was on the way.

We are now applying to skyscrapers, landscape gardening, coast-to-coast highways, and things more bordering on the social rather than the scientific life, the genius of Jefferson, not that of Edison. We are just beginning to graduate into the former's mellow type of Virginia versatility. We are becoming Randolphs.[17]

The twentieth century Randolphs who inspired the architects of Springfield 2018 were Louis Sullivan (1856–1924) and Frank Lloyd Wright (1869–1959). Springfield's buildings seemed "to live and breathe" for they were effective products "of the school of Louis Sullivan and Frank Lloyd Wright," the original practitioners of "Organic Architecture," a theory of unifying the inner and outer worlds through buildings whose usefulness, comfort, and beauty made for "the beauty of human lives," [18] and whose form followed the function of social utility. In 1918 Sullivan had only six years of life left, but he was expressing himself as forcibly as ever about the inextricable association of democracy and national architectural patterns, which was one of his perceptive contributions to American architectural theory. He defined architecture as "the great creative art of upbuilding a chosen and stable civilization with its unique culture"; and therefore concluded America's need of an indigenous architectural style which would express "the deep, the sincere, the wholesome aspirations of our people, and of our land," [19] a style which would be applicable to houses, shops, factories, and schools, and not merely to showpiece buildings. His other major contribution to American architectural thinking was to take the lead in breaking away from the acceptance of the city as a solely commercial proposition for commercial intercourse. His Wainwright Building in St. Louis, the first steel frame skyscraper (which he followed in the 1890s with the Gage, Stock Exchange, and Auditorium Buildings in Chicago) declared war on the city of stiflingly packed skyscrapers, heavy blocks of masonry which eliminated light, air, and space, and only made sense in terms of property manipulations. He substituted his concept of a city in which the spaciously located skyscraper, slender and soaring, was an aesthetic and social structure, opening up new and increasingly egalitarian patterns of work, play, and everyday life. Understandably he was a legendary figure in the Chicago which was Lindsay's local metropolis, and where, as an art student, he was especially aware of Sullivan.

Sullivan's rationalization of the skyscraper to some degree resolved the city dilemma, and enabled his pupil Wright to go ahead and envisage whole new city formations. Many of Wright's books did not appear until after Lindsay's death, and the complete model of his urban blueprint, Broadacre City, was not exhibited until 1934. But both men were in Chicago during the first decade of the twentieth century. Wright lectured to, and Lindsay attended Hull House; and Lindsay also came to know Wright's buildings in Springfield and Chicago. From 1900 to 1920, in articles, drawings, and speeches Wright publicized what were later to be integrated as components of Broadacre City: an interfaith cathedral, skyscrapers in green settings, and air, road, and rail transport which were sculptured, swift, and silent. Lindsay transposed these components as a unit into Springfield 2018 in a correct anticipation of their significance not merely as separate projects but for overall city planning. They were related manifestations of that modern beauty and controlled technology which Wright thought would make for contented, equable inhabitants of his "City of Democracy"; and in so far as Springfield 2018 approached a more real egalitarianism than twentieth century America, it was largely due to the Wrightian environment.

The city-country placename "Broadacre City" echoed Lindsay's urbanized "village"; and similarly a key characteristic of Wright's city was the integration of nature and man-made constructions. "Broadacres would be so actually built in sympathy with omnipresent nature that deep feeling for the beauty of terrain would be fundamental in the new city building," Wright explained. He planned to do Sullivanesque justice to the skyscraper by locating it in its own small park, and rhapsodized about exuberantly modern "shafts rising above greenery,"

tier on tier of glass used as screen-walls, golden with sun on the shining steel of copper-sheathed frames, each tier with its own flower- and vine-festooned balcony terraces. Such tall buildings would stand in irridescence of vivid color in the landscape set up in spacious blossoming grounds[20]

—hence the "orchard city" of 2018, with its "sunset towers" of glass and steel, and its many parks.

Wright intended Broadacre City to utilize intelligently all "modern gifts, steel in tension, steam, electro-magnetic sciences, chemistry, new atomic dissonance, alchemy." It was the kind of city that Lindsay had envisaged in "On the Building of Springfield" in his 1909 "Gospel of Beauty" trilogy: "Let Science and Machinery and Trade/Be slaves of her and make her all in all." As if to strengthen such invisible ties between himself and Lindsay, Wright found he could explain his architectural theories most easily in terms of poetry.

Architecture speaks as poetry to the soul. A good building is the greatest of poems when it is organic architecture. The building faces and is reality and serves while it releases daily life; daily life is better worth living and all the necessities are happier because of useful living in a building none the less poetry, but more truly so. Every great architect is—necessarily—a great poet.[21]

In some measure the converse was applicable to Lindsay, great in architectural perception, if without technical architectural ability. The two men were bound together by their utilitarian yet transcendental conception of the effect of art. It was almost inevitable that in twenty-first century America Lindsay should be looking for "a ripe architectural genius" like Wright, technically excellent, and who also related architecture to human growth, community spirit, and the realization of American democracy, an architect

who will gather to himself all that can be known of beam and girder and truss, of foundation and wind pressure, and the distribution of light, all that can be learned about brick and tile, of pillar and elevator and fireproofing. He will understand the chances peculiar to his materials and town. . . . He will have visions of welded steel that will put all men to shame but the builders of the Parthenon, the hewers of the Sphinx. There shall be no borrowing from Paris or Rome.[22]

Two lesser architectural progenitors of Springfield 2018 were Ebenezer Howard and Ralph Adams Cram. Lindsay expressed the hope[23] that *The Golden Book of Springfield* would lead Americans to investigate avant-garde prototype cities like Howard's Letchworth Garden City scheme in Hertfordshire, England. Like Broadacre City, the Garden City concept unified city and country. It was a city in a garden and of gardens, with wide, tree-scaped streets, and a five-to-one proportion of green land to built-up areas. Howard had also evolved a plan for a grouped unit of Garden Cities with access to a larger, mother city, metropolitan, but itself a Garden City: his solution to the search for a design capable of reproduction on a nationwide scale. Wright's solution was a virtual one-city nation, with numerous Broadacre Cities merging into the great community of Broadacres, a solution which Lindsay reproduced somewhat confusingly in a Springfield which was both Springfield and America.

In an essay about "Springfield's Ancient Mariner" (himself) Lindsay admitted that

in some ways he agrees with Ralph Adams Cram, as to what should be the typical future American City . . . he pictures a walled town with a gigantic cathedral, a city which will seem to some mediaeval.[24]

Cram (1865-1942), a devout Catholic, was strongly opposed to the impersonalization of the big society and big business; he imagined that basic human contacts and values could be reinstated in a community which he called "vill" and "commune." He attributed to it the unity of outlook, simplicity of function, and religious atmosphere of Lindsay's village, though Lindsay could not approve the detailed structure of this community, which, in its determination to eliminate all uncongenial labor, cut out luxury items, excluded industrial and mechanical benefits, and reduced existence to a primitive simplicity. But Cram's passionate, religious concern for a better way of life and a beautiful environment—"beyond a certain point man cannot live in and with and through ugliness, nor can society endure under such conditions"—was a general inspiration of Springfield 2018, which Lindsay acknowledged by giving Springfield a set of city walls named after Cram. The walls also expressed for Lindsay the idea of integration characteristic of medieval towns like Nuremberg, "cities which were nations within a nation, and in which citizenship was indicated by a flag and badge and costume representing a special honor and protection." [25] It was this idea which led Lindsay to formulate the concept of a network of World's Fair cities across America, cities striving for excellence in all spheres, and developing into centers where individual integrity, community spirit, and patriotism were highly regarded.

THE WORLD'S FAIR CONCEPT

World's Fairs and large expositions were increasingly prevalent in Lindsay's America. More than a dozen were held between 1893 and 1915, and they took on a relative importance in national life, especially for the literary and architectural sectors of the community with which Lindsay was affiliated. For Louis Sullivan the Chicago World's Fair of 1893, for which he designed the Transportation Building, had an undeniable and undesirable significance. "Here was to be the test of American culture, and here it failed," [26] he commented; for the only architectural advance consisted of a swing from Romantic to Classical devotee-ism. Foreign visitors found nothing remotely indigenous about the Fair's architecture except Sullivan's building, a plain, purposeful form with a touch of exotic prosperity in a richly decorated doorway. He had had the building sprayed gold in defiant contrast to the all-white World's Fair City on Chicago's Lake Front. Let America be her idiosyncratic, materialistic self, his building seemed to say, and cease to make even the monuments of her characteristic affluence plaster imitations of old Europe's marble. After all, the Chicago World's Fair did call itself the Columbian Exposition, and was supposed to celebrate Columbus's discovery of an altogether New World.

Lindsay visited that same Columbian Exposition. (There is no evidence that he visited any other World's Fair.) His diary for the period shows a schoolboy's reactions to lions, Turks in fezzes, and Grace Darling's boat. But from the subsequent formulation of his World's Fair theory it is clear that the event had a lasting impact on him. He succumbed emotionally to the fascination of World's Fairs, and his later theorizing amounted to an intellectual coming-to-terms with this fascination. Sullivan had noted a World's Fairs' magic, but with reservations: "Dreamers may dream; but of what avail the dream if it is but a dream of misinterpretation?" [27] He did not allow for the inspiration of his own buildings and ideas, which enabled a Lindsay to visualize in *The* Golden *Book of Springfield* a thoroughly American city, "a national dream, a music, a hope and the best place for dreamers in America." [28] And like Lindsay, others saw beyond the almost totally unoriginal shell of the Fair to the exciting idea of collecting the qualities and achievements of a civilization under one roof, of sampling what society had achieved, and of suggesting in which direction it might move. Hamlin Garland felt at the Columbian Exposition that "an era of swift and shining development" had been dramatically summarized; and E. L. Masters regretted the closing of that Fair, which for him symbolized the "glory and freedom of the Republic."

Here indeed was an emotion and an event to capitalize on; and Henry Adams, deeply concerned for America in his involuted way, seized on the possibilities of the Chicago World's Fair which "asked . . . for the first time the question whether the American people knew where they were driving." The Fair seemed to him to have managed to express American heterogeneity as a homogeneous unit, and in admiring acknowledgement of this seemingly impossible achievement, he "professed the religion of World's Fairs." [29] Lindsay was similarly converted, and he believed it possible "to enlarge this proclivity [for expositions] into a national mission in as definite a movement as carefully thought out as the public school system . . . [and] the Steel Trust." He envisaged a permanent, coast-to-coast, Panama-Pacific Exposition, with cities as pavilions: Chicago—Transportation (a tribute to Sullivan's Transportation Building as well as a characterization of Chicago's perpetual motion); Kansas City—Agriculture; Denver—Mining; Jacksonville—Horticulture.[30] Such a permanent national World's Fair would be a source of employment and profit to Americans, and was therefore a realistic proposition. But it would also be a national social achievement: Americans working for, creating, and enjoying an object to which they could all contribute and from which they could all derive. They would unconsciously train themselves in the qualities and logic of good citizenship.

Lindsay also hoped that a regular influx of foreign visitors would foster a spirit of internationalism in Americans, and make them admit the universality of habits and aspirations (though it was more likely that his World's Fair concept would stimulate chauvinism!). Consequently he imagined as one of the desirable trends of the twenty-first century an American World's Fair in which Springfield was the Architectural Pavilion, and he looked forward to America becoming a pavilion in a Universal World's Fair.

PRESENT AND FUTURE

In 1920 Lindsay sent out a pamphlet about *The Golden Book of Springfield* to the sponsors of his recitations, to national networks of clubs and organizations, and to civic authorities. The statements he made in the circular, "A Letter for Your Wicked

Private Ear Only," showed how firmly he considered the book to be rooted in his own times. He claimed that it was relevant to all American cities and civic leaders, and that he wanted to speak about it to "the entire inner machine of the town, all types of kinds of chieftains . . . who were responsible, for instance, for the Billy Sunday campaign . . . and all the Liberty Loan Campaigns"; for he wanted the book to be applied as well as read. It was not as conceited as it sounded, for he hoped that cities and citizens would adapt his book to their own situations, put their own glosses on it, and only refer to it as "a kind of temporary sketchy Civic Koran" "till the town can build its own Alhambra and Taj Mahal, and write its *own* Arabian Nights (and forget mine)." [31]

Lindsay's intention was to rouse the public to action by showing what could be achieved in American cities with a little imagination and foresight, and with not too radical a disruption of human stolidity and conventionality. He hoped he had the appeal of reason, for there was no remotely perfect person or institution in Springfield 2018, and no completely successful project. The picture he drew was one which the most dour man-in-the-street could identify as a potential America, with its assets—an increasingly beautiful environment, controlled mechanical aids, growing social and religious brotherhood, tentative international cooperation—and its liabilities—ugly, dominant mechanization, rampant materialism, and a fissiparous and belligerent world developing combatively alongside. There were elements of fantasy in the story line of the book, which Lindsay had originally intended as a series of essays, but which his publishers had insisted he fictionalize; his own dream came through, but he did not describe a dream society, a utopia.[32] *The Golden Book of Springfield* was neither a holier-than-thou comparison of what was with what ought to be, nor a sanguine description of a startlingly better community; nor was it an unrelievedly gloomy picture of the inevitable decay of civilization, an anti-utopia like Edward Shanks' *The People of the Ruins,* also published in 1920. Lindsay's book was a purposely tentative delineation of those trends of his society, hopeful and discouraging, which he thought would survive into the twenty-first century, purposely tentative because he did not believe that human beings could make confident predictions and because humanity had deserted ethical predictability for a state of chaotic uncertainty.

He made the point of intentional indefinitiveness through his use of golden imagery in the book. The original Golden Book which appeared supernaturally to the characters of *The Golden Book of Springfield* was an unadulterated text of Religion, Equality, and Beauty. The glass and steel skyscrapers of Springfield 2018 ran the gamut of golden sunset colors, the "pure" gold of St. John's New Jerusalem, which had the purity of glass (and vice versa). Reflecting and filtering light, they made the streets seem like carpets of dandelion and goldenrod. Art and nature had arrived at a golden indistinguishableness. But a hard, crude yellow-gold was the color used by the imperialist aggressor in 2018, the "yellow peril" Singapore (a choice of menace dictated by color symbolism and not by racialism)[33] for its drug-selling Yellow Dance Halls and for its warring airplanes.

This ambivalent use of golden imagery was Lindsay's way of conveying the paradox of the American way of life. Gold, part of creation, was intrinsically good; good, too, was the American promise of an ideologically new society, purged of social and political impurities. Gold in the hands of men unable to leave well enough alone aroused possessive instincts, and produced a cut-throat society; man's perversion of the American promise was an unprecedented display of the capacity to ignore ideals and to indulge acquisitiveness. Even for himself, Lindsay admitted, gold was both God and Mammon; and on several occasions he broke the book's narrative to explore "Map of the Universe" territory, worlds outside time and space, to find reassurance about his reform aims. Each time, however, he succumbed to the temptation to admire himself in glittering pools of "devil's gold" and he failed to conquer his self-indulgent, materialistic streak. Even the fantasy of *The Golden Book of Springfield* was rooted in reality, the reality of self-analysis, and the whole book was rooted in the limitations and possibilities of America and its men and women.

CHAPTER SIX

2018

O N THE TITLE PAGE OF *The Golden Book of Springfield* Lindsay
explained he had written "the review of a book that will
appear in the autumn of the year 2018, and an extended description
of Springfield, Illinois, in that year."[1] This Golden Book was a
heaven-sent textbook of the good society; it appeared miraculously
to various citizens of Springfield 2018 (transposed citizens of 1918)
who had strong views about the kind of future they wanted for
their city and their country. Few of them could agree on a description of the book's cover or its contents; after all, Lindsay pointed
out, in some places south of Mason and Dixon's line the story ran,
even in history books, that Grant surrendered to Lee. To represent
the diversity of human and national reactions, the variety of social
goals and of projected means of reaching them, he peopled his
book with a cross section of Springfield society.

The dream-visions of the people to whom the book appeared
were twentieth century dreams "writ" large. The correspondence
lent realism to the different Springfields they saw, though for
Lindsay, himself, the original Golden Book, the most apparently
unlikely part of his story, was ultimately the most realistic of his
creations. It was a reminder that man's best resort and essential aid
is God. But his was only one interpretation of the Golden Book,
and many others were forthcoming when a small group of friends
met at the Leland Hotel, Springfield, on All Saints Day, 1918, to
discuss the question of whither Springfield, whither America? The
group discovered that the previous night each of them had seen
"vistas of the future of their city"[2] in a dream. Each had been

transposed into an inhabitant of Springfield 2018 in a form congruous with his twentieth century occupation, and each proceeded to describe his dream to the other members of The Prognosticators Club.

THE PROGNOSTICATORS CLUB

One of the leading members of the Club was David Carson, in 1918 a Campbellite minister, and in 2018 St. Friend, a Catholic priest and the town's most notable religious figure. The Golden Book appeared to him in his great Wrightian interfaith cathedral of St. Peter and St. Paul as a "book of air, gleaming with spiritual gold," flying through the walls as if they were shadows. It was bordered and illuminated like a medieval manuscript, and its teachings consisted of vague prophecies about the coming of a half-millennial Springfield. Nathan Levi, a young Jewish pawn-broker, found himself transformed into another of 2018's religious leaders, Rabbi Terence Ezekiel. When he came to open the Torah he found instead a book of "Air and Wonder" [3] which predicted that Springfield was about to become a human unit with a common soul instead of a congeries of people. Neither Rabbi Ezekiel nor St. Friend were especially religious interpreters of the Golden Book. Although they were allies, and in that sense progressive churchmen, their revelations were platitudinous. There was no wholly integrated or logical figure in 2018, any more than in 1918, and Lindsay left it to a person for whom he had rather less liking, the raucous Baptist Daisy Pearl Johnson, in 2018 a revivalist Negro leader, Mary Timmons, to find a relatively simple Golden Book, wafted on enormous feathers, with doves and robins flying around it, to be the Bible, open at the Beatitudes. This interpretation for Lindsay was undoctrinaire teaching, straight from a New Testament whose truth he did not doubt, and unadulterated by any sectarian interpretation. But he did not expect to find any member of the Prognosticators Club, or of American society, reflecting his views. Mary Timmons put her own perverse gloss on the Bible, thinking she discovered interpolations specifically commending the emancipation of the Negro, and urging the immediate elevation of

Negro leaders in all walks of life.[4] There were other equally partisan interpretations of the Golden Book. A Christian Scientist reading *Science and Health* saw it turn into a plain, unwinged, silver book which emanated a purifying white light; it prophesied the glorious rebuilding of the city's decaying First Church of Christ Scientist and the subsequent conversion of the whole town to the teachings of Mary Baker Eddy. A pantheistic florist saw a boulder which was being removed from the Governor's yard struck by a thunderbolt, and a book fly forth preaching the panacea of contact with nature and quoting Swedenborg.

The Prognosticators Club had many nonreligious members with nonreligious reactions. For Eloise Terry, whose organizing abilities as a 1918 hostess had turned her into Patricia Anthony, a 2018 factory inspector for the Telescope and Microscope Company (and who came across the book while checking supplies), the book was economic, with citations from Adam Smith, Karl Marx, Henry George, and the twenty-first century economists Joseph Bartholdi Michael II and Black Hawk Boone. The head of an expanding color printing firm envisaged an indestructible book of popular sayings, which, even when burnt, rose again four times as big; it was mass-produced for America, Europe, and Asia, and rendered the original superfluous (and at the same time lessened its impact). A scenario writer gave Lindsay's comment: in the course of watching the first takes of a film about the founders of Springfield, he saw a book flashed onto the screen which seemed to everyone present to depict, with irresistible beauty, their own church.

Lindsay was no less judicious in his breakdown of the opposition to a reformed Springfield. In its ranks was an artist, John "Sparrow" Short, who, like all citizens of Springfield, but somewhat more than most, mixed virtue and vice. He had been a tremendous force for good in American art; he had taught over a thousand pupils to liberate themselves from European influences and had sponsored artists until he became penniless himself. But he was an apolitical pacifist who believed in the integrity of isolation, in unwritten but binding diplomatic understandings, and in the possibility of instant world peace without an accustoming period of authoritative enforcement. Similarly, he saw no need for rules and laws in Springfield. His philosophy ran "be yourself completely. Utter your soul, regardless of cost," a dangerously libellous viewpoint which from time to time landed him in prison. There he found among his reading material a Golden Book which urged the dissolution of all forms of official international government and a "return to the glory of the ancient time of the unchained nations,"[5] that era of peace and goodwill when the Czar instituted the Hague Tribunal and Andrew Carnegie introduced peace lectures.

Sparrow Short's was a mistaken idealism. A less excusably perverse interpretation of the Golden Book was that of Cave Man Thomas, formerly a dubious evangelist, and in 2018 Vice President of the Springfield Athletic Union. His bent for channeling crowd hysteria was an asset to the antireform elements in the city. In the course of going through the President's desk after that individual's mysterious demise, he came across a cheaply printed, yellow-backed book, rather like the local *Spaulding's Athletic Guide* in appearance. This paperback preached eternal hellfire and a temporal beating-up for all who dared to disagree with the sacred trio of God, Mayor, and Doctor: a triune authority based on the unthinking, unassertive citizen's fearful respect for the representatives of power over life after death, day-to-day survival, and community status. Lindsay conceived this unattractive character to be an American type!

Most of Lindsay's debunking comments on the opposition to the new Springfield were about the city boss, Mayo Sims, who in 1918 was a financier, John Fletcher. He represented that impregnable commercial class which Lindsay detested, and which worked on the assumption that "politics is business and business is politics and the only worth while citizens are those that 'get the money.'" Fletcher-Sims was appalled by the idea of "any clan wanting anything except well-dressed bank accounts to rule the city." His belief that "every large bank account is automatically moral, that every small one is almost moral, and the one crime is to be without money"[6] showed his adherence to the Gospel of Wealth. Religion entered his life on Sundays only, from eleven to twelve-thirty, and he put liberal ideas equally firmly in their place by blandly interpreting the Emancipation Proclamation to mean that he should be exempt from criticism. With his powers of self-deception it was not surprising that Fletcher-Sims, who explained Christ and Mohammed as epileptics,[7] dreamt of a book of chronicles and parables which taught the heresy of economic leveling, but which was utterly rejected by the mass of citizens. He recollected that one tattered, wingless copy with a cheap gilt cover was passed around for a time, but it was soon dropped into an abandoned coal shaft. It had been written by sociologists from the University of Springfield, who for the anti-intellectual city fathers were prime suspects as critics of social and economic privilege.

Lindsay's idea of a new, heaven-sent textbook of government and morality may well have originated in the story of Joseph Smith's discovery of the Book of Mormon. Smith, aptly, was part of Illinois' history. In 1839 the Mormons had made their third attempt at settlement at Nauvoo, Illinois, before their final migration to Utah in 1846; Smith had been lynched in jail in Carthage, Illinois, in 1844. Contemporary testimony about his discovery of the Book of Mormon in Ohio in 1821 reads as if Lindsay were putting words into the mouth of a member of the Prognosticators Club.

He said there was a book deposited, written upon gold plates, giving an account of the former inhabitants of this continent. . . . He also said that the fullness of the everlasting Gospel was contained in it.[8]

The Book of Mormon appeared as mystically as the Golden Book. Smith was led by an angel, Moroni, to a hillside where he excavated the book from among earth and rock. The eight-inch square, thin gold plates which were the pages, and the sword-breastplate-spectacles contraption which had to be worn to decipher the book were in the spirit of the paraphernalia which were present when each Prognosticator found his book. The parallel between Smith and the Prognosticators underlined what Lindsay was trying to say through the device of the Club: that each man gropes for a definitive order with an infallible set of rules, though the end product is intensely subjective. But Lindsay's *Golden Book of Springfield,* unlike the American commandments of Smith's Book of Mormon, and the numerous Golden Books of 2018, was not dogmatic. While it became obvious as the book progressed that Lindsay ranged himself with the would-be reformers of 2018, his reservations about their aims and methods were such that he welcomed the existence of an opposition to prevent them from substituting one unsatisfactory tyranny for another. The Prognosticators Club of 1918, which attracted the custodians of the status quo as well as the advocates of change, was a club of friends. Lindsay accepted a partial irreconcilability of human attitudes, though he certainly hoped that they could be modified to the extent of allowing a little more social cohesiveness at home and a little more political unity in the international sphere.

His plastic, inclusive philosophy was emphasized by his own variety of functions in 2018. Sometimes he was a 1918 style Vachel Lindsay, mockingly and pityingly treated by a Springfield which still expected a conventional day's work from every man; at other times he was a city hall stenographer to an antireform Mayor; a clerk to St. Friend's associate, John Boat, J.P.; and a servant in the house of a statesman from the World Government's most hostile opponent, totalitarian Singapore. In each of these roles the "millennial chameleon" saw with the eyes of those he served. The demands on his capacious tolerance and understanding were nevertheless painful, and he still found the inertness and conservatism of other Americans hard to accept. He described his own passage into the future in physical terms which conveyed the depth of struggle accompanying reform aims taken seriously.

There is deep darkness and time passing by without end, and shade. There is the fear of moles that will not leave me alone, who make nests of alien dust, beneath my ribs. And my bones crumble through the century, like last year's autumn leaves. Then there is, alternating with drouth, [*sic*] bitter frost. And roots wrap my heart and brain. And there is sleep.[9]

CITY BEAUTIFUL

Lindsay's first impression on waking was that little had changed in Springfield. He picked up the *Illinois State Journal* which had the same layout and the same advertisements. Springfield seemed, as of old, "a travelling man's home city, a retired farmer's place of sleep, a state official's paradise. Agricultural experts, coal mining experts, would-be statesmen of the middle west, have the same general relation to the city about them that they had in the ancient days of the horse-cars, and the Sangamon County Fair. The town has many of its ancient types." [10]

But a closer familiarity made him qualify this judgment, and only his own house on South 5th Street finally seemed the same to him. For while he could identify shops and department stores, they were characterized by a formerly unknown pride in a service scrupulously performed. Trades and crafts had adopted insignia and flags which they displayed in their shops and premises as tokens of their immaculate professional and ethical standards. There had been a general release of decorative civic energies. "Our city is indeed a flying, fluttering place," Lindsay found; and in an anticipation of latter-day beflagged drive-ins and musical ice cream vans, "confectionaries, auto trucks, popcorn vans, pleasure machines, and the passing crowds are decked with ribbons and streamers." [11]

Bunting and badges were surface indications of a move toward a functional beauty, a move more fundamentally evidenced by the wholesale replanning of the city which was taking place under the direction of two young architects, a Thibetan-American (nameless) and a Negro, John Emis. They had based their design on the star of the American flag, and had erected a five-pointed system of double walls, Cram's Walls, within which was a network of avenues and boulevards leading to the points of the star. The star-plan network connected and unified a complex of "exquisite and slender sunset towers of the school of Louis H. Sullivan and Frank Lloyd Wright." [12] In the center of the complex were seven rainbow-colored towers, grouped around a central white Truth

Tower, known as the Edgar Lee Masters Tower: a tribute to Masters' *Spoon River Anthology* which seemed to many people a courageous, accurate criticism of American sloth and corruption. Set into the outer sides of the seven steel and glass towers were approximate glass reproductions of the Springfield flag, a red star surrounded by white stars; at night spotlights poured through these murals. The seven rainbow towers themselves formed the hub of a complex of ninety-two other skyscrapers, making a vast sweep of color shading from white in the center through grey, rose-grey, and grey-gold to rose-gold on the perimeter.

The stress laid on red, gold, and sunset colors was part of an association by Lindsay of this color range with the founder of Springfield, John "Hunter" Kelly. In 1832 Kelly had been largely responsible for the choice of Springfield, not Decatur, as the site for the removal of the State capital from Vandalia (by leading an inspecting delegation on an intolerably circuitous and muddy route to Decatur). Few facts or stories survived about Kelly, and so Lindsay, following in Percy Mackaye's footsteps, wove a meaningful legend about Springfield's founding father. In this legend Kelly was inspired by his teacher and friend, Johnny Appleseed, and by his own dog-eared copy of St. Augustine's *City of God* to found a city which he thought of as an apple tree, firmly rooted, producing both blossom and fruit and growing heavenwards. He chose a spot in Sangamon County, Illinois, but before he could plant the seed he was apprehended by the devil, and forced to undergo a form of probationary torture to ensure that Springfield would come into being. He was buried a few feet below the surface of the soil with the roots of the apple tree city entwined in his living skull and heart. Yearly the city grew out of him, and yearly the devil dug him up to test his determination, but Kelly never let pain make him relinquish his mission. At the 1918 ceremony, thinking America would now reflect at home the sobering compassion she had learned abroad (one instance in which Lindsay used Springfield and America synonymously), he drove the devil away and retired to a cell in heaven. He found, however, that he had misconstrued American reactions, and that his work was perilously incomplete. It was he who compiled the original Golden Book, red-gold, the color of the blood with which he ritually dedicated Springfield.

The color range of the buildings and the star system of Springfield 2018 were Lindsay's own carefully constructed symbols, but he had taken to heart Sullivan and Wright's dicta about the relationship of architecture and democracy. Wright had noted the need for "a break-through to sunlight, sky, and air, or we will have a communist factory hand instead of a democratic citizen . . . in a land of opportunity for that worker";[13] and Lindsay described Springfield's architects, John Emis and the Thibetan Boy as "crusaders for democracy," whose buildings were "soldier-machines of liberty." Since they were used by everybody for everything—as schools, homes, shops, restaurants, factories, and recreation centers—they were throwing the community together and making it an egalitarian in-group. Community contacts were thought out with exaggerated care. The walls of the restaurants, for instance, were single sheets of glass so that citizens, whether sitting inside, walking by, or flying past in airplanes which were as ubiquitous as cars, would remain unfragmented. Aesthetically, the skyscrapers expressed as much as Hunter Kelly's tree city concept the humanistic attempt of man to reach up to new worlds, and to God. By contrast, Lindsay noted, despotic Singapore refused

to use the Sunset Towers, when they build their new cities in their battle for world supremacy, and even by that they are doomed. The houses and commercial palaces and temples of Singapore crouch little and low, like huts in a forest, or glass pagodas in little stage comedies. They are fearful of the incantations hatched in our hives of electrical flame that shine on to the glory of Louis H. Sullivan and Frank Lloyd Wright, who planned the first ones, a century ago, and the Thibetan Boy and John Emis who build them today.[14]

But Springfield was not yet thoroughly Wrightian. Many of its inhabitants still lived in individual houses, and would continue to do so until succeeding generations came to prefer the communal egalitarian life, as Lindsay, hoping for egalitarianism and believing

in Wright, assumed they would. Black and white were still segre-
gated, and this separatism too militated against a democratic
Springfield. But the Negro architect John Emis, who was only
allowed a free hand in his own district, managed to make the
small houses of the Negro ghetto as gorgeous as the sunset towers.
He was gradually patterning them in a flower town, a magnified
design of violet petals, and coloring the buildings a reproachfully
dignified purple.[15] Nevertheless, he was patronized far more than
the white Wright had been (Broadacre City never got off the
drawing board); and he was even getting a chance to put something like Broadacres into operation. From the top of the Truth
Tower Lindsay saw with excitement that "Springfield extends
over the whole county [Sangamon County] through the taking in
of countless groves, orchards and aviation fields"; and further ex-
ploration showed him that the whole of Illinois was on the way
to becoming a state of Springfields.[16]

The total environment of the immediate city of Springfield
2018 was benefiting from a refined technology. The streets were
vacuum cleaned and "with no soot and no coal dust and no factory
grime people can be dressed all day for a party if they choose."
Quiet and efficient automation was taking over such routine jobs
as bricklaying. As for transportation facilities—to Lindsay's eyes airplanes seemed like delicate, shining dragonflies, trains like elegantly
slung chariots and proud, devouring "corn-dragons." He was
present at the official start of the first journey of one splendid corn-
dragon, decorated with a plume motif, which had been designed
by a ploughboy (there were still some, apparently), and he was
inspired to imagine that those who saw it, whether city or country
dwellers, would "catch the original vision" [17] of engaging art and
life, and themselves contribute to man's ease and pleasure by in-
venting ways of containing and expressing energy.

Springfield was appreciatively exploiting nature as well as
architecture. The flower town was a miniature garden city, within
an orchard city, landscaped with magnificent trees to complement
the sunset towers. Lindsay especially noted gigantic blossom trees
—Hunter Kelly's Apple-Amaranths,[18] and Golden Rain Trees

from New Harmony, Indiana, symbols of Robert Owen's attempt to refresh democracy. All the skyscrapers were surrounded by parks named after figures significant for Lindsay: Carl Sandburg, another Illinois poet, and one who had sensed unique urban beauty in Chicago; Joyce Kilmer, a poet whose death during the 1914–18 war gave Lindsay a noncombatant's guilt; Louis Untermeyer, a comparatively understanding critic of Lindsay's; and Springfield's Lincoln. Camp Lincoln was the calisthenic, drill, and assembly center of the city, organized around a revolving, irridescent, semi-hemispherical building the size of the Taj Mahal,[19] painted outside like a globe. The citizens of Springfield were thus reminded that they belonged to a nation committed to the World Government.

THE CITIZENS OF SPRINGFIELD

The Michaels were one of the most important families in Springfield. Called after the St. Michael of the Roman Catholic liturgy, "defender in the day of battle," who "stands at the right hand of the altar of incense," they were guardians of civil liberties and disciples of the incense-spirit of ecumenism. By trade they were traditionally blacksmiths, and they personified Lindsay's concept of Blacksmith Aristocracy.[20] The founder of the family was Joseph Bartholdi Michael I, named for the biblical workman Joseph and for Bartholdi, the designer of the Statue of Liberty. Joseph Bartholdi Michael II was another Ephraim Frazee, an aristocratic democrat. While he represented America in the 2018 World Government, and was the author of *Paper-Made Nations,* the basis of international aviation law, in recess he returned to his blacksmith trade, and to the manufacture of his father's invention, the Avanel Blade,

waspish and supple, all-conquering in body and soul. Sideways it can be wound like watch spring steel, or even a coil of narrow ribbon. Edgewise it can cut more human flesh and bone than the heavy guillotine. It can cut straight through an iron or granite block of any thickness, as though it were cutting snow.

Lindsay was not advocating the development of an invincible military technic when he attributed this lethal weapon to the Michaels; he was symbolizing the devastating, miraculous effect of the forces which the Michaels stood for: moral principle, justice, and democracy. Extending the symbolism he described the Michaels' regiment, the Horse Shoe Brotherhood, which had fought at the Meuse-Argonne "when the American First Army cut like magic swords through those four intricate systems of German defences," [21] a regiment of people in a momentarily sustained crusade of right against might.

Lindsay tempered nicely what might have been an insufferable romanticization of this crusading family by revealing that it intended to impose its decisions on the town regardless of majority inclinations. But there was another family in Springfield, the Boones, who had an identical conviction of its own indispensability as "the sole saviors of defiant democracy." There was little ideological difference between the two families (the Michaels were perhaps more loyal internationalists), but their interest in reform was more than a little bound up with an interest in spearheading reform, and hence their controversy.

The head of the Boone family was Black Hawk Boone, a descendant of the pioneer Daniel Boone and the Indian chief Black Hawk. Black Hawk had waged war against the American government in an attempt to prevent his tribe being moved from its traditional lands in Illinois and Michigan. His was a stand against greed, cruelty, injustice, and the rough-riding impulse of Manifest Destiny, qualities which Daniel Boone to some extent exhibited. But Daniel Boone also personified the all-conquering frontier spirit that Lindsay wanted to see channeled into an other-regarding fierceness. Lindsay's attribution of such composite origins[22] to the Michaels and the Boones was meant to recall the melting pot, and taken with his delineation of their mixed motives suggested the "typical" American, ambitious to the point of ruthlessness and dedicated to his own personal America.

The Michaels showed their concern to foster Americanness by bringing out a pageantry calendar of local and national history for annual enactment; they also contributed heavily to the backing for the project. The Boones took a more directly critical view of the American experience in their extrovert acknowledgement of Indian ancestry;[23] they and their followers dyed their left hands crimson and grew their hair Indian style. Only Boone's daughter, Avanel, stood out against this rite, and refused to participate in an action of inverted snobbery which she felt set the Boones unnecessarily apart. Her name, that of the Michael's sword, was a reminder of the fundamental unity of Springfield's leaders, whatever their apparent divergences. She led the Boone forces and a special troop of Amazon cavalry which exercized at Camp Lincoln and swore fealty on Daniel Boone's hunting knife. Avanel admitted that it was no historic weapon, but, with Lindsay, who was at times her companion in the twenty-first century, she felt that reiterated symbols met an unconscious American need for roots and traditions.

To Lindsay's mind a fine woman was the highest form of human being, and one progressive characteristic of the New Springfield was the increasingly important role of women, an increase which might have been expected to follow female suffrage, but which failed to develop. Theoretically it would seem that women have some special instinct to bring to politics, and Lindsay found that in the twenty-first century they were shrewd judges of municipal affairs who could recognize responsible or crooked housekeeping. Although a minority of women worked, the scope of their jobs was rapidly extending from doctors and billposters to locksmiths. Avanel was as eminent as any man. Senator Joseph Bartholdi Michael II acknowledged her to be the rising young leader of Springfield when he ceremonially shoed her horse on one of his return visits from representing America in the World Government. On that momentous occasion the Golden Book came once more out of the sky to be read by her in its most nearly original version, as quotations from Lincoln's writings and speeches.

The suitors of this modern young woman were men whose occupations emphasized the growing egalitarianism and machine-mindedness of Springfield 2018. They were an aviator, an engineer, and a truck driver. They represented the new aristocracy of Springfield, which would be recognized in years to come from photographs of twenty-first century ancestors in working clothes, whereas the early twentieth century fun-seeking, belligerent aristocracy posed "in the midst of their athletic sports, at the race track, or playing golf or croquet, or in soldier's uniform." [24] The group photographic contrast gave an instant image of a difference of outlook in the two centuries that Lindsay would have liked to see.

Avanel was an important part of the everyday pageantry of Springfield, drilling her Amazons daily. They wore a trapper-style white uniform: coonskin cap, fringed suit, moccasins, and leggings made of fur-trimmed leather. Slyly Lindsay pointed out that "their faces are not masked as were those of the ancient Ku Klux Klan but the costume is indeed, as singular." For although he was one of Avanel's suitors, he was wary of any attempt to regiment and indoctrinate—even when the teaching was democracy, and the motives apparently less partisan than the Klan's—in the self-righteous and militaristic way that Avanel adopted. If *The Golden Book of Springfield* had a heroine it was Avanel, but "dear me, what stubborn material for a heroine," Lindsay acknowledged. Her didacticism made her a species of ideological snob, and she had no patience with those who bore abuses uncomplainingly. Her comment on John Emis' beautiful Negro quarter was that most of its houses "still hold slack colored people." She fulminated against her father and St. Friend for being "narrow as mousetraps," [25] but she had her own rubber-stamp ideas.

St. Friend was a partial supporter of reform in Springfield. Lindsay made him the successor to a St. Scribe; and while he was subsequently non-Pharisaical, he was out of touch with reality. He veered from revolutionary support for virtually sexless comrade-citizenesses (a species which appealed to no one else) to conservative opposition to motion pictures (though the Springfield Survey had recommended the motion picture house as a powerful alternative to the saloon). He also opposed the new educational methods which Lindsay felt had such significance for America, and urged a return to the regime of book and blackboard, almost disappeared in "the presence of the protean triumphant films, of the street pageantry, the training of skilled labor in the high schools, of the oral, the phonographic, telegraphic and telephone methods applied to all forms of teaching." It is remarkable how persuasively Lindsay could express views not his own; as usual, he was not prepared to deny a modicum of truth to anyone, and, while making his own position clear, he had fair success in standing at a distance from issues.

What spoke well for St. Friend was the supervisory care he took for the subclass of society: the defectives and drug addicts, the unemployed, and the discriminated against. He himself had set the example by adopting the Thibetan Boy and was the permanent leader of Associated Charities. He instituted graded Orders of Blessed Bread—Strict Observance, Liberal Observance— in compassion for the varying strengths and weaknesses of men, and in the wishful thought that the symbolic sharing of the staple of life would have a beneficial effect on the individual and a cohesive effect on the community. Avanel commended him, with generous condescension, for his subscription to "the idea of thousands of laymen, that few priests have represented:—the . . . idea of religion . . . with no theological or creed fences . . . the blessed company of all faithful people";[26] but while he conveyed this concept effectively in conversation with her, the average citizen of Springfield could not comprehend it or reconcile it with his Catholicism.

Lindsay did not succeed in making St. Friend a particularly interesting character. His exemplary saintliness lacked color. It may well have been an intentionally flat delineation of a personally intense religiosity which was a-communal. St. Friend inspired reverence, not confidence; he never convinced Springfield of his practicality. In the light of Lindsay's gospel it would have been a non sequitur for him to make priests effective social leaders; the very existence of his gospel indicted the clergy. The gulf between the two men was apparent in Lindsay's caustic comment on the pledge to lead a good life that St. Friend drew up for a repentant high-liver. In a pinch Lindsay could accept that certain specific promises—no alcohol, no Yellow Dance Halls, no motion pictures —could be kept. But he had to reject the illusory general terms that Surto Hurdenburg promised to fulfil; for example, that he would

faithfully observe and keep inviolate the moral laws of the community . . . carefully and faithfully observe my duty to my neighbor, recognizing his rights at all times . . . exercise . . . rights of franchise . . . to bring about the best results for clean and honest government and . . . devote as much strength as possible to the study of civic reform, examining at all times the opinions of clean-minded radical citizens, and acting on them according to the dictates of . . . conscience.[27]

What a spiel for a working-man, and how little related to political realities! It hardly amounted to the constructive planning Lindsay was working for, nor did it correspond to his assessment of city politics.

CITY POLITICS

Springfield's progressive faction, headed by the Boones, the Michaels, St. Friend, and Rabbi Ezekiel (the last barely delineated), was opposed by an equally dashingly named assortment of rivals: the Mayor, named for his deviousness Slick Slack Kopensky; the boss, Dr. Mayo Sims; and their underlings, Drug Store Smith, Cave Man Thomas, and Coffee Kusuko. (Coffee John, of "The Shame of Minneapolis"?) This American racial complex in miniature formed a clique which monopolized city government and ran it for their own benefit, in so far as it could be monopolized when the city's commission government put substantial powers of overseeing and redress in the hands of the electorate. But although brazen illegality and graft had become more difficult, the sustained reform impulse in the community-at-large on which successful commission government depended, proved to be fitful, and Kopensky's clique (seven out of the eleven commissioners) flourished on covert and occasionally overt chicanery. Kopensky himself had the advantages of a McKinley-style geniality, and the braggadocio and romance of his followers' names and postures made them attractive voting propositions for the youth of Springfield. Moreover, the city hall clique was in monopolistic control of certain pivots of the American city: Cave Man Thomas, the entertainment sector and the sporting facilities; Coffee Kusuko, the coffee shops and restaurants; Drug Store Smith, the "pharmacy-post-office-street-car-station-patent-medicine-confectionary-cigar-stand-and soda-fountain establishments." [28]

Lindsay was charitable to this official opposition, though it led to all kinds of policy clashes, for example, on the Board of the University of Springfield of which Boone was President, but where Sims and Kopensky could heel a number of votes. However, Lindsay felt reasonably confident that it would be difficult for any governing body to perpetuate retrogressive policies in the face of an already highly educated university intake (the age for leaving high school had been raised to twenty-one). Intensive teaching and a syllabus which probably included World Religions, Beauty, Equality, and Internationalism had made the schools into "battle-tanks" [29] for New Springfield.

Another bone of contention between the two factions was the sale of liquor. Prohibition was still in force, but it was suspected that Kusuko spiked his coffee and his twenty-first century versions of Bevo and Coca-Cola. But in spite of such problems Lindsay gratefully tolerated "the City Hall gang" for keeping "our more angular truth-telling moods from torturing the town beyond reason." [30] Boone and Avanel and St. Friend were righteously intolerant reformers, embryonic dictators; and the effective city hall opposition staved off the excesses of puritanical or religious tyrannies, which, in Lindsay's view, would simply militate against any more altruistic reformers who might arise.

Lindsay did not expect danger to a reasonably harmonious Springfield to come directly from a clique which was conventionally and predictably shady, but from the opportunity to foster discord provided by its slackness and corruption. He had in mind the world menace of 2018, Singapore, whose ultimate aim was to win antidemocratic and would-be plutocratic elements to its side in a world war of aggrandizement, but which started with small international pockets of disruption: through Springfield's Yellow Dance Halls, for example, which it indirectly owned with the connivance of Kopensky and Co., and to their financial advantage. The Yellow Dance Halls sold drugs which inculcated the habit of heedless self-indulgence, and which created a desperate interest in making the sort of money that would buy drugs. This subversion was the thin end of the wedge; the next ominous step was to induce open violence in Springfield between the selfishly individualistic and the community-conscious, between the materialists and the idealists. It took the form of an aerial war between two sets of youths.

The airplane in 2018, like the automobile in 1918, was an incipient status symbol. The city authorities had already forbidden the private ownership of planes, which they saw as a symbol of blatant inequality; but the children of wealthy parents found lessons in aviation and the renting of planes much easier than the less well off, who qualified more slowly, in fewer numbers, and who hired the cheaper, slower machines. An aerial war of nerves, skill, and numbers broke out between the hundred percent Springfield youths and the children of plutocratic, reactionary parents, educated away from the contagion of Springfield's "infamously democratic atmosphere" [31] (though the city had not been democratic enough to give everyone free lessons, or to institute a means test for instruction and renting). The latter group of young people almost had a corner on the rented planes at the Springfield airport, and their leaders, patrons of the Yellow Dance Halls, acolytes of Singapore, gilded their machines and plastered them possessively with their names. They called themselves Snobs, the advocates of the artificial, of what could be bought, for they had been indoctrinated by Singapore with the teaching that everything and everyone had his price. They attacked the hundred percent Springfield youths (the standby pilots of the World Government's mail and aid planes), who, in turn, were quick to acknowledge their loyalties to principles befitting creatures of God by adopting the name Robins. Eventually the machines were declassified, and given uniform rentals, and limitations were placed on how frequently they could be rented, but existing rifts in the social fabric had been unforgettably accentuated in Springfield, and in many world cities. A chain of unrest was set in motion; the violent opposition of group interests became habitual; and an international coalition lusting for power, territory, and wealth waged war against the protagonists of democracy and world brotherhood.

The Snobs-Robins conflict expressed Lindsay's attitude to the machine age: good if properly used, dangerous, or marvelous. He saw the destructive possibilities of the airplane together with its potential in breaking down the barriers of international distance, and in taking succor to the hungry and deprived. He made the same point when, in the subsequent world war, he attributed to Singapore a weapon called a Lens Gun, made with lenses illegally sold by the Springfield Microscope and Lens factory. But he indicted men rather than their inventions. Springfield had lacked the logic to follow up its ban on the sale of planes; it lacked the logic to see that the good things it produced were not abused. But the indictment of Springfield was directed less at basic human nature than at the corrupting and debasing effects of exclusive practices and artificial social distinctions within the community. Lindsay listed accusingly the materialistic inequalities which had led to the Snobs-Robins conflict, and which allowed devilishly brutish elements to "escape the leash":[32] the Kopenskys and Simses who had acclimatized America to corruption, however mild; the old world of orthodox selfishness, however apparently respectable; the misconceved inactivity in international affairs of self-styled American patriots. The young Boones put up a group of grotesques on pedestals—a featherless chicken, a trousered pig, a dragon with a duck's head, a three-legged bulldog in a plug hat—as a memorial to these attitudes. The central pedestal was inscribed:

To the corner stones of the town; to the newspaper and motion picture and stage censors; to the respectables, the lady bountifuls, the so-called senior families; to the Sons and Daughters of the American Revolution; to the Sons and Daughters of the Ancient Democrats and the Sons and Daughters of the Ancient Republicans; and in general, to the dragon-quack worm of respectability, that dieth not.[33]

The struggle was not only against Singapore but against meritless opposition to change in any form, against the intolerant mentality which could not comprehend the erection in the interfaith cathedral of statues to St. Francis, Swedenborg, Johnny Appleseed, Emerson, Mary Baker Eddy, Eugene Debs, John Brown, and Karl Liebknecht. It was a struggle against all those who lacked the goodwill to acknowledge other men's idiosyncratic manifestations of goodwill.

SPRINGFIELD AND WORLD GOVERNMENT

Springfield was part of an America which was represented in a World Government, an organization of whose constitution and function Lindsay gave scarcely any details. On the one hand he was trying to indicate the lack of impact of the World Government on Springfield and America, and on the other his allegory had gotten out of hand. He could imagine and vividly convey the essence of a prototype city which was based on material and concepts close to him, but he floundered in the specialist intricacies of speculative world politics. The only way in which he could cope with the concept of world government was to use Springfield as an international microcosm, a parallel which re-emphasized the shakiness of international political cooperation.

In one outstanding sense, however, Springfield "afforded a symbol of desirable world conditions": by setting an example of racial harmony. The city's development into an architectural World's Fair City had brought her worldwide eminence; as a focus of international interest and a convention center she had decided to turn herself into a World's Fair University, encompassing all disciplines and cultures, each with its own regularly updated exhibit. The success of this experiment in promoting racial understanding had led people from all nations to want to become residents in such clamoring numbers that the city had instituted an entrance examination. But, in a typically Lindsayan reversal of the usual assembly line product envisaged in communitarian experiments, and conjured up by the word "exam," Springfield's exam aimed at peopling the city-university-fair with a diversity of nationalities and types and interests. Every school of philosophical and aesthetic thought could be found in a Springfield which had become "as much a Hobby Horse as a [universal] University Fair." [34]

The mixture of race strains in this World's Fair city had made "an elastic, resilient type that is one with the city's suddenest moves": a new Springfield strain which was the product of disproved fears, abandoned prejudices, and intermarriage. Like America and her hyphenates the community retained its racial and religious divergences, and made them such vital contributions to the city's personality that the loss of a sect or a national group would mean a vacuum in society. In Lindsay's eyes it was a significant step toward making world trust, world peace, and therefore world government possible; for he believed the racial prejudices and hostilities which in turn raised sexual and religious hackles to be the basis of humanity's internecine struggles. He used Sake Shioya, an elder statesman of Japan and visiting head of the department of Asiatic Art at the World's Fair University, as his mouthpiece for putting this view forward, and for divining that twenty-first century Marxians were as divided on a racially hostile basis into "the Purple Flag Marxians of Japan, the Yellow Flag Marxians of China, the White Flags of Thibet, the Black Flags of Russia, the Red Flags of Central Europe, the Gray Flags of America." [35]

The twenty-first century had apparently seen an increase in the number of Marxist societies, but Lindsay hoped that Springfield, with the World Government following suit, would pass beyond that state to become

the dream of a human beehive far from the Marxian society. It is something on the newest New Harmony model, a Springfield that is democratic, artistic, religious and patriarchal, and therefore following many of the most ancient forms and metaphors of orthodoxy.

With the passage of time the revolutionaries of total change and nonconformity were reemphasizing the immemorial values which were politically as well as individually important—the values of Lindsay's gospel. Their aim had become the consummation of old and new, a politics of vigilance and maturity which Lindsay likened to "an electric light . . . softened and given its final character by the shell of an ancient horn lantern." [36]

But not all nations, and not all Americans were agreed on the political pattern which Lindsay sketched with such tantalizing brevity. The World Government was like the early American federal experience, a substantial advance on the separatism of its member states but a Union which required at least one Civil War to solder it together. America herself was posing the threat of "World-Anarchy" [37] in her occasional reassertion of the principles of Washington's Farewell Address and the Monroe Doctrine; and other member nations of the World Government, like Singapore, were claiming the right of secession in order to perpetuate their slave-owning societies and their aggressive international policies. Lindsay compared Singapore with South Carolina; and American racial prejudice also seemed relevant to the disintegration of the World Government, as an example of the superiority complex which made wars likely. The self-righteous Boone whipped up race prejudice in Springfield by comparing Singaporians to superstitious blacks, and by suggesting that the anti-Singaporian forces wear white, a token supremacy almost enough in itself to defeat Singapore. He reactionarily suggested that if Springfield had been painted an all white city instead of her golden self, the complicating World's Fair University of blacks, browns, and yellows, and the troublesome presence of Singapore would never have come into the city. Shades of Chicago in 1893, and the unyielding forces of conservatism against the flexible forces of idealism and advance!

Boone's reaction showed Lindsay the intolerant limitations of Springfield's reformers, though even he was hard put to find a redeeming feature in Singapore. But he did point out that the talent and drive of that polyglot city, though for the moment misused, were the remarkable products of a racial amalgam: an English admixture had given Singapore an insight into the Western mind; a Chinese streak had given her patient one-hundred-year plans; an Arab undercurrent had made her capable of the decisive gesture. She had bought independence from Britain and had made herself into the world's greatest port. Gradually she acquired more territory, and with it more power. All the islands north of Australia and south of Japan, including the Philippines, had become hers, a repetition on an international scale of the short-term gains which led Kusuko and Co. to allow the Yellow Dance Halls into Springfield.

Lindsay symbolized Singapore's threat to world peace in the shape of a "Cocaine Buddha," [38] a somewhat inadequate attempt to suggest how easily apparent stability could be undermined, and how craving for pleasure opened the door to dependence on the source of that pleasure. The Cocaine Buddha was also an intended personification of those forces of evil which were apparent in the "Map of the Universe" heaven, and which were capable of abusing religions of integrity on earth. More effective was Lindsay's characterization of the dignified, quietly powerful Man from Singapore, a delegate to the World's Fair, who inspired the Snobs-Robins conflict, and his daughter, Mara, who ensnared Joseph Bartholdi Michael III. They were a rarely seen but continually felt menace in Springfield, and until Singapore openly defied the World Government they had to be tolerated while known to be stimulating antiprogressive discontent. But in his transformed state as a Malay servant in their house, Lindsay found himself in the possession of ideas and thoughts which had never before occurred to him, and which occurred to no one else in Springfield 2018. He was impressed by the formidable Eastern culture, outstripping anything in America; he found Boone and Avanel whey-faced and physically repulsive. His openmindedness alleviated what, in its final stages, had become neither successful fantasy nor meaningful allegory.

The conclusion of *The Golden Book of Springfield* was disjointed and incoherent and as undefinitive as the outcome of the World War. Burma, Indo-China, and South China joined Singapore, but the World Government's reaction to their declarations of war was patchy, with "strange hesitancies in Europe and South America . . . [and] rumors of World Treason, even among

American officials of the World Government." [39] Singapore and her allies apparently affected a Munich-style fait accompli. Events in Springfield mirrored the uncertain state of world affairs. There were outbreaks of irresponsibility on both sides: Smith and Kusuko were poisoned and Boone lynched. Springfield, America, and the embryonic international community remained disappointingly imperfect societies, poised between advance and retrogression. Symbolic of this uncertain state was the task that Avanel was left with as the book ended, a task mystically entrusted to her in "the jungles of heaven": the ever-recurring one of sowing "the torturing thistle of dreams," tormenting young citizens so that "they will build things greater than Springfield has yet looked upon, people's palaces as yet without a name." [40] The spirit of youth, the power of beauty, and the inescapable conscience of the divinely created human being were, for Lindsay, the perpetual and only hopes of mankind.

CONCLUSION

Out of context the characters of *The Golden Book of Springfield* seem to inhabit a knights and dragons, trappers and Indians, space fiction world. But Lindsay managed to bring a delicate and serious touch to the creation of an allegorical whole, a whole which is solidly American in the tradition it draws upon, and yet singularly American in its unique amalgam of hope, suggestion, and realistic prophecy.

The incongruous elements in *The Golden Book of Springfield* —the adventures of Avanel and Lindsay in space, the sometimes painfully obvious nomenclature, the artificial pageantry of the city —and its inadequate ending, were partly due to the fact that Lindsay had been working on the book for six years, and had been mulling over the project for twenty. It had become one of those too dear projects which so often fall short. The sensitive imagination which enabled him to be accurately selective of trends which could for good or ill prevail had worked overtime, and could not stop working. The clarity of what could have been an impressively prosaic delineation of the future was clouded by his emotional preoccupation with man's blindness to things divine and America's failure to follow her best traditions.

The semireligious ceremonial and the paraphernalia of frontier Arthurianism with which he surrounded Hunter Kelly, the Michaels, and the Boones were symptomatic of his attempt to underwrite the American experience, and also of the idealistic streak which regularly underlies apparently despondent and cynical theories. Such thwarted and unfulfilled idealism, though concealed under layers of acquired defensive unexpectancy, can emerge, sometimes forcibly and unmistakably, like Lindsay's in *The Golden Book of Springfield*. He continually and intentionally erred on the tentative side, never admitting that the improvements of 2018 were secure or permanent, never underestimating opposition. But in the ritualistic and courtly aura with which he encircled his characters, and the innate chivalrous uprightness with which he imbued them, his dormant belief in good human instincts and in some unforeseeable, but not impossible realization of American potential sprang into life. The significance of his religious and historical nomenclature, of his lyrical descriptions of the new race of architects, and of the incidence of earnest civic leaders was that he admitted the existence of sources of social and national regeneration.

The main threads of *The Golden Book of Springfield*—transferred twentieth century trends, created Springfield legends, and a linking story-fantasy—were tangled with a network of ideas and symbols. Lindsay's vibrant and almost uncontrollably receptive mind produced an idiosyncratic tour de force, and not the popular, thought-provoking book he had hoped to write. But though the diversity of material made the book demanding and sometimes confusing reading, it also contributed to its ideological challenge. And in an odd way, Lindsay's technical shortcomings served his purpose; smoothness of execution might have detracted from earnestness of intention. Moreover, the elimination of incongruities, while making stylistically for a more satisfying narrative, would have minimized the type of society he intended to depict. The necessity of divine intervention in an otherwise calamitous world, a purposefully cultivated sense of community and tradition, and the failure to resolve international political issues were features that he intentionally attributed to society in 2018. They were the liabilities of society which had as its assets orchard cities, Wrightian architecture, civic and vocational pride, better racial understanding, and an increasingly intelligent use of machines.

From a literary point of view there is no choice but to deplore anachronisms and sketchy treatment of themes. Lindsay was frank that the book was "a great deal duller than it should be . . . full of awkward English, incredibly awkward." He wondered if it would ever read well: "I have to revise it twenty times before it is prose and I suppose fifty times before it is poetry."[41] But this did not deter him from considering it his major work, for his criterion was the idea expressed, not the mode of expression.

Poor as *The Golden Book* may be, it is the effort of my life, and I hope that my method of trying to apply it to your town will not be considered lightly, seeing that it represents an idea that may be traced through my eight books for twenty years of writing.[42]

To see the book with Lindsay's frankness, in its personal and ideological contexts, is to accept, even appreciate its flaws for what they are—the fumbling attempts of a man to whom subtlety and an oblique approach were entirely foreign to formulate his obsession with America's future as a literary tract. The often trite framework on which far from trite ideas were exhibited was typically Lindsayan. No one could veer from the sublime to the ridiculous more quickly than he, not only through an irregularly flowing literary talent, but through his mistaken conviction that in pulling out every available stop he would reach his largest audience and swell the numbers of potential civic converts.

Lindsay managed a partial adjustment to the anticlimactic reception of *The Golden Book of Springfield*. He came to accept that the book had immediate appeal to a small minority, and that most people's interest was limited to the short-lived, emotional experience of his recitations. "The very public that rejects with scorn the High Mass and Incense of this book [its rituals, Catholicism and catholicity] clamor for my poem on the ghost of Abraham Lincoln. . . ." In a live-for-today America, a book that was "all tomorrow, and the day after tomorrow, and the day after that" was unpalatable. Lindsay wrote to John Drinkwater that

they [the public] will see in the air the picture they love, otherwise a blank. I should have had Confederate flags and Union flags marching through the air in this book.[43]

Yet with all his reservations about his achievement and his audience, he still hoped that the book would "work in the background for a long time." He could not conceive the extent of the general American public's incapacity for introspection and self-criticism, nor the degree to which self-satisfaction had blunted responses to reform needs. Had he known that America would refuse to look honestly at itself he might have been too depressed to realize the implication that such voices as his were all the more vital; he might have wondered whether to persevere. For there were not so many ways in which he could alter *The Golden Book of Springfield*. As it was frankly propaganda, catchy devices of form and style were only sensible, but the message to America to look ahead and plan had to remain unchanged. And although he had plans to revise the book to make it more readable, he was never able to carry them through; he was too involved with it.

What I am lies between the lines of *The Golden Book of Springfield* . . . this is the private self that I talk to and consult, this is the set of nervous habits . . . that are the actual basis of my motions.

He doubted if "three living creatures ever read [it] in the true Henry James way, between the lines." [44] But in a partly unintended way, *The Golden Book of Springfield* did expose Lindsay: the man of technic and style submerged by the enthusiastic proselytizer, yet emerging in the more than occasional fine phrase and paragraph; the man of ideas overcoming the confused structure of those ideas by the compelling realism of his conception of the future. The exposure was cruel; but it was accurate.

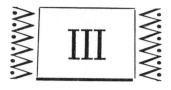

An American Entity

Wherever I wander, beggar or guest,
The soul of the U.S.A.:—that is my life-quest.
—LINDSAY, "Doctor Mohawk"

"Nothing yet is fixed in America, all, all is yet possible for our land."

"I see this whole land as a unit. I have traveled over it so much, and a thousand songs and drawings have almost reached the surface about it. . . . I just can't help it, and I see that whole land as a unit from the very beginning."

—EDGAR LEE MASTERS, *Vachel Lindsay*

CHAPTER SEVEN

The American Past

FACT AND FICTION

L INDSAY'S ENTITY was a mixture of history, myth, and vision; it was an attempt to provide a framework for American identity. America and Americanness existed, but only patchily, and often regrettably; Lindsay was trying to create conditions for their proper realization through the mental and physical breakdown of group and regional hostilities, and through the reinvigoration of tradition. With the warp and woof of celebration and admonition he wove together what he considered to be significant strands in the American experience: some cautionary (the unresolved Negro problem), some hopeful (the occasional leader of caliber, the bountiful West), and some regretful (the failure to use Indian tradition intelligently). He could not indiscriminately glorify the fabric of America's past and present any more than he could its future, but he could describe arrestingly what was and what could be the stuff of America; he could stimulate the grand American design.

He tried to extract from America's past—and if necessary write into it—characteristics which would make Americans ambitious to live up to their heritage. The result was not strictly historical. Sometimes Lindsay thought that he could make American self-analysis more rewarding, for example, by ignoring discrepancies of character in Bryan and Theodore Roosevelt, and by embroidering legends. He was "not trying to please the kind of historians that fight over a comma or a phrase," but to give an impression of what he could approve as Americanness. His approach to the past was "a work of the imagination, somewhat in the spirit of state house and court house and dollar bill mural paintings"; and consequently he used myth freely. Like William Carlos Williams he believed that fabulae possessed a kind of reality, that they were part of the national idiom, and had entered the national psyche. Williams' *In the American Grain,* 1925, was an attempt to achieve in one book what Lindsay insidiously fed into all his writings, a concept of Americanism; but while Williams disclaimed any attempt to explain the past, Lindsay set out to indoctrinate with the American ethos, to bring Americans "nearer . . . to exactitude in United States Citizenship." [1] He wanted America to nationalize, as well as to denationalize; to replace many histories by one.

The legends surrounding American folk figures, however fictional or distorted, have expressed genuine processes and types: Daniel Boone, the pioneer who was always moving away from the encroaching Western thrust of civilization; Jesse James, the good-bad man whose code was a product of the exigencies of Western life. Occasionally American legend has been a reflection of how a people wishes to see itself: as a Bunyanesque race of physical supermen, for example. Such complexities make it hard to distinguish between historical myth and historical fact, but what is certain is that events as they happened and as they are now interpreted, and myth in its factual origins and as it has been filled out, have become inextricable in the American mind.

Lindsay recognized the curious myth-fact amalgam of American history, and reflected its characteristics of fabrication, folk-lore and hero-worship. In one sense the territory of the cumulative American imagination was the real America, not what the past had been, but how people chose to remember it, and in some cases Lindsay was content with what people chose to remember. He merely revived, though forcefully, and often beautifully, conventional images of Washington, Jackson, and Johnny Appleseed. Washington and Jackson were the American promise and its interim fulfillment; Johnny Appleseed was the representative of a Western process which augured well for the resources and character of the nation. The picture he drew of Lincoln, however, was unconventionally somber: the picture of a reproachful reminder that America was not justifying her auspicious and morally overladen beginnings, that the concept of Manifest Destiny—potentially useful if seen as an end to work toward, and not as an excuse for fatalistic inaction—involved not only the material concept of an ever fertile Virgin Land, but the moral concept of a good society. In the "The Golden-Faced People" Lindsay used Lincoln to draw a cautionary parallel between the impossibility of white isolation in America and of American isolation in the world. It was a reasonable piece of historical application, but the same can hardly be said of Lindsay's treatment of the American attitude toward the Indian.

AMERICA'S INDIAN PAST

Lindsay attempted to create the factually groundless tradition of a vital Indian contribution to America's past, when the prevalent conception of the Indian remained that of an inferior branch of the human species, of a no-class citizen. The take-over of Indian settled land and the demolition of Indian society were actions for which Americans felt justification, rarely unease. Helen Hunt Jackson's sympathetic review of *A Century of Dishonor,* 1888, had been influential only among a small minority. In the absence of cultural or racial assimilation by the Indian (the process being reversed, if anything), and in view of the lack of physical remains of even a crumbled civilization, Lindsay's picture of a revered, ancestral Indian race seemed absurd.

But Lindsay himself was mesmerized by the romance of the noble savage; he liked to think that he had that kind of Indian blood.[2] He did not merely cast around for a plausible starting point for his entity; he was involved in an idealization which made him flout fact and emotion. Even so it was with a belief in symbols rather than nationwide miscegenation that he wrote

> *We here renounce our Saxon blood.*
> *Tomorrow's hopes, an April flood*
> *Come roaring in. The newest race*
> *Is born of her* [*Pocahontas'*] *resilient grace.*

The immemorial dissolution of Indian bodies into America's soil had indianized her crops (hence consumers) and building materials; and so, Lindsay argued, it was the Indian, not the white pioneer who was the original conditioner of American character.

> *John Rolfe is not our ancestor.*
> *We rise from out the soul of her*
> *Held in native wonderland,*
> *While the sun's rays kissed her hand,*
> *In the Springtime,*
> *In Virginia,*
> *Our mother Pocahontas.*[3]

In a physical sense, then, Lindsay saw the Indian as a possible symbol of a common antecedent for a racially diverse America; as a unifying allegiance for a polyglot people. Spiritually, from childhood fascination with " 'Heap-big-chief-the-Mohawk,' with eye like a tommyhawk/Naked in war paint, tough stock and old stock" he drew the picture of the Indian as the symbol of American difference.[4] He accepted certain qualities attributed to the Indian—stoicism, fearlessness, loyalty, principle—not for identical reproduction (for he cannot have been unaware of a code of retribution and rights abnormal in a largely Christian society) but which, as abstract, sterling virtues, could help form a backbone of national integrity. And even when abused in a "Babbitt Jamboree,"[5] the Indian could mold America, as reparation for such indignities would have to be made to the accompaniment of a healthy amount of national soul-searching.

Lindsay was obviously one American who was troubled by the fact that the American Indian, if anyone, was the rightful owner of the continent, and he channeled his disquiet into another of his indictments of the moral dubieties underlying and permeating American society. In "The Ghost of the Buffaloes" he imagined the vengeful demolition of a usurped America by its natural heirs, who, like the young, he saw as righteous rebels.

> *The city was gone.*
> *My home was a hut without orchard or lawn.*

It was mud-smear and logs near a whispering stream,
Nothing else built by man could I see in my dream . . .
Then . . .
Ghost kings came headlong, row upon row,
Gods of the Indians . . .[6]

Lindsay's America, increasingly emotionally, racially and historically rigid, did not respect the Indian even theoretically, and was content to accept both his exploitation as entertainment and his economic, cultural, and political subjugation; Lindsay's attempt to elevate the Indian to the national pantheon went to the other extreme. He suggested that America could purge herself through the election of an Indian president,[7] an absurd suggestion then in the light of national prejudice and the average Indian's level of education and citizenship, though in view of the widening spectrum of dissent and reaction in America, all shades of events seem possible. But though such theories as Lindsay's were contextually ludicrous, they were acute comments on the bulldozing American process, and on the nation's sins of omission. Regrettably, she had been no more than spasmodically conscious of her need of oneness, and of the part that history and myth could play in the creation of an American entity and American maturity.

JOHNNY APPLESEED AND
THE WESTERN ETHOS

Johnny Appleseed was the nickname of a nomadic Massachusetts man, John Chapman (1774–1847), who spent his life moving west, planting fruit seedlings in areas into which he anticipated a flow of population. His familiarity with little known territory, and his conscious attempt to show that America was a land of natural plenty combined to make him a gift to myth makers. He was a real concomitant of western expansion who had also become a legendary representation of America's benevolence and fecundity, and of dedicated citizenship.

Chapman was germane to Lindsay in several ways. He was a practicing Swedenborgian; he used to separate the chapters of

Swedenborg's books, and on each trip shuffled them around the houses he called at like mobile books-in-parts (each household reading the book backwards). He subscribed to the Science of Correspondences, seeing, in Lindsay's words

> *A ballot-box in each apple,*
> *A state capital in each apple,*
> *Great high schools, great colleges,*
> *All America in each apple.*[8]

Lindsay also felt affinity with Chapman's lonely, dedicated life; they were both acolytes at the consecration of the American entity. In "Johnny Appleseed Speaks of the Apple-Blossom Amaranth that Will Come to This City," and "Johnny Appleseed Speaks of Great Cities of the Future," Lindsay made him a denizen of the heaven of the "Map of the Universe," who walked in the Jungles of Heaven. Seven of his eight poems on Chapman indulged this fantasy that the countryman Chapman had been as city conscious as himself, an idiosyncratic slant that made their content no more suited to a national entity than the "Map of the Universe" was to a national religious revival. But the one poem in which he treated Chapman traditionally, "In Praise of Johnny Appleseed," more than compensated the entity for the existence of the other seven. Lindsay faithfully identified Chapman and the Western ethos; he memorably brought his own America face to face with the best in pioneer spirit, and with the almost mystically inevitable Western bent of everything in America. First

> *Dust and ashes,*
> *Snow and sleet,*
> *And hay and oats and wheat,*
> *Blew west.*

Every creature and every plant had a reason for migration: for colts "gastronomic revelations," for chickens, escape from "farm-yard congregations." With historical inaccuracy, but with mythical effect, the first white infiltration occurred when

A boy
Blew west,
And with prayers and incantations,
And with "Yankee Doodle Dandy,"
Crossed the Appalachians,
And was "young John Chapman,"
Then
"Johnny Appleseed, Johnny Appleseed." [9]

This sequence of penetration of the West, with its symbolic climax in Johnny Appleseed, was Lindsay's version of Turner's history of the conquest of the frontier by buffalo, Indian, fur-trader, settler, soldier, and merchant. "In Praise of Johnny Appleseed" showed that Lindsay, like Turner, subscribed to the Western ethos. The push west was inspired, inevitable, entailing a missionary compulsion to convert to domestic uses the farthest stretches of land; it was permeated with strains of the assertive patriotic song of the American Revolution; it acted as a catalyst on the frontiersman.

Lindsay was well within the visionary and literary traditions of the West. Just as Whitman had celebrated the Passage to India and the Suez Canal—"the earth to be spann'd, connected by network" —so Lindsay celebrated "all windings and unwindings of the highway/From India across America," [10] and the Panama Canal. He also subscribed to the "garden of the world" metaphor, to the West of "To-morrow's peaches, pears, and cherries/To-morrow's grapes and red raspberries"; and he saw the West in Turneresque terms of regeneration. On his second tramping expedition in 1912 he noted in his diary: "I have crossed the mystic border, I have left Earth. I have entered Wonderland . . . I am in the West." [11] His use in *The Golden Book of Springfield* of the Western hero-figure Daniel Boone to represent a promising strain in American life demonstrated his belief in the uniquely adventurous, resilient, and practical characteristics that Turner suggested the West produced. But his qualified approval of Boone and his family reflected his qualified approval of the frontier process. He regretted its restless, rarely satisfied settlers, pioneers whose constant mobility was a retreat rather than an advance, who went "West, to escape from Western ways." [12] To flourish in any but the crudest senses men had to face the reality of less romantic frontiers than the West; and Lindsay echoed Turner's thesis that the end of the physical frontier would mean the creation of new ones, that "masters of industry" were "pioneers under changed conditions," [13] and more demanding ones. The premise of *The Golden Book of Springfield* was that man is forever creating frontiers, and is perpetually his own frontier, a point that Lindsay also made about Johnny Appleseed: "The real frontier was his sunburnt breast." [14]

THE TRIUMVIRATE—LINCOLN, WASHINGTON, AND JACKSON

Springfield, Illinois, Lindsay's home town, was the city in which Lincoln lived and practiced law from 1836 to 1860, and where he was buried. Lindsay's home, 603 South Fifth Street, had been owned by a sister of Mary Todd Lincoln, Mrs. Cyril M. Smith. Lincoln had often been entertained in its front parlor, which had been the scene of a memorable party before he left for Washington. Lindsay had no option but to grow up with the shade of Lincoln; he was inevitably Lincoln-conscious and Lincoln-conditioned. In the local "Lincoln House" museum he remembered seeing "the cartoons of his enemies, showing the alleged rank, slack, ungrammatical, sweating, thieving person" and "the cartoons of his friends which expressed every kind of devotion to the railsplitter and the lawyer from the vast prairie circuit." At home too, he was bombarded with conflicting views of Lincoln, his mother giving a Unionist and Abolitionist interpretation of the Civil War, but his father relating that, in Lindsay's words,

Once upon a time a certain Abraham Lincoln came, with many soldiers. According to this tale they stole all the horses from my Grandfather Lindsay's estate, drove off all the negroes forever (my grandfather's personal property and mine), burned the crops, and then, in a way not mentioned, stole the farm, and left us all to begin again by studying medicine by a solitary candle. And as for Harriet Beecher Stowe, any one who would read her book was worse than an infidel.[15]

Lindsay also associated Lincoln with the Western ethos. Some of the terms which he used to define the essence of Lincoln could equally apply to Natty Bumppo:

> *That which is gendered in the wilderness*
> *From lonely prairies and God's tenderness.*
> *Imperial soul, star of a weedy stream,*
> *Born where the ghosts of buffaloes still gleam,*
> *Whose spirit hoof-beats storm above his grave,*
> *Above that breast of earth and prairie-fire.*[16]

Here was Natty's solitude-induced philosophy; his observance of the morality of what, in spite of an often adverse natural world, he felt to be a benign, profuse God; his feeling for a personal frontier empire; his affinity with the Indian essence of America. Lincoln's own log cabin and homesteading experiences, his desultory employment in and around the small Illinois village of New Salem, and his rise to the rank of lawyer in the state capital was a frontier process comparable with Bumppo's progression from a creature of nature and an independent hunter to official scout with the British forces at Oswego on Lake Ontario. Lindsay was full of admiration for a country like America in which Lincoln, a man who "was born, with tears, in the dust," could rise to the highest post in the land.[17]

Lindsay was perhaps more sympathetic toward Lincoln than toward any other American, but for once he did not overwork his interest in his writings. Lincoln escaped over-emphasis because he was a perpetual, implicit part of Lindsay's Springfield. His overt role in Lindsay's writings was effective for its brevity and memorable for its intensity. Apart from the Lincoln stanza in "The Litany of Heroes," Lindsay's only substantial poetic comment on Lincoln was in "Abraham Lincoln Walks at Midnight." Written shortly after the outbreak of the first World War, the poem described the shade of Lincoln walking at night through Springfield, remembering the first terrible modern war that America had given the world, and unable to rest while its successor pressed on with destructive momentum. Apart from two evaluative lines at which he might have quibbled—

The quaint great figure that men love,
The prairie-lawyer, master of us all

—Lincoln would have been recognizable to himself in the poem. For his physical presence Lindsay was able to consult people in Springfield who had known him—hence the shawl; for his prescience Lindsay simply stated the compassion and conscience of a provincial, American, universal man.

His head is bowed. He thinks on men and kings.
Yea, when the sick world cries, how can he sleep?
Too many peasants fight, they know not why,
Too many homesteads in black terror weep.

The sins of all the war-lords burn his heart.
He sees the dreadnaughts scouring every main.
He carries on his shawl-wrapped shoulders now
The bitterness, the folly and the pain.[18]

Lindsay dealt with his own and Lincoln's concern for the Negro and the Union in a short story "The Golden-Faced People," published in *War Bulletin No. I,* July 1909. Racial questions must have seemed more poignant and have loomed larger in Springfield, Illinois, than anywhere elsewhere in America, especially to a proselytizing adherent of Lincoln. Lindsay always maintained that the Negro population of Springfield was 20 percent when it was actually 6 percent. Even *The Times,* London, overdramatized the issue of race in Springfield. After a minor race riot there in August 1908, in which two Negroes were lynched, the paper ran daily rebukes to "American civilisation . . . disgraced by . . . criminal hysteria." [19] Lindsay's reaction was his story, a painstaking allegory, which, for its honest and penetrating treatment of the inhumanity of the Negro's situation, is in a class of its own in white literature on this theme.

"The Golden-Faced People" envisaged white Americans in a state of subjection comparable to that in which they held the Negro. To give his story full point Lindsay did not reverse situations and make the Negro a master-figure—a state of affairs ludicrous even to "enlightened" whites, who could tolerate the Negro as an equal, but could not conceive of him as a dominant element. He chose instead to tell a story of the Chinese conquest of white America, a choice of race which seems apt in the light of today's Chinese menace. The theme of conquest could have only limited impact on an America generally convinced of its impregnability, and beginning to feel itself decisive in world affairs; but Asia, if anywhere, was regarded as the source of a potential menace, particularly in view of the manifestations of Japanese naval strength in the Russo-Japanese war (1904–5). Asiatic immigration, and the unassimilated Chinese concentrations in California had inspired early nativist sentiment, the Chinese Exclusion Act of 1882, for example. Alfred Thayer Mahan had warned that "free Asiatic immigration to the Pacific coast, in its present condition of sparse population would mean Asiatic occupation—Asia colonized in America." [20] But in "The Golden-Faced People," China did not constitute a Yellow Peril warning of Asiatic territorial designs on America, though existing phobias motivated and helped to intensify Lindsay's cautioning; as a colored race, and one culturally superior to white America, it supplied the physical and cultural analogies Lindsay needed for his story.

The only other comparable use in literature of the theme of a Chinese conquest of America was in *Looking Further Backwards,* (1890) Arthur Vinton's reply to *Looking Backwards*. Vinton was not warning America of potential Chinese aggression either, but was trying to paint a gloomy picture of the sort of thing which might happen if a cooperative, egalitarian society such as Bellamy envisaged, came into being. Vinton argued that the isolationist, pacifist, and cooperative characteristics of Bellamy's so-called "Nationalism" would have made strong leaders, international awareness, and an adequate defence policy redundant, and would have ironed out strength of character along with inequalities. As a consequence of debilitating "Nationalism," he imagined America crumpling under Chinese invasion, and becoming nothing more than the Chinese province of North America.

Lindsay, like Vinton, thought that the Chinese analogy might startle Americans into thinking, but he used the theme of Chinese invasion to point home a racial moral, not to combat egalitarianism. In "The Golden-Faced People" he went forward to the Springfield of 2909. The day was the hundredth anniversary of the emancipation of white man by the Chinese leader Lin Kon. (The translation seems ingenious or crude according to one's degree of fellow feeling with Lindsay—the day was really the two hundredth anniversary of Lincoln's birth.) At a meeting celebrating the anniversary, a speaker recalled the history of white servitude. The superiority of the Chinese had stemmed from their command of resources and education, which had enabled them to control the political, social, and industrial mechanics of the country. The white man had been circumstantially, not intrinsically inferior. But however specious the Chinese assumption of a superior intelligence, a convinced inferiority came to characterize white Americans. Whatever whites might have had in the way of their own forthright culture (in architecture, Lindsay mentioned, they surpassed the Chinese), they were made to feel apologetic for by the production of the dazzling textile, the subtle ceramic, the antique bronze, and other manifestations of a level of civilization immediately unattainable by them. In slavery and in legal freedom alike they were politically and culturally submerged and exploited. With what was probably a dig at the democratic travesty of Reconstruction, with its buying and selling of votes, Lindsay, a twentieth century observer in 2909, noted:

In the presence of the well-rounded daily life of China, how brash seem the unclothed inventions of this whey-faced democracy where the weakling and diseased are tolerated for their votes and praised for their perverseness.

They were a race of sapped energies: "They moved about, aenemic and restless like the petted white monkeys that eat sweetmeats in the palaces of India." [21]

The simile was not exact, but Lindsay had caught the lethargy and hopelessness, the shambling indifference of so many Negroes of the deep South, and their counterparts among better-off northern Negro workers. He had caught what, in spite of an element of militancy, was perhaps the numerically dominant mood of the Negro, whose independent culture and self-confidence had been insidiously undermined, and whose one remaining bastion was his religion (this could still be true of the Black Power Negro). The whites of "The Golden-Faced People"—the twentieth century Negroes—had benefited very little from Lin Kon's campaign for equality before the law for white and Chinese. Lin Kon remained a martyr—a saint—to the whites. They relished the legend of a man who had been born "on the hardy plains of central China where people had a rough sort of equality" (frontier Kentucky?), who had seen state auction blocks and white men sold, and who had been assasinated for his efforts on behalf of the whites. But after a hundred frustrating years the white man had given up hope of the fulfillment of the corollaries of legal equality in the United States of China; like the Negro he could count it a privilege to be left in peace. Madison Grant, in his nativist classic *The Passing of the Great Race,* 1915, stated:

The native American has always found and finds now in the black men willing followers, who ask only to obey and to further the ideals and wishes of the master race, without trying to inject into the body politic their own views, whether racial, religious or social.[22]

Lindsay had really gotten into the nativist skin when he had his white Negro say

. . . we do not want social equality, neither do we want the color line rubbed out. Our highest dream is that by patience and dignity, by more care for ethics and ceremony, by a sweeter Christianity, to attain a sort of spiritual rank with the conservative everlasting race that still dominates.[23]

Pathetically, even in the sphere of religion the white Negro abased himself. Was this the one point on which Lindsay's allegory fell down, or does the Negro think that while he will enjoy the "nigger heaven" and would be out of place in the white one, qualitatively pleasure is more intense in the latter?

Lindsay's allegory posed the crucial question of the forms that integration might take at a more than legal level. Given that white opposition could be made quiescent if not cooperative, given an increasing number of militant, educated, would-be-integrated Negroes, how can one bring about the rehabilitation of the passive majority as positive personalities, as caring citizens, how can one substitute community action for individual lethargy, interest in America for subversion and apathy? Once established, should a community of constructive Negro feeling be directed toward the accommodation of Negroes in white society as if they in no sense differed from whites? (One implication of integration movements is that Negroes alone cannot achieve a satisfying life, that they need white influence and contact, and want to emulate whites.) Or should Negroes aim for an equal yet distinctive society, characterized by assimilation in schools, jobs, and residential areas, yet remaining a group within a nation, their civil rights observed and their human dignity and equality taken for granted, like other racial groups in America?

Lindsay endorsed the latter aim, not in the extreme forms advocated by self-appointed Black Messiahs as Marcus Garvey, from 1915–27 president of the Universal Negro Improvement Association, who saw in "Back to Africa" the means by which the Negro could regain his hypothetical national stature; nor in those now adopted by Black Power and Black Muslim movements which preach the millennium of black supremacy in America (ironically, the "golden-faced people" strongly resemble Malcolm X's "white devils"). Lindsay's stand was for quiet pride in negritude, for the acknowledgement of Africans as brothers in spirit and color, and of themselves as black, as Africa in America. Presciently, he looked to black Americans to aim at the "commercial equality" which would allow them to take or leave the corollaries of that equality.[24] But Lindsay's consciousness of the almost immediate reorientation and elementary training in the capacity for independence that the Negro needed that led him into Booker T. Washington's camp rather than into W. E. B. Dubois'. He dedicated a trilogy of poems to Booker T. Washington: praising Negro dignity in "King Solomon and the Queen of Sheba," lamenting the immoral prosperity of "Simon Legree," and in "John Brown" showing his approval of Washington's and Brown's attempts to gain legal and human equality for the Negro. He used the imagery of the psalms to convey his and heaven's approval,

> *I saw the harp and psalt'ry*
> *Played for old John Brown.*
> *I heard the ram's horn blow,*
> *Blow for old John Brown.*
> *I saw the Bulls of Bashan—*
> *They cheered for old John Brown.*

When Lindsay hoped that John Brown had helped to "Set God's Israel free," Israel was both Black America and the whole of America. Action on behalf of the Negro meant that America might become a better approximation of the Promised Land.[25]

Any analysis of Lindsay's attitude to the Negro is usually based on "The Congo," which is seen as an appreciation of a raucous Negro subculture, an amused delineation of Negro antics. He did characterize the Negroes for "their basic savagery," "their irrepressible high spirits," and their unashamedly emotional religion, but he was at the same time voicing his witness to an alien, but undeniable civilization. He was swept away in spite of himself.

> *THEN I had religion, THEN I had a vision.*
> *I could not turn from their revel in derision.*

"The Congo" embodied Lindsay's hope that Negroes would be racially confident in their ambitions, that they would accept as an ultimate aspiration

> *A negro fairy land . . .*
> *A minstrel river*
> *Where dreams come true,*

an Afro-American dream in which

> *The ebony palace soared on high*
> *Through the blossoming trees to the evening sky.*
> *The inlaid porches and casements shone*
> *With gold and ivory and elephant-bone.*

He hoped that from choice they would integrate only to an extent consistent with the retention and promotion of their racial identity.

But without prior knowledge of Lindsay's belief in racial equality and in negritude, "The Congo" was easily misunderstood. Segregationalists welcomed it as a good-humored, burnt-cork burlesque; militant Negroes considered it deprecated Negro potential. They did not relish references to a past of voodoo and cannibalism, to "the boom of the blood-lust song/And a thigh-bone beating on a tin-pan gong," nor to a present of the juba, cakewalk princes, raucous revivalism, and "fat black bucks in a wine-barrel room." [26] Lindsay and Du Bois clashed about the poem; and a revealing exchange of letters about it took place between Lindsay and Joel E. Spingarn, after the first Amenia conference at Troutbeck in 1916, to which Lindsay, with other prominent white and colored men of reasonably liberal persuasion, was invited to discuss the Negro question. Spingarn, the white collaborator and echo of Du Bois, wanted Lindsay to write about black men as if they were white; Lindsay, who was celebrating negritude, though somewhat naively, could not see what in his poem was a source of displeasure and shame to the Negro. The letters show the same difference between Spingarn and Lindsay that existed between the early Du Bois and Booker T. Washington: imitation of the white man to the extent of racial assimilation versus race survival and reconstruction.

SPRINGFIELD
ILLINOIS
November 2, 1915

MY DEAR MR. SPINGARN:

Last August when I was away and my mail was being dammed up here in Springfield, your letter to the Amenia conference arrived . . .

I send my belated thanks. . . . Be sure I was with you in spirit. My "Congo" and "Booker T. Washington Trilogy" have both been denounced by the colored people for reasons that I cannot fathom.

As far as I can see, they have not taken the trouble to read them through. The third section of "The Congo" is certainly as hopeful as any human being dare to be with regard to any race, and the "John Brown" is not an unsympathetic poem, and "King Solomon and the Queen of Sheba" is a prophecy of a colored Utopia. Yet *The Crisis* took the trouble to skin me not long ago. This is in face of the fact that they had published with great approval my story of "The Golden Faced People" in *The Crisis* of November, 1914. That is the index to all subsequent work. . . .

And after you have read this letter, I would appreciate it if you will send a copy to the editor of *The Crisis,* to be printed, if he cares to do so [he did not]. Personally Mr. Du Bois has been most courteous, but I cannot understand his editorial attitude.

Very sincerely

NICHOLAS VACHEL LINDSAY

AMENIA

N.Y.

November 6 1916

MY DEAR MR. LINDSAY:

I wish you had been able to attend the Amenia Conference, and perhaps then you would have understood the difference between a poet's pageantry and a people's despair.

No colored man doubts your good intentions, but many of them doubt your understanding of their hopes. You look about you and see a black world full of a strange beauty different from that of the white world; they look about them and see other men with exactly the same feelings and desires who refuse to recognise the resemblance. You look forward to a colored Utopia separate and different from the hope of the white man; they have only one overwhelming desire; and that is to share in a common civilization in which all distinctions of race are blurred (or forgotten) by common aspirations and common labors.

Your poetry is wonderfully beautiful, and the poems on black men and women are no less beautiful than the rest. How can we fail to be grateful for all this beauty? But somehow we feel (and I say "we" because I share the feelings of the colored race), somehow we feel that you do not write about colored humanity as you write about white humanity. We remember your poem on John Altgeld (to mention only one) and realize that your heart goes out to—

"The widow . . .
The mocked . . ."

but somehow we feel that for you, black men and women are not like others who have been mocked and scorned and wounded, but beings a little different from other sufferers who do not share the same ancestry and the same color of skin.

Faithfully yours
JOEL E. SPINGARN[27]

Lindsay wanted to wedge George Washington more tightly into that neat myth which made him the aloof recipient of national glory, a figure who in his personal and historical distance and grandeur fulfilled a need that the human, Republican Lincoln could not. It is impossible to imagine fluctuation in what is subsequently likely to remain Washington's historical-mythical primacy. He combined too well a usefully imponderable symbolism with an unexceptionable matter-of-factness; he was safely situated in a section of the past which Americans manage to find a source of comfort and pride, and not a reminder of their national shortcomings. He was a successful general, a founding father, and a respected president: a faultless combination.

The Gilbert Stuart portrait of Washington's "mountain-dignity"[28] epitomized the superior, impenetrable Washington that Lindsay wanted remembered. In this sense he was fighting a battle already won, for that was the image of Washington that was becoming commonplace through its circulation on postage stamps and currency. But Lindsay made two original contributions to the Washington myth. First, he suggested that Washington was a physically conditioned American in the same mold as the American Indian. The soil

had given him its special vitamins, the blood of its wild animals; he was acquiring a tomahawk skull and cheekbones; a fact that distinguished him forever from the Englishman, and a tomahawk way of thinking [the famed American forthrightness?] that distinguished him forever from Europe, and made him no longer a colonist.

Whether Lindsay believed this of Washington or was trying to tie him in with his definition of Americanness is not always clear, but it was his way of paying a compliment, and he did manage to tinge Washington and his campaign with an Indian stolidity.

There were many times when the Revolution consisted of George Washington on horseback riding toward the enemy slowly and magnificently, and looking impregnable; shot at a thousand times and always missed; while the patriots were somewhere back there in the nearby woods, invisible, but bushwacking according to the Indian code.[29]

Second, in *The Litany of Washington Street,* Lindsay evolved the composite image of Washington Street, which symbolized his updated conception of the founding fathers' implicit promises. Ideally it was the antithesis of Main Street; factually it was a street which in many towns "has grown dim and dingy . . . but when it was named, it was with a magnificent intention, as the Via Appia was named for Appius Claudius."[30] (Springfield's Washington Street was the center of Salvation Army activities.) It was a symbolic highway, both wooded and residential, echoing with poetry and politics, stretching from Atlantic to Pacific. On this street Lindsay imagined Washington, Jefferson, and Hamilton riding abreast, Washington in the middle keeping the truce. Here was a representation of a golden era in politics, when faction could exist, gain a hearing, and receive arbitration. Lindsay did not know, or did not admit, that Washington had virtually become a Federalist in the latter part of the 1790s, and that in the eyes of many he was a partisan, not a dispassionate President. He did not discuss whether Washington's attributed qualities were the genuine article, or poses, or the expression of the need of the people for a focal image of altruistic rule. Whatever the historical truth, inconvenient facts could be passed over with resignation and satisfaction projecting to an already convinced public the personification of American dignity and vocational principle.

Washington's indigenous, selfless "grand style" was the only kind of built-in authority that Lindsay, as an American, could accept. It was an authority "Cold and mighty as his name/And stern as Freedom's story." Washington Street government was the only nondemocratic sovereignty that Lindsay found palatable: "Washington . . . was our first and last king, and let us face that." [31] Lindsay exemplified many Americans' conviction that, the right man forthcoming, one-man rule is attractive and effective; he had reservations, however, about "King Andrew."

It may seem strange that Andrew Jackson and not Thomas Jefferson formed the third member of Lindsay's triumvirate. Washington, Jefferson, and Lincoln constituted the conventional triad of great Americans. Lindsay had enormous admiration for Jefferson, as author of the Declaration of Independence, as a pioneer in the social application of scientific inventions, and as a Virginian. The exclusion of so politically able and influential a president, who embodied, if anyone did, that artistic leaven that Lindsay thought would produce better government, is superficially puzzling. But in all probability, the sheer complexity of Jefferson's image, the diverse interpretations put on his words and actions, and the tendency of every party at any given period to claim to be the rightful repository of the principles of Jeffersonian democracy, left Lindsay with the feeling that historians have today, that Jefferson still evades definition, and that, as Lawrence Chamberlain has said, "the search for his proper image has become indistinguishable from America's search for her own image." [32] This search is beyond most historians, and certainly beyond Lindsay; and lacking a clearcut and recognizable essence, Jefferson would only be an encumbrance to Lindsay's carefully delineated corps of American leaders.

Jackson did not exemplify Lincoln's high principle or Washington's political polish; different qualities made him round off Lindsay's triumvirate aptly. He was not a symbol of American independence and stature like Washington, nor a symbol of American unity and moral principle like Lincoln; he was a symbol to identify with, not for looking up to—the American people in their own imagined likeness. From the war of 1812 a residuum of insecurity hung over the people; Jackson's defence in 1815 of New Orleans, symbolic of victory, coupled with his colorful association with an Expansionist policy which was broadly supported throughout the country, had given him the rank of American savior. His popularity was unprecedented; his nickname, Old Hickory, suggested how firmly rooted he was as an American institution. With Jackson such appallingly trite phrases as "the common man believed implicitly in him" [33] have to be taken at their face value. He was the democratically logical phenomenon of the election of a hero, who represented, though in a crasser, less Athenian sense than Lindsay would have wished, the national realization of the principles of the Declaration of Independence.

It was this Jackson of the people, not a historically dissected Jackson that Lindsay wrote about. As in the cases of Lincoln and Washington, he assumed that analyses of the motivations and achievements of the American presidents could only blur the outline of the emotionally coherent entity he wanted to create.

> *Do you think I want some fool*
> *Statistical,*
> *To picture that second inaugural*
> *Who has read all the diaries of the day*
> *And all that the Adamses have to say?*
> *And the speeches of Calhoun, of Webster and Clay?*

He wanted instead to project the naturalistic image of Jackson handed down from his grandparents. "I will think of you"

> *Old turkey cock,*
> *On a forest rock,*
> *Old buffalo, knee-deep in the weeds,*
>
> . . . .
>
> *I will think of you when I harvest again,*
> *I will think of you when the woods are cut—*
> *Old, old Andrew Jackson.*[34]

This Jackson, from the back country of South Carolina and Tennessee, the West of his day, symbolized backwoods America, American innocence, and the rough true virtues of the West. He was "the frontier brought to its place of power." Yet while Lindsay was celebrating the valid image of Jackson as "Democracy irresistible" he was not unaware of an often glossed-over paradox. When the people, through democratic processes, raise up such a champion as Jackson, to some extent they are expressing a wish for despotism, one initially of their own choosing, but whose specific formulation is left in hands they admire so much as to consider infallible. Though at the time of Jackson's elections in 1828 and 1832, it may have seemed like "London Tower fallen" or the fall of the Bastille ("gone were the blasphemous breeds/Mankind was made new"), Lindsay at least realized that one form of tyranny had merely been substituted for another:

> *The only crown was Democracy's crown*
> . . . .
> *And Jackson was king of it, too.*

Lindsay tried to set out an American mythology in terms of its heroes and its ethos to give a sense of continuity and responsibility to a century in which precedents tended to seem irrelevant. He assembled diverse materials from the past and showed them to be historically and mythically coherent; he made the kind of general statements—"Log Cabins mean Andrew Jackson" [35]—which historiographically seem more valid in America than anywhere else.

Lindsay did not, then, distort the American past beyond recognition; but did he succeed in crystallizing a national mythology of his own choice? He was clearly convinced that there were good (nationally constructive) and bad (nationally hazy) myths, and that more often than not good myths reflected a degree of historical truth. For instance, he would not accept the essentially human (though extremely virtuous) Washington that Weems depicted, that "vague general demagogue made of clouds and cotton batting." [36] And however Washington's character has subsequently been analyzed, it was his transcendence rather than any humanity that constituted the prevailing impression he made on his contemporaries. And while Lindsay's myths might be emotive, they were not unjustifiably sentimental. In spite of his feeling for Lincoln he toned down the Christ-like figure whose birthday Whitman celebrated thus:

Today, from each and all, a breath of prayer—a pulse of thought
To memory of Him—to birth of Him[37]

and tried to reinstate with plainer emotion the image of an irresistibly humane man.

Lindsay's entity was bound to hold together shakily when it was scattered through his writings and not collected. But however organized, a paper entity will not produce the hard-to-define, atmospheric unity of national spirit and tradition which must be socially motivated. Only if such motivations came into serious play might Lindsay's synthesis of the American past acquire the full significance he attributed to it. But the vivid and evocative poems he wrote in the course of brooding on the past—for example, "In Praise of Johnny Appleseed," "Abraham Lincoln Walks at Midnight," "Old, Old, Old, Andrew Jackson"—arouse personal pleasure and national pride in many Americans who read them; no mean achievement even for as nationally concerned a writer as Lindsay. Historians may dismiss him, but he recreated the atmosphere which, it can be argued, is as valid, and as evasive a part of history as the historical fact.

CHAPTER EIGHT

Regionalism

THE PUBLICATION in 1930 of *I'll Take My Stand,* a book in which twelve Southern intellectuals supported a "Southern way of life against what may be called the American or prevailing way," marked the beginning of a spate of reports, surveys, and speculation about political, economic, and sociological balances within America. Lindsay was dead before the debate on American regionalism was thoroughly under way, but his theory of Regionalism was part of the prelude to the debate.

Frederick Jackson Turner, in his essays "Section and Nation," 1922, and "The Significance of the Section in American History," 1925, had already explored a new dimension of regionalism. American history, Turner proposed, was not only the history of the frontier, but of the section. Based on geographic regions, the concept of the section entailed

a geography of political habit, a geography of opinion, of material interests, of racial stocks, of physical fitness, of social traits, of literature, of the distribution of men of ability, even of religious denominations.[1]

While diversity was natural and welcome, Turner felt that sectionalism had its undesirable manifestations—North-South and East-West hostilities—and that it was acquiring overtones of isolation, self-sufficiency, and selfishness. American regions were becoming transatlantic versions of European nation-states. Protagonists of regionalism—Turner himself—were torn between advocating regional development as a means of retaining and furthering folk, cultural, and natural characteristics, and cautioning against a process that might undermine a hard-won degree of national solidarity and uniformity.

Lindsay's attempt to plan a civic unit capable of reproduction on a nation-wide scale related him to the latter school of negative regionalism. Aggressive regionalism was an obvious barrier to an American entity. And yet, Lindsay was a constructive regionalist. Just as he argued that in human relationships differences of character did not preclude compatibility, so he felt a fuller, tensile unity could spring from regional diversity. He bridged the approaches to regionalism by celebrating each part of America for its unique ambience, not for its controversial claims. If, on his travels he could appreciate "Florida moss, Georgia violin, a New Jersey orchard in the spring . . . a California orange grove," the odor of coffee in New Orleans, and eating breakfast on the roof of Texas hotels,[2] and think that these experiences had created his own high pitch of Americanness, regionalism was not only desirable, it was vital.

A map Lindsay produced to confront an English reporter from the *Observer* in London in 1920, when the reporter's questions irritatingly seemed to indicate that the English thought New England and America were synonymous, showed he had made some changes in the traditional regional divisions of America.[3] To the six New England states he added New York, New Jersey, and Pennsylvania, and continued to call the region New England. The Old South was unchanged; the Midwest was diminished by the loss of the eastern parts of Montana, Wyoming, and Colorado; the Far West was reduced to California, Nevada, Washington, and Oregon, and renamed New Italy; and a new division, comprising Arizona, New Mexico, Colorado, Utah, Idaho, Wyoming, and Montana was created and christened New Arabia.

It was no novelty to celebrate the individual beauties of these regions; to that extent Lindsay's treatment was unoriginal. What was remarkable about his theory was his success in being unpartisan about the Midwest to the extent of being virtually hostile to the region, and the allocation of responsibility he made for national essentials: character—the Old South, culture—New Italy; unity—New England; urban beauty—New Arabia.

NEW ARABIA

New Arabia was Lindsay's most original redefinition of American territory; it was made by splitting up vertically a generously conceived Far West (New Italy and New Arabia) to create a region dominated by Santa Fe and running from the Canadian border down to Mexico. In this region, he said to the *Observer* reporter, lay "the future of America." [4] He meant not the cultural future—that was to be divided between the east and west coasts —but the social and physical future, the future of housing, employment, and shopping centers, of transport and recreation in an integrated environment. As Lindsay never showed interest in Arabian desert society, only in Egyptology, his description was probably spontaneous, impact-produced rather than reasoned, but it was none the less apt. New Arabia was largely desert, and the desert image expressed Lindsay's overall vision of America. It provided a contrast to disorderly urban proliferation, and suggested a national panorama potentially as ordered as the desert. As it stood, it comprised "illimitable fields," but it could acquire less oceanic expanses and more frequent towns.

Lindsay chose Santa Fe as the heart of New Arabia because it was on his tramp along the Santa Fe Trail in 1912 that he felt he had memorably seen how "the United States goes by." Clouds raced along the sky, cars along the road; nature and artifice progressed together. He associated New Arabia, Santa Fe, and the Trail with the continual juxtaposition of extremes in America:

> *Cars from Concord, Niagara, Boston,*
> *Cars from Topeka, Emporia and Austin.*
> *Cars from Chicago, Hannibal, Cairo.*
> *Cars from Alton, Oswego, Toledo*

jostling with the countryside, *"land that restores us/When houses choke us. . . ."* He looked forward to the day when the Santa Fe Trail, "now nothing but a well dragged road" would "assume the dignity and granite setting of a Roman highway." He wanted a New Santa Fe Trail, a New Arabia—modern, beautiful, convenient. He felt some "private griefs" at the obliteration of rural America, but he was excited and committed in spite of himself.[5]

Another aspect of New Arabia which led Lindsay to call it "the American Splendor"[6] was its complex of national parks. He had tramped with Stephen Graham in Glacier National Park, Montana, in 1921; he honeymooned there in 1924, and revisited it in 1925. From 1923 to 1928 he lived in Spokane, Washington, primarily to be near the park, which was of particular significance to him because of the ease with which he and Graham had crossed the border into Canada and the Waterton Lakes Park in 1922. "We crossed a Canadian American line almost obliterated. Every line should be like that."[7] The experience seemed to him an anticipation of the day when a fraternal international community could dispense with physical and emotional barriers.

Lindsay relied on national parks—particularly Glacier Park— as a personal panacea. On July 16, 1931 (he committed suicide on December 5) he was still saying "All I need is a change and a rest, a new sight of the park."[8] His own experience of pleasure and refreshment in national parks led him to think of them as an antidote for national ills: "Only the deserts and mountains of America can crack the business hardened skulls of the East," he brooded in Glacier Park in 1922. The Parks represented the Western essence of the United States as opposed to a Europeanized, disparate America: "If in America one does not have the West-going heart, the thousand little nations that are the countries of Europe pull one away from our great National Parks."[9] He thought they might provide a means of permanent regeneration for a society to which the great outdoors was becoming increasingly foreign. Renewal was particularly necessary for the governors of the country, to maintain, or if necessary, create, an awareness of natural America and the unfathomable, mystic element in her destiny (though one doubts if Theodore Roosevelt had himself in mind when he promulgated his conservation policies).

Lindsay laid too much emphasis on National Parks as repositories of Americanness, and perhaps on the West as the key ingredient of American difference. But it was part of his concept of American lacks and needs to embalm as a permanent point of reference an unsettled frontier and an area of natural beauty. They do have a certain emotional and physical function, but they hardly constitute a "spiritual lodestone" [10] for America generally and for America's leaders in particular.

NEW ITALY

The name "New Italy" recalled the ideas Lindsay had propagated about an architectural and cultural renaissance in the communities of the New Localism (though their model was as often Athenian as Italian). Geographically New Italy consisted of California, Nevada, and most of Washington and Oregon; emotionally New Italy encapsulated Lindsay's concept of an American artistic outburst, precipitated by the growth of the motion picture industry in California. The motion picture could be the first predominantly American art form, and it could also disseminate knowledge of other arts. With these considerations in mind, Lindsay wondered, in the first edition of *The Art of the Moving Picture,* 1915, if, "in the next decade, simply from the development of the average eye, cities akin to the beginnings of Florence will be born among us." [11]

Because of his hopes that through informative, educative films culture consciousness would spread through America, California and Los Angeles temporarily became the most important areas of America to him, the ultimate in the continent's frontiers, the West's West. America's disproportionate puritan hangover and her English ties had, he felt, made it difficult for a fresh and vital culture, expressive of her scale and energy to spring up. People like himself

who revere the Pilgrim Fathers of 1620 have often wished those gentlemen had moored their bark in the region of Los Angeles rather than Plymouth Rock, that Boston had been founded there. At last that landing is achieved.

He accepted as a fait accompli (minimizing Midwestern achievements) that Boston had "appropriated to herself the guardianship of the national text-books of Literature," but he expected that Los Angeles would "lay hold of the motion picture as our national text-book in Art." [12] In the 1920s the orientation of the American film industry to sensation-seekers disillusioned Lindsay about the foreseeable realization of a New Italy; but in 1915 he indulged, unusually for him, in almost Whitmanesque admiration of the Average Californian, magnificent, like eucalyptus and pomegranate (ready for the cultural picking?).

California also appealed to Lindsay in the traditional Far Western sense of plenty, for its lushness, more obvious than anywhere else in America. The state was to him what Texas is to the Texans: biggest and best. Flowers did not just open, but "burst like bombs in California"; cattle and pigs had "ears of silk and velvet," "tusks like long white poles." California was an almost over-fecund "garden of the world"; Lindsay teased that whales were fed there with

> *Boatloads of citrons, quinces, cherries,*
> *Of bloody strawberries, plums and beets,*
> *Hogsheads of pomegranates, vats of sweets.*

While he was amused at the exaggerated abundance of California—

> *There are ten gold suns in California*
> *Where all other lands have one,*
> *For the Golden Gate must have due light*
> *And persimmons be well-done*

—he did feel it was a rare region, which in its natural state was an Eden.

It has not the sordidness of gold, as has Wall Street, but it is the embodiment of the natural ore that the ragged prospector finds. The gold of California is the color of the orange, the glitter of dawn in Yosemite, the hue of the golden gate that opens the sunset way to the mystic and terrible Cathay and Hindustan.

But its brilliance was vice as well as virtue. The gold rush, for example, brought national appreciation of California's rare scenery and climate; it also demonstrated the state's intrinsic materialism, which in part caused, and in part was caused, by the gold rush, and which colored mind and matter.

> *Oh the flashing cornucopia of haughty California*
> *Is gold, gold, gold.*
> *Their brittle speech and their clutching reach*
> *Is gold, gold, gold.*

In keeping with the golden imagery of *The Golden Book of Springfield,* Lindsay used the transformation of a naturally golden California into a cruelly imaginative paradise to symbolize the failure of the American promise. He saw Californians, like the original forty-niners, and many pioneers, as pathetic mixtures of self-indulgence, gusto, and bounty.

> *They drink, these belly-busting devils*
> *And their tremens shake the ground.*
> *And then they repent like whirlwinds*
> *And never were such saints found.*
> *They will give you plug tobacco.*
> *They will give you the shirts off their backs,*
> *They will cry for your every sorrow,*
> *Put ham in your haversacks.*[13]

A relation of Lindsay's on his mother's side, Frances Frazee Hamilton, in "Ancestral Lines of the Doniphan-Frazee-Hamilton Families," 1928, suggested that there was Spanish blood in the family through the marriage of Lindsay's great-great-great-grandfather to Susan Doniphan, the descendant of a Don Alexander Iphan. But whether Frances Hamilton was accurate in her genealogy is not important; what matters is that Lindsay, aware from his early days of family legend, found it easy to believe in a

> *. . . Spanish ancestor,*
> *The mighty Don Ivan, Quixotic explorer:—*
> *Friend of Columbus, Queen Isabel's friend,*
> *Conquistador!*
> *Great-great-great-grandfather.*[14]

Columbus had been an early agent of Manifest Destiny; a Californian impetus might help to realize the cultural dimension of his mission, so Lindsay was eager, and able, to identify himself with Spanish America. But just as he was scrupulous about guarding against an addiction to the Midwest, so he did not let his emotional affinity with California prevent him from looking elsewhere for the source of regeneration when his plans for California, explicitly put forward in the little noticed *Art of the Moving Picture,* failed to germinate.

THE OLD SOUTH

Following the still poor reception of his image of New Italy in the second edition of *The Art of the Moving Picture* in 1922, Lindsay tried to stimulate interest in another vitally American region. This sounds like and was an artificial process: Lindsay was prepared to be flexible in the construction of an American entity, and to play on any principled part of the imagination which would respond to him. Ironically, his ease of transition from one valid American image to another reflected the key hindrance to a would-be entity: racial and religious groups, all with plausible bases for the conviction that they alone embodied the real American spirit. The notion of an entity which, however composite, might take away their uniqueness, was resented.

It may have been an increasing awareness of the odds against this entity that brought forth increasingly controversial theories from Lindsay. He called on the South, the Old South, to put nonracial, nonsectional backbone in the nation. He avoided using the term "New South" current around 1900; like Thomas Nelson Page, whom he regarded as an encouragingly liberal Southerner, he realized the new south was "simply the Old South with its energies directed into new lines." [15] A contemporary regionalist, Howard Odum, wrote of the immoral morality and moral immorality of the South; and it was this residual, predictable, and responsible code, which had existed in spite of, and because of, slavery, that seemed to Lindsay a not undesirable standard for national character.

He chose the state of Virginia to characterize this South of permanent, old-fashioned values. In his poem "Virginia," 1926, he reversed his Californian thesis that the farthest West, most un-English region should be the starting point of the American entity, and saw that the American experience could have gone another way. Virginia, as he symbolized it, could have been what all men went to America for, and what they should have been satisfied with. Although in retrospect interest, glamor, and admiration attached to the frequently grim push west, although it was picturesque,

> *They took their schoolbooks and their wagons,*
> *They took their scythes, their rakes and flagons,*
> *They took their fiddles, Bibles and guns,*
> *They took their sons, and their sons' sons,*[16]

it was a wrongly motivated, self-defeating movement. Lindsay could express only modified approval for what amounted to a search for unformulated ends and an attempt to satisfy unascertained urges. Of course population increases would have made the movement a physical necessity as well as an emotional fact. Lindsay was not regretting that all America could not live in Virginia, but that defects of American society and character had grown out of the western movement: a lack of stability, an inability to sit tight and take stock, the conviction that things would automatically happen right. What from one angle appeared to be foresight and the destined take-over of the continent, from another seemed a barely understood, instinctive process, ingrained by the time the physical frontier was exhausted (c. 1890), and likely to go on manifesting itself in an agglomeration of subjective individuals, loosely bound together by a memory of what America had been ("Remembering daguerrotypes, tintypes . . ./That once came from Virginia"),[17] and by physical circumstance, but with no conception beyond the material of what America could be.

Lindsay's own perception that the western process had produced a formidably individualistic outlook which ran contrary to his entity was not sustained. He found it as hard as anyone to stand back from the accepted romantic, formative period of American history; where would his entity have been without it? "Virginia" was keen comment, but it involved substituting Lindsay's romance of history for traditional romance. In "Virginia" Virginians had been nebulous but commendable spiritual citizens of the

> *Land of the gauntlet and the glove,*
> *Virginia, Virginia,*
> *Horseback land of sash and plume,*
>
> . . . .
>
> *Virginia, Virginia.*[18]

In "The Virginians are Coming Again," 1928, they had become the people to alleviate the American process of "killing off souls and dreams."

> *Thin-skinned scholars, hard-riding men,*
> *Poets unharnessed, the moon their abode.*
> *With the statesman's code, the gentleman's code.*
> *With Jefferson's code, Washington's code*
> *With Powhatan's code.*

Virginians, Southerners—Lindsay was by now using the terms interchangeably—were men of stature and diverse abilities; and Lindsay, taken with his characterization, decided that "Virginian" could describe any American who was nature's, and nature's God's gentleman, in fact, any American who in Lindsay's eyes had outstanding individual or national merit. Helen Wills, Gene Tunney, and Charles Lindbergh were all Virginians in this sense. As early international successes in tennis, boxing, and aviation, they had ignored the logic of isolationism, and had looked beyond small-town ambitions. So Lindsay's concept of the Virginian progressed to that of an affirmative American and a potential world citizen (Lindbergh proved an unlucky choice!). The Virginian-American was the opposite of

> *Babbitt, [whose] . . . tribe is passing away.*
> *This is the end of your infamous day.*
> *The Virginians are coming again.*[19]

It was in the context of Virginia and as the supreme Virginian that Lindsay considered Jefferson. Unfortunately for literature, he wrote about him not in some stirring "Old, Old, Old Thomas Jefferson," but in the politically and stylistically wooly *The Litany of Washington Street,* 1929. In verse it has been left to Stephen Vincent Benét to express Jefferson's versatility; it is sentimentally satisfying that he wrote in Lindsay's colloquial style of

> *The big hands clever*
> *With pen and fiddle*
> *And ready, ever,*
> *For any riddle.*
> *From buying empires*
> *To planting 'taters,*
> *From Declarations*
> *To dumb-waiters.*

Lindsay said the same thing—in less effective prose. "The list of the contrasting things he did superbly well would shame a Florentine of the Renaissance";[20] he combined the qualities of philosopher and politician, aristocrat and democrat, cosmopolitan and American. On a bigger scale he was Lindsay's grandfather Ephraim Samuel Frazee, "The Proud Farmer"; so perhaps the Virginian *was* a national type.

Lindsay's sole interesting and original approach to Jefferson was to compare him with Edgar Allan Poe. According to Lindsay, Jefferson had conditioned Poe's talents: first, by helping to create the Virginia in which Poe periodically lived, and second, by founding the University at which Poe studied. Jefferson's influence, Lindsay argued, emanated not through the education which the University provided (Poe only spent one year there, 1826, and that mainly gambling) but through "Jefferson's architectural genius [which] became a part of Poe's visualizing power. Just as Poe mixed the classic and the wildly unknown and original in order to achieve a new order, so did Jefferson in the drawing of . . . buildings and in . . . landscape gardening." (Jefferson designed both the buildings and the grounds at the University of Virginia.)

This combination of convention and innovation had first been attributed to Jefferson in William A. Lambeth and Warren H. Manning's *Thomas Jefferson as an Architect and Designer of*

Landscape (1913), and in Thomas Fiske Kimball's *Thomas Jeffer-son and the First Monument of the Classical Revival in America* (1915). These writers concluded that Jefferson's outlook was one of "retrospection and of science";[21] that his architectural style was distinctively American, classic but modern in the circumstances of the time; and likewise his landscaping, a mixture of the natural and the rococo. Whether Lindsay was familiar with these writers is not known, but he came to the same conclusion. He tied it up with the fact that Poe harked back to classical imagery and nomenclature in his poetry while striking out into new dimensions of imaginative fantasy in his short stories. In their respective spheres the two men were of seminal importance for America: "the mind of Poe in the arts is as . . . pervasive as the mind of Jefferson in politics." [22] The old and the new, the conventional and the innovatory, the bedrock and the fresh formation: this was a rationalization of what Lindsay wanted for America; this was why Virginia, and the old South, excited him.

NEW ENGLAND

"In infancy I never heard of New England. I heard of Europe every day." Lindsay's words, written in 1925, reflected the hostility toward New England which was part of his upbringing and which he felt throughout his life. In Hiram's magazine *The Spider Web,* 1899, he had mused, with more envy than pity: "Consider what a curse it is to live down the Harvard label." "So Much the Worse for Boston," 1923, indicted

Proud Yankee birds of prey, overshadowing the land,
Screaming to younger Yankees of the self-same brand.[23]

He carried this hostility over into his career. Although he was as much in demand in New England as elsewhere, and was "fashionable" at Ivy League universities, his audiences were somewhat inhibited, hardly liking to admit they were moved. John Dos Passos, a student at Harvard in 1915, expressed the reserve and the superficial sophistication which Lindsay did penetrate, but which he was unaware he had broken through. Many years after

1915, Dos Passos admitted "we went to kid, but were very much impressed in spite of ourselves." But sometimes Lindsay and New England were undeniably poles apart. In 1921 he wrote a long, sentimental "village apocalypse" eulogy about Governor Taylor of Tennessee, "Bob Taylor's Birthday," as the Phi Beta Kappa poem for Harvard's Commencement Exercises; as one commentator summed it up: "The oratory which would have soared under Chautauqua canvas sank in the Harvard Yard." East coast sophisticates did not appreciate what Lindsay himself called his "'log-cabin' way of reiterating the dogmas of Walter Pater" through the medium of Governor Taylor in "his giant chair of sky and dreams/Of the Great Smoky Mountains and East County Streams."[24]

Culturally Lindsay had an inferiority complex about New England. He conceived of a Western renaissance in defensive terms.

The western farms, though scarcely settled, have the Chautauqua, which is New England's old rural lecture course; the temperance crusade, which is New England's abolitionism come again; the magazine militant, which is the old *Atlantic Monthly* combined with the *Free-Soil Newspaper* under a new dress, and educational reform, which is the Yankee school-house made glorious.

Western and Southern culture were meritorious because they were "richer and broader and deeper than New England"; a "worth-while" American culture, to be thoroughly representative, would have to take on a cruder form than the cultivated "prunes and prisms of Boston." Lindsay apparently saw his own work, and that of his fellow Midwesterners, as inferior by absolute cultural standards, but superior in the context of the demands of American culture.[25]

Although he was annoyed by New England's exclusive intellectualism, Lindsay was not part of any tradition of antiintellectualism. He had the non-New Englander's suspicion of an erudite cabal, but believed New England and the rest of America to be potentially complementary areas which could learn from each other. He would have liked to experiment politically, to "put all the Boston and New York people out . . . on the plains and let the plain men run the east." Culturally he had the splendid idea of getting the imposing, impossible-to-ignore Amy Lowell to tour and thoroughly observe the South and West. If she could be convinced of their potential, she would "proceed to educate the east." He urged a friend to "move Heaven and Earth to make a westerner and southerner of her, and . . . she will then proceed to send all Boston and all the aesthetes of [New] England West and South." To interchange ideas was vital; no region could go it alone. "Believe me, the West and South need the East and North. Each is suffering for lack of the other." [26] A toughened up East and a refined down West could mean the beginning of American homogeneity, in which New England had a vital psychological role to play by denying her superiority and affirming the regional doctrine of different but equal. Even here Lindsay was almost unconsciously looking to New England to supply her traditional leadership.

THE MIDWEST

Lindsay was remembered by contemporaries as a Midwesterner par excellence. To Harriet Monroe he was a man of the prairies. "From Lincoln's own country a poet of Lincoln's own breed" and to Percy Mackaye he seemed a Midwestern country boy.[27] It is perhaps the crowning irony of Lindsay's career and writings that in spite of an unmistakably Midwestern presence and speech, and although he always went back to live in Illinois, he created the picture of a Midwest without a commendable identifying characteristic—except its partially dubious revivalism—the only region in his entity to lack such a characteristic. So eager was he for a visible impartiality to swell his audience that in the Midwest he created an America limbo, a region of corn and Cadillacs, with unchanging material essence, and ever-changing materialistic expression. The Midwest might be east of the cowboy, west of the forests, and north of the Negro, but it remained its conservative, reactionary self, populated by self-satisfied Midwesterners, who had "too much to eat, too many automobiles, too easy communication, too rich soil, and often an outrageous complacency"[28]—solid obstacles to Lindsay's entity.

Nevertheless, the physical Midwest conditioned Lindsay in his passionate love of nature; he never ceased to "faint with love/till the prairies dip and reel";[29] and the ubiquitous activity of religious sects in the region led to his incessant awareness of man's inadequate response to the demands of religion, intensified his concern for justice and morality, and kept spiritual goals before him. And although the Midwest figured in a minor way in his explicit regional picture of America, it had already been implicitly incorporated in *The Golden Book of Springfield*. The Midwest was Springfield; it was the Illinois which by 1920 was the third most populous state in America and which in 1910 had boasted eleven cities in the 25,000 to 100,000 population range. Its phenomenon, Chicago, razed in 1871, and by 1900 the second biggest city in America, with over a million inhabitants, had played host to a World's Fair, and had become the hub of a literary renaissance. Lindsay had lived in Chicago from 1901–1903 and he had seen in it the symbol of American resilience and perseverance, cultural vitality and architectural possibility. He had also seen written large in that city the American order of ruthlessness and materialism, ranging from the incongruous elite empires of the Palmers, McCormicks, and Pullmans to the equally incongruous congestion of poverty and hardship. The Midwest—the home of the bloody shirt and Haymarket justice, the home of Altgeld and Wright— was for Lindsay "typical America,"[30] whose challenge he had met and whose essence he had captured in *The Golden Book of Springfield,* a regional-national set of hopes and fears. With its cross section of native and immigrant elements, old and new hostilities, it was also the region in which he felt American racial and political divisiveness most clearly. His father had been one of the few militant Democrats in Republican Springfield, and as a child Lindsay felt his father's isolation. "The inexplicable Mason and Dixon's line, deep-dyed and awful, ran straight through our

hearts": a piercing experience, but one which made a compensat-
ingly positive contribution to Lindsay's internationalism.

It seems to me Mason and Dixon's line runs around every country in
the world, around France, Japan, Canada or Mexico or any sovereignty.
It is the terrible line that should be the line of love and good-will . . .
but may be the bloody line of mis-understanding.[31]

Not only was Lindsay more critical of Midwesterners than of
any other regional type, he did less than justice to the wealth of
literary talent endemic in the Midwest and converging on Chicago.
Chicago provided a home and an inspiration for nearly thirty years
(c. 1890–1920) to the avant-garde of America's literary talent, many
of them Midwesterners: Hamlin Garland (Wisconsin), Henry
Fuller (Chicago), Frank Norris (Chicago), Theodore Dreiser
(Indiana), and Sherwood Anderson (Ohio). Through piece-meal
and painstaking research one can establish—what one would any-
way have assumed—that Lindsay knew, and read these men; but,
with the exception of his appreciative references to Hamlin Garland, his sponsor through thick and thin, their existence does not
seem to have affected Lindsay personally, or his search for healthy
mental and artistic stirrings in the regions. He dissociated himself
from much of the poetic dimension of the Chicago renaissance,
particularly from Imagism, Imagisme, and the European oriented
Little Review. It is understandable that he could accept Masters
and Sandburg for American culture, and not Pound—but why
not Anderson, Dreiser, and Norris?

The answer is that he did not wish to be coupled with what
the public construed as this serious prose revolt against the
region, its towns, its villages, and its inhabitants. The concept of
such a revolt, stretching from E. W. Howe's *The Story of a
Country Town*, 1890, through to Sherwood Anderson's *Tar, a
Mid-West Childhood*, 1926, is suspect; for with the exception of
the strong regional roots of Willa Cather and Joseph Kirkland,
Midwestern self-criticism was part of what Ford Madox Ford
described as ". . . a world movement . . . an enormous disil-

lusionment"[32] with universally oppressive and repressive human qualities. The Midwest might be the scene; the universal dilemma of being was the subject. But however mis-coined, "Midwestern rebel" was too limiting and too extreme a label for Lindsay's taste. It invited superficial dismissal, and precluded his acceptance as a national theoretician. Paradoxically, in depth, and without overtones, the label was not inapt; Lindsay was more Midwestern and more rebellious than he chose to appear.

Lindsay's theory of regionalism was characteristically idiosyncratic. He attributed to his regions qualities which at first sight seemed wrongly distributed: New Italy—aesthetic leadership, the Old South—moral and intellectual fiber, New Arabia—town planning of distinction, New England—tolerance and cooperation. He was certainly urging the possible more than celebrating the actual, and perhaps, in his own almost imperceptibly humorous way, he was trying to startle Americans into new activities and different thoughts. Whatever the balance of speculation and challenge in his theory, it has worn increasingly better. New Italy has provided, in poetry and theater, an indigenous and unprecedentedly popular culture. The Kennedy New Frontier was a New England sermon —perhaps the first of many—on transregional and transworld cooperation. All America is a New Arabian desert of highways and oases. As for the Old South—its present conditions and its everpresent past fit it to produce a depth and intensity of mind impossible elsewhere in America.

But in spite of Lindsay's implicit suggestions of how the American regions fell short of their potential, he considered himself his own sort of hundred percent American nationalist, not in a Rightist, Know Nothing sense, nor in the sense that he believed that America was, or ever would be, the best or the perfect society, but in that he drew the line at a certain style of criticism.

I am a 100% American in deadly opposition to George Horace Lorimer and H. L. Mencken. The magazines *Saturday Evening Post* and *Smart Set* represent the most distinctive forces against which I am most definitely and clearly in opposition, and whose opposition makes my own position clearer.[33]

In stating his opposition to Mencken, Lindsay highlighted his weakness and Mencken's strength as surveyors of the American scene. Mencken's caustic commentary on American life was often iconoclastic for the sake of iconoclasm; he was contradictory, contemptuous of democracy as "government by orgy, almost by orgasm," [34] and yet critical of American poets (except Lindsay) for not being democratic poets, of and for the people. But his cynicism was a healthy outgrowth in the frenetic conformities of the twenties, and for many his slashing technic was an impetus to improvement. The fact that "he calls you a swine and an imbecile . . . increases your will to live," [35] wrote Walter Lippman in 1927. By contrast Lindsay's writings seem full of unspecific diatribe and overtentative suggestion, though he felt that if ever there was a case in point of destructive versus constructive criticism, it existed in the contrast between Mencken and himself. Every word that Mencken wrote seemed to Lindsay to cut away America's already loose and inadequate underpinnings. In fact, they were comparable realists, one showing his feelings with brutal directness, the other obliquely. Mencken thought the Virgin Land was best cultivated through a ruthless pruning, while Lindsay advocated the loving, selective encouragement of its best blooms.

CHAPTER NINE

The American Present

LINDSAY VIEWED the events of his lifetime with overall perspective and rarely with detailed close-up. For a curious audience this seems an imbalance in Lindsay's analysis of America, but for him it meant he had achieved that detachment from current manifestations of problems which would enable him to see the problems in their fundamentals. Of course he was involved, ultra-sensitively, with national and local affairs—were they good or bad omens for his theories? But he commented on them obliquely as part of the total experience which led him to say to America: your progress is unsatisfactory—rethink and replan; you are a new nation—put down roots and grow together; you are drifting spiritually— remember the validity of religious and ethical concepts.

Lindsay's remarks on the contemporary scene became fewer after 1920. He generally worked from notes; his minimal backlog was ten years; he died in 1931. He was also devoting his time increasingly to drawing. But his paucity of comment was primarily due to the fact that he was hard put to see any healthy trends in the twenties; and since he felt that an American entity was best served by concentration on acceptable elements (which was its own selective form of indirect criticism) and undermined by unrelieved invective, he kept largely silent. When he did comment directly on current affairs it was either to celebrate—instinctively and calculatingly—figures whom he felt should become a part of American hagiology, or to express himself on issues which had become personal.

JAZZ, JEZEBELS, AND LIQUOR

In his authoritative *Prohibition: The Era of Excess,* Andrew Sinclair pointed out that the crusade against drink enlarged into a crusade against other forms of excess, among them new styles of dancing and jazz. He attributed this antipathy to the release of inhibitions to the extreme drys. Lindsay, who drank the occasional glass of wine, was never an extreme dry, never a Prohibitionist. He worked in and around Springfield for the Anti-Saloon League from 1909 to 1911, a time when the League's aim was not national Prohibition, but the abolition of the saloon. He did, however, fit into the extreme dry convention of opposing any visible lack of restraint as abandoned and libertinist. He lumped together jazz and intoxicating drink as factors which contributed to lax national morals, and he was afraid that they would undermine the pre-marital celibacy that he was retaining with difficulty.

Lindsay seemed never to have overcome a warning from his father against three evils—venereal disease, drink, and tobacco. In 1903 he took home from the Chicago School of Art drawings he had made from the nude. His father was outraged and made him leave home immediately. Lindsay apologized in terms which from another man would have been tongue-in-cheek; coming from him they were painfully sincere and naive.

My dear Papa, I am very very sorry. . . . I am not going to the bad. . . . Viewed theoretically, I do not like the nude much better than you. I am going to neglect it all I possibly can. I am going to study hard on draperies and conceal my ignorance all I can by them.

Dr. Lindsay believed that sex was very much all right, in its place. Lindsay remembered his (Dr. Mohawk's) advice:

> *When you take your bride*
> *Be a bull of power*
> *Be an eagle*
> *Flying over red-eagle,*
> *A whirlwind*
> *Going up a flower.*

But anticipated fulfillment was poor consolation to Lindsay. As he wrote to Harriet Moody in 1914: "I have the spiritual hungers of a Franciscan ninety years old, yet I am suddenly loaded with a flowering outer self, and a blood heat more like twenty than thirty-five." [1] When he finally married in 1925, aged 45, he was publicly ardent to his wife in a way embarrassing to everyone except themselves.

Before marriage anything aphrodisiac was taboo to Lindsay. Jazz he found an inescapable sexual incitement. Scott Fitzgerald, the expert of the Jazz Age, described jazz as "first sex, then dancing, then music," and to Lindsay it was "midnight dirt and a sad morning after." [2] He lived in the Davenport Hotel, Spokane, from July 1924 to May 1925, and from the fringe of the ballroom he was disturbed by what for him were erotic foxtrots and tangos; he was haunted by the earthy note of the saxophone. He would have answered in the affirmative the question the *Ladies Home Journal* asked in 1921: "Does Jazz put the Sin in Syncopation?" and would have agreed with the dry Dr. Henry Van Dyke that jazz was "a sensual teasing of the strings of sensual passion." [3]

In the Davenport Lindsay wrote "The Jazz of this Hotel." The poem began with a frank question—"Why do I curse the jazz of this hotel?"—but evaded the sexual issue, and concentrated on the musical one.

> *I like the slower deeper violin*
> *Of the wind across the fields of Indian corn;*
> *I like the far more ancient violincello*
> *Of whittling loafers telling stories mellow.*

In another poem he wrote there, "A Curse for the Saxophone," his abhorrence for jazz was blown up into an obsession. He depicted the saxophone as an immemorial cause of evil. Devised by Cain, it had provided the theme for the lives of Jezebel, Judas, Henry VIII, and John Wilkes Booth. At Booth's death Lindsay imagined

> *Twenty thousand pigs on their hind legs playing*
> *"The Beale Street Blues" and swaying and saying:—*

"John Wilkes Booth, you are welcome to Hell,"
And they played in on the saxophone, and played it well.
And he picked up a saxophone, grunting and rasping,
The red-hot horn in his hot hands clasping,
And he played a typical radio jazz,
He started an earthquake, he knew what for,
And at last he started the late World War.[4]

This was the kind of imagination that went with fanatical prohibitionist mentality: the psychology of the have-nots wanting to impose their restrictions on others. It was a frightening phenomenon; as Sinclair said, "with a terrible faith in equality, the prohibitionists often wanted to suppress in society the sins they found in themselves."[5] Sinclair emphasized that the antisocial motivations of this outlook were unconscious, that people genuinely believed in their mission to free not only America but the world from debilitating evils. This point can be, and was reached in prohibition; but universalizing a temptation in order to make it a communal bogey is surely a second stage in a mental process which originates in disconcertingly honest self-analysis. It was certainly so in Lindsay's case; preceeding the publication of his ward-off-jazz, ward-off-sex poems, he was privately writing verses expressing his longing for a "little sweetey,"[6] physically fascinating, mentally vacuous.

Marriage in 1925 brought a partial satisfaction of his longings, though its total success is hard to judge. His young wife, Elizabeth Conner, who taught English and Latin, was a remarkable woman, a strong personality, intellectually talented, and not the least remarkable because she nevertheless remains a self-contained, hard-to-evaluate figure. She was the daughter of an independent minded Presbyterian preacher, the Reverend Franklin T. Conner, who had drawn his own map of biblical prophecy, not unlike the "Map of the Universe"; and, with Lindsay's urge to communicate, he had it painted on the walls of his church. Elizabeth Conner, sensitive, contemplative, devout, and not unecumenical—she became a Catholic after Lindsay's death—could also match Lindsay in his love of walking (they had a tramping honeymoon in Glacier National

Park), and she too published the occasional poem and short story. They seemed ideally suited; though with Lindsay's health and career past the point of recall, marriage was no panacea.

Perhaps, too, Elizabeth sank her own personality in Lindsay's too deeply, and in trying to gain him audiences and encourage him to believe in himself in the adverse climate of the twenties when his own health was breaking down, she may have underestimated the strain on his nerves and stamina of constant itinerant recitations to audiences demanding the same few poems, and unwilling to listen to his theory of American civilization. She enrolled Lindsay with a brisk commercial agent, William Feakins, to replace his previous manager, the intellectually sympathetic A. J. Armstrong, Professor of English at Baylor University, Waco, Texas; she told Lindsay "I'm going to get behind you and push till you just can't bear it." [7] But though she may have organized him beyond his endurance (one of his hallucinations was that she sent him on tours so often because she had a lover), and though by his code matrimony was a sanctified state which precluded complaint, she remained on her pedestal of physical importance as probably the only woman he had slept with, and of mental importance as a Londonesque soul-mate, who, in the words of one of her closest friends, was characterized by

a sort of exaltation about things and toward ideas which moved and inspired her. It had something to do with faith; it very much had to do with the frame of reference within which she lived and moved. I think both Vachel and Elizabeth Lindsay were capable of this exaltation, and for many of the same reasons.[8]

Marriage brought Lindsay a partial escape from prohibition mentality. In 1925 he was able to state that "it is a mistake to make me out a steady, orthodox established official Anti-Saloon League worker." [9] He had come to terms with himself—but he was also dissociating himself from a movement whose original campaign for local option had been transformed into a crusade for an international millennium of peace and purity. Lindsay could not subscribe to such utopianism, nor to the black and white conflict of exclusives, wet versus dry. He wished to make it plain that he was not in accord with the League's blanket hostility to the city, nor with one of its logical, wasp developments, the Ku Klux Klan, which was riding high in the mid-twenties. His disclaimer was especially necessary since, during the years he had lectured and distributed leaflets for the League, he had incorporated a fair amount of League propaganda in his writings. Thinking in terms of purity versus impurity, virtue versus vice, he had compared the Anti-Saloon League with "King Arthur's men [who] have come again," with "Cromwell's men," and "Lincoln's men": the personification of principle and uprightness. His idealization of women and children had left him defenceless against the ubiquitous parades of Anti-Saloon League girls, dressed in white, with their sentimental vocal appeals to men's "best instincts"; he determined to work to the end that "no way of thorns/Shall snare the children's feet." [10] Perhaps the fact that he continued to include such poems as "The Trap," "Galahad, Knight Who Perished," and "King Arthur's Men Have Come Again" in *Collected Poems* indicated that as well as intensifying his own best interests, marriage had come too late to dispel all his frustrations or their lively memory.

He was bound to retain an interest in the Anti-Saloon League, moreover, since it provided him with an argument in favor of the motion picture industry, whose productions he regarded as America's first potential mass art. Prohibitionists envisaged the movie as a vehicle for dry propaganda, and 1908 saw the release of such admonitory films as "The Saloon Dance" and "The Saloon Keeper's Nightmare." Lindsay, however, was thinking in terms of the motion picture house as a replacement for the social functions of the saloon: as a center of warmth, comradeship, and communal entertainment. The proprietor could play host; nonintoxicants could be served; the audience could comment during a silent film, or after a talkie. Americans en masse could respond to art; they might even be intellectually or creatively stimulated. For in the first two decades of the twentieth century, the cinema, whose sheer novelty attracted large audiences, did seem to rival the saloon. An Anti-Saloon League report summed up the potentially wholesome influence of motion pictures: "If you want to see the motion-picture business flayed alive, and its skin hung up to dry, talk to a saloon-keeper or a pool room attendant." But the enactment of Prohibition not only created a vogue for drink among those who could afford it, it brought into being risque entertainments which catered to a popular determination to be bold and bad in spite of and because of the legal dourness of the twenties. A typically enjoyable film for Middletown audiences in 1925 was "Flaming Youth." A press advertisement described its contents (and its audience): "neckers, petters . . . pleasure-mad daughters, sensation craving mothers."[11] Nothing could have been more execrable to a man like Lindsay. The Anti-Saloon League was forced to campaign for the censorship of a medium which glamorized "licentiousness": Lindsay was forced to admit disappointment that the motion picture had proved not to be the immediate answer to mass culture-hunger, but an extension of saloon mentality.

The opening of "A Curse for the Saxophone" showed the close association Lindsay made between jazz, eroticism and promiscuity.

When Jezebel put on her tiaras and looked grand,
Her three-piece pajamas and her diamond bosom-band,
And stopped the honest prophets as they marched upon their way,
. . . .
She licked her wicked chops, she pulled out all her stops,
And she ordered the saxophones to play.

He shied away from a more realistic description of jezebels. Probably he knew none and tried not to think of them in flesh tones. They were the vaguely delineated madams of the red light district of Springfield 2018—Velaska, a woman of sin, for example—earth mothers run amok. He diverted his fears and aversions into an exaggerated attack on the jezebel by default, the irresponsible, slapdash woman who had not taught her daughter "the worth of the bridal bed," who "failed to tell/The maze of heaven and hell." He considered such women to be responsible for prostitutes

As good as chained to the bed,
Hid like the mad, or the dead:—

The glory of endless years
Drowned in their harlot-tears:
The children they hoped to bear,
Grandchildren strong and fair,
The life for ages to be,
Cut off like a blasted tree,
Murdered in filth in a day.

The virulence with which he indicted the clients and promoters of prostitution as "Lust-kings with a careful plan/Clean-cut, American," was part of an intensive attack on all expressions of lax morality, an attack he hoped would highlight the cumulative corruption which followed wide-scale self-indulgence.

What shall be said of a state
Where traps for the white brides wait?
Of sellers of drink who play
The game for the extra pay?
Of statesmen in league with all
Who hope for the girl-child's fall?
Of banks where hell's money is paid? [12]

His intensity also communicated his genuine compassion for the unwilling loss of innocence, and his genuine wrath at the blind eyes turned. But the ranting rhetoric of his verses suggests that the attempt to get his desires out of his system had gotten the upper hand, and it seems to have been as much his psycho-sexual pattern as his concern for America and her morality which led him to write directly on the contemporary issues of jazz, jezebels, and liquor. In doing so, he mirrored the complexities of Prohibition psychology so exactly as to present Sinclair with a case in point.

THE WAR, THE LEAGUE OF NATIONS, AND WOODROW WILSON

Lindsay reluctantly seceded from pacificism to register for the draft in September 1918, two months before the Armistice was signed, sixteen months after the United States entered the war. He had voted for Wilson on his 1916 "keep us out of war" platform; and while he believed Wilson declared war against Germany not as a press-ganged pacifist, but as a neopacifist finally convinced of the tragic necessity of violence, he was unsure about supporting America's declaration of war. On the day of the declaration he wrote:

My heart is very sad tonight about the war—I have not the heart to challenge Wilson. I voted for him, and cannot regret it—yet Jane Addams' dauntless fight for peace goes home to my soul. I feel with her—and with him—and am all torn inside.[13]

Like his friend Jane Addams, chairman of the American women's peace party, and organizer of the Women's International League for Peace and Freedom, Lindsay was sure that "no war ushers in the perfect state";[14] but while he admiringly celebrated her pacificism in "Speak Now for Peace," he himself felt able to accept the concept of a just war. Nor was he unwilling to believe that bloodshed, however terrible at the time, could act as a partial purge.

His thoughts about war, and about the First World War, can be traced in a series of poems. In "The Tale of the Tiger Tree" he outlined in extensive metaphor an ineradicable struggle between war and peace.

The Fantasy shows how tiger-hearts are the cause of war in all ages. It shows how the mammoth forces may be either friends or enemies of the struggle for peace. It shows how the dream of peace is unconquerable and eternal.

Even near Springfield, which Lincoln's memory should have made a symbol of peaceful coexistence,

> . . . the Tiger leaf is falling around
> As it fell when the world began:
> Like a monstrous tiger-skin, stretched on the ground,
> Or the cloak of a medicine man.
> A deep crumpled gossamer web,
> Fringed with the fangs of a snake.
> The wind swirls it down from leperous boughs,
> It shimmers on clay-hill and lake,
> With the gleam of great bubbles of blood,
> Or coiled like a rainbow shell . . .

The Tiger Tree was a twentieth century edition of the biblical tree of the knowledge of good and evil: beautiful in itself, but whose fruit, when tasted, originated murderous and acquisitive instincts. "Lord of the race since the world began," Lindsay's Tiger Tree symbolized perpetual conflict; while one group resolved to "hew down every Tiger Tree," "a million new tigers swept south." [15]

From this theologically conventional but forcefully expressed view of war as an extension of the Cain-Abel conflict, Lindsay moved on to apportion war-guilt for the 1914–18 hostilities. His attitude was a national one. Before and after their brief intervention Americans regarded the war's archducal inception and autocratic conclusion (which swept minority rights by the board) as the logically chaotic outcome of the immoral rule of kings, of decayed European feudalism, and of the lack among the combatants of American-style democracy. In "A Curse for Kings" Lindsay struck an archetypal American war attitude in attacking

> . . . *each king who leads his state,*
> *No matter what his plea, to this foul game,*
> *And may it [Lindsay's curse] end his wicked dynasty*

and the old world diplomacy of balances of power and spheres of influence.

> . . . *Fiddling, twiddling diplomats,*
> *Haggling here, plotting and hatching there,*
> *Who made the kind world but their game of cards,*
> *Till millions died at turning of a hair.*

Wilsonian diplomacy, much of it traditionally devious, and anti-German discrimination in America were to cut away Lindsay's righteous indignation; and he was more accurate in the sobering thought that there were (and are) sections of the community, regular army material, who enjoyed war as a manly occupation, a moral sport, and a hierarchical privilege. These representatives of a powerful, medieval, militaristic mystique were (and are) European rather than American types;

. . . sleek lords with their plumes and spurs,
May Heaven give their land to peasant spades,
Give them the brand of Cain, for their prides' sake,
And felon's stripes for medals and for braids.[16]

Lindsay was conscious that the 1914–18 war had not only the historical and psychological continuum of all wars, but novel features: the immense financial benefits accruing to armaments and general supplies manufacturers, for example, though these had been anticipated in the Civil War. (Writing in 1914 he referred to Krupp's profiteering, not the economic boost that war was just beginning to give to the American economy.) He saw the clinching importance of mechanical and scientific aids, and that the possession of new weapons of destruction could transform dormant belligerence into confidently undertaken wars. Consequently he excoriated

. . . the men who make and sell iron ships,
Who walk the floor in thought, that they may find
Each powder prompt, each steel with fearful edge,
Each deadliest device against mankind.

He was particularly bitter that "Science towers above . . . /Science we looked to for the light of life." [17]

What excruciated Lindsay about war between nominally Christian powers was the subsequent ridicule of Christianity. He called the perversion of Christian precepts "The Unpardonable Sin," "the sin against the Holy Ghost." A Catholic conception, it is the gravest of sins committed by those both within and without the Catholic faith who are arrogantly self-reliant, and who believe in their independent rightness. To sin in ignorance is remediable, but the knowing sins of presumption and self-sufficiency are grave. The warmonger's pretensions to truth and self righteousness, "to speak of bloody power as right divine,"

To go forth killing in White Mercy's name,
Making the trenches stink with spattered brains,
Tearing the nerves and arteries apart,
Sowing with flesh the unreaped golden plains.

In any Church's name, to sack fair towns,
And turn each home into a screaming sty,
To make the little children fugitive
And have their mothers for a quick death cry,—

This is the sin against the Holy Ghost.[18]

In this poem, "The Unpardonable Sin," and in "Who Knows" Lindsay represented the American approximation of an English tradition of wartime poetry in which religiosity and humanity survived, and compassion produced and overbore virulence. Wilfred Owen, for example, might seem an unlikely poet to compare with Lindsay, who was of an older generation, never a combatant, and unable to parallel the realism of experience which Owen expressed. But their poetic content was analogous: it expressed agonized Christianity. Lindsay, like Owen, was something of a "conscientious objector with a very seared conscience," a believer in the intrinsic evil of war, yet doubting his right to express a view about it if he did not commit himself to one side. Owen's "At a Calvary near the Ancre" and Lindsay's "The Unpardonable Sin" were comparable expressions of the shame that war had brought on Christianity. "In this war He too lost a limb," Owen wrote. Both men attacked an Old Testament God. In the spirit of Lindsay's "The Scissors Grinder" Owen described a "Soldier's Dream" in which Christ put all weapons of war out of commission, but when he woke, he found God had "seen to our repairs." Yet ultimately both men accepted that the war was man-made, not God-given. In "Where Is the Real Non-Resistant?" Lindsay unfolded his belief that the unsurmountable obstacle to peace and Christianity was self-will. Owen reached the same conclusion: "Already I have comprehended a light which will never filter into the dogma of any national church: namely that one of Christ's essential commands, was Passivity at any price!"[19] Their war poetry was distinctive for its combination of simple, emotional reaction, and adult, objective analysis.

Carl Sandburg and Robinson Jeffers typified the American school of war poetry to which Lindsay did not belong. Sandburg's war poems were effectively Whitmanesque (cf. "Murmurings in a Field Hospital" and "Salvages"), but he had not Whitman's consolation that it was an American war; he found little comfort in nature, no prospect in the future, and could only miserably, savagely write of death and battlefields and envy the dead. Jeffers pushed his logic further; "The Double Axe" and "I Shall Laugh Purely" were powerful statements of nihilism. His post-war prediction was: "all will be worse confounded soon." [20] Lindsay's less personally conceived themes did add another dimension to American war literature, which was not present elsewhere in American poetry. Joyce Kilmer had his emotion but not his analytical depth. Nor was Lindsay's stance to be found in the subjective expressions of general disillusionment with twentieth century society, which the war precipitated, but did not originate, in the novels of e e cummings, Ernest Hemingway, and John Dos Passos.

If the 1914–18 war was the nadir of fruitful international cooperation, it at least gave rise to the zenith, the League of Nations. Lindsay was realistic about the limitations of such a League, and in *The Golden Book of Springfield* had indicated his expectation that the indifference of nations to the League concept and their self-interest made further world wars almost inevitable. His canny view of human nature and human intentions equipped him somewhat better than his contemporaries to sustain the secondary treatment that Clemenceau and Lloyd George, reparation and retribution bent, gave to the fourteen points of the nation that had won the war. Nevertheless, the League was bound to rivet the attention of a dedicated internationalist, an opponent of hostile national borders, and an advocate of world government, just as Woodrow Wilson, the prime architect and proselytizer of the League, was inevitably a hero of Lindsay's. Wilson's decline in status from an international moral figurehead to a nationally humiliated president and a broken-down man and politician seemed good material for Lindsay's often sentimental pen. But philosophically, and without fuss, Lindsay saw the end of Wilson's career as part of the trying pattern of greatness. No more than Lincoln, no more than Socrates, should Wilson have expected to see his ends attained in his lifetime;

it was enough that he had been able to state them. It was his cup of hemlock to see a League of Nations in existence without American membership.[21]

In the process of thinking that Wilson should be stoical, Lindsay exaggerated his actual stoicism. Defeat did not bring out Wilson's good qualities; he was palpably resentful when the Senate refused unconditional ratification of the Treaty of Versailles which contained the League Covenant, for a League without America and without himself was a travesty of what he had envisaged. At the other extreme Robinson Jeffers[22] saw in Wilson's collapse proof that his high-flown tenets hid shallow ambitions. But Wilson was not as politically petulant as he appeared. Naivete and excess of principle led him to overlook real difficulties in the way of American membership in the League. The tradition of American isolation, for example, remained strong; Republican leaders aroused a near-the-surface national eagerness to be free from Europe's troubles. And by gambling the League and his reelection on one throw, Wilson may have helped the League. American lip-service would have increased the League's flimsiness and diminished its expectations, and in 1920, would the United States have been an active and useful League member under any president but Wilson?

Whatever considerations Wilson weighed to be sure he was right, and that right would prevail with the electorate, was myopic. As the fourteen points had already been modified at Versailles it was realistic to be prepared for a further paring down. But for Lindsay, Wilson's apolitical tenacity confirmed his image as a man of principle. In Wilson he admired a man more idealistic than himself, the personification of the inflexible ideals behind the variable mechanics of the League. He saw merit in being

> . . . *like stern Woodrow Wilson*
> *Drinking his cup as such proud men have done*
>
> . . . .
>
> *Staking his last strength and his final fight*
> *That cost him all, to set the old world right.*[23]

In a curious poem, "The Bankrupt Peace Maker," Lindsay seemed to fuse himself and Wilson. The poem discussed the viability of pacifism and idealism, and acknowledged that neither man had been sufficiently strong to withstand the pressures of patriotism, militarism, and the hope of arriving at peace through war. Lindsay imagined himself crucified on his bookcase (representing his paper contribution of peace?) "to end war for good" (to make the world safe for democracy?) His crucifier, the devil, questioned his right as a noncombatant to advocate one course or another: "You are voting for talk with hands lily white" (you must enter the war to determine the peace?) In the poem Lindsay failed in his sacrifice for peace. He held out for three years only (1914–17?); the effective peacemaker, he discovered, would hang for three hundred (the length of time he set for nations to subscribe sincerely to international government?)

Lindsay assessed himself harshly in the poem. It was his "own cheap bankrupt soul" (characteristically disguised as a "lady of sin")[24] who had tempted him off the abstraction of his bookcase-cross. He had disappointed himself by arriving at the conclusion that world order was "worth all our blood."[25] The future was paramount to him, and the war brought forward into his lifetime an irresistible prospect of unity which he had dated eons ahead. But at the back of his mind was the fear that he had been seduced from a moral, Christian vision of the future into supporting a war, which, although it had made possible an international League, was unjustified in terms of human suffering. The League idea had impelled a cautious Lindsay into advocating the use of what he had regarded as "improper" means for "desirable" ends; it shook Wilson out of political loftiness into the recognition and practice of real-politik. Wilson retreating from optimism surely arrived at the same qualified conclusion as Lindsay advancing from pessimism: "The League of Nations course is yet to run."[26]

A LITANY OF CONTEMPORARY HEROES

Names, slogans, and catch-phrases are components of the American tradition of declamation that stretches from stump to senate, and the evocative power of verbal symbols has been, in the words of Denis Brogan, "one of the chief means of uniting the United States and keeping it united." [27] The names of John Peter Altgeld (1847–1902), Williams Jennings Bryan (1860–1925), and Theodore Roosevelt (1858–1919) were three of Lindsay's incantations. As men and politicians they were his personal heroes. They seemed to conceive of problems and issues in his terms; their words had an excontextual validity for him; and he felt a rapport with them which overcame the fact that their ideas, with the exception of Altgeld's, were frequently at variance with his own. They were modern, manifest, and potentially inspiring carriers of the American entity: Altgeld in its humanitarian sense, Bryan in its egalitarian sense, and Roosevelt in its political sense.

The dark places in government and civil affairs are now festering with wrong; let the sunlight of eternal truth and justice shine on them and they will disappear. . . . That man will render mankind the great service who, recognizing this fact, will help the race onward to this place of eternal sunlight.[28]

These words of Altgeld's illustrate the wavelength of communication that Lindsay felt existed between himself and his heroes. The words could be his: exhortatory, sermonizing, seeking after morality and honest relationships. To Lindsay, Altgeld was the essence of compassion that America failed to cultivate, "The Eagle That Is Forgotten." His rise from farm laborer in Pennsylvania to Illinois' first foreign-born governor (he came from Germany) was an American process, and a form of proof that some assimilating entity existed. As a success story, Altgeld's career was not unique. What differentiated him for a few admiring, important contemporaries (like his secretary Brand Whitlock, and Henry Demarest Lloyd, for example) and for a large number of faceless Americans, was that he succeeded Lincoln as the great humanitarian. For Lindsay, whose home overlooked the Governor's residence, and who often saw Altgeld, he had a special value as a fitting resident and a further symbol for Springfield. His significance for the American entity was that he exhibited unflinching concern for, in his own words, "those that are fighting an unequal fight in the struggle for existence";[29] he was modern America's conscience; he was a self-conscious American.

From 1886 to 1892 Altgeld was a member of the Superior Court of Cook County, Illinois, and played an active part in Chicago's politics. He governed Illinois from 1892 to 1896, and then returned to Chicago's affairs. The period of his political activity coincided with a transitional stage in American history (c. 1885–1900) when a complex of problems involving labor, trusts, currency, and immigration were springing out of rural depopulation and urban aggrandizement. His reactions to issues in this time of flux rarely coincided with those of less altruistic individuals and national authorities, and as governor he was involved in a number of controversial actions.

In 1892 he pardoned the foreign-born "anarchists" who had been convicted of responsibility for the Haymarket Riot of 1886. His thorough, ruthless inquiry proved that there were no grounds at law for conviction, and that bribery, corruption, and racial and political prejudice had been rife among judge, jury, and police. The graft-ridden establishment quivered and began a campaign to stigmatize Altgeld as—no matter if the terms were incompatible—socialist, radical, anarchist, and disruptive alien. The campaign stopped only at his death. Another example of that independence of his age which endeared him to Lindsay was Altgeld's condemnation of Grover Cleveland's dispatch of federal troops to Chicago to put down the peaceful Pullman strike in 1893. In part it was a states rights issue, but Altgeld was trying to scotch the unscrupulous tactics of government and big business who found it in their common interests of finance and status to keep wages and workers down and to smear strikers and socialists and humanitarians as dangers to the lives and liberties of Americans.

The third national episode in which Altgeld figured was Bryan's nomination as presidential candidate at the Democratic convention in Chicago in 1896. Altgeld was opposed to Bryan's candidacy; he knew that behind a silver tongue lay neither knowledge nor experience, nor potential statecraft. But the organs of wealth and power, and the men who stood to lose by a more egalitarian democracy, managed to believe otherwise. No charge was too steep, no rumor too malicious for them to believe it of Altgeld. The Bryan landslide was obviously, or so the *New York Herald Tribune* thought,

conceived in iniquity and . . . brought forth in sin. . . . It has been defeated and destroyed because right is right and God is God. . . . He [Bryan] was only a puppet in the blood-imbued hands of Altgeld, the anarchist.[30]

Altgeld's infamous reputation in high places was matched by the respect and affection of the underprivileged for him. With the slow turn of the progressive tide it became fashionable after Altgeld's death in 1902 to speak well of him:

They made a brave show of their mourning, their hatred unvoiced.
They had snarled at you, barked at you, foamed at you day after day.
Now you were ended. They praised you. . . .

But he belonged to the people, to

The others that mourned you in silence and terror and truth,
The widow bereft of her crust, and the boy without youth,
The mocked and the scorned and the wounded, the lame and the poor.[31]

Altgeld's militant humanitarianism at all levels was visible in his books *The Cost of Something for Nothing* and *Live Questions: including Our Penal Machinery and its Victims.* The titles indicated his bias; he was concerned for the conditions of every individual life. He discussed passionately issues ranging from the compulsory arbitration of strikes, pensions for soldiers, the dilemma of the immigrant, and "slave girls of Chicago," to anonymous journalism, the eight hour movement, and judicial and penal reform. His solutions, based on a belief in the dignity of man and the determination to see that the American combination of "the best fiber of all nations" [32] resulted in a unique material and cultural civilization, invariably benefited the underdog. Muckraking, Roosevelt's tempering of the trusts, and civic reform movements were all corollaries of Altgeld's stand. Lindsay recognized that Altgeld was not consciously remembered as a progenitor of sociology, that even those who benefited directly from his child labor, sweatshop, and factory legislation (which Henry Demarest Lloyd described in 1893 as the best statutes of their kind in America), even they

"That should have remembered forever, . . . remember no more." [33]

But, as Waldo Browne, his biographer, concluded,

In some degree his voice still speaks in every programme of political or social reform; the work of every earnest man or woman who would alleviate the ills under which humanity suffers has been made easier because of his efforts.[34]

Lindsay lifted this assessment from the mundane: Altgeld had fathered a new race.

> *A hundred white eagles have risen the sons of your sons,*
> *The zeal in their wings is a zeal that your dreaming began*
> *The valor that wore out your soul in the service of man.*[35]

Altgeld has grown in stature for intellectuals and historians and has shrunk from the prominence he had in American folklore when he released the anarchists, opposed Cleveland, and at his funeral, which was attended by everyone who was no one in Chicago. Lindsay perceived no irony in this. Altgeld was the most fulfilled of his heroes. He could

> *Sleep softly, . . . eagle forgotten, . . . under the stone,*
> *Time has its way with you there and the clay has its own.*
> *Sleep on, O brave-hearted, O wise man, that kindled the flame—*
> *To live in mankind is far more than to live in a name,*
> *To live in mankind, far, far more . . . than to live in a name.*[36]

To see in his lifetime a reincarnation of Lincoln's spirit was immensely satisfying for Lindsay, and grist to his entity. In "The Eagle That Is Forgotten" propaganda and truth were synonymous. They fused into a tribute which captured the struggle of Altgeld's life, the acrimony he met, and his posthumous triumph. The poem is one of those rare recreative, evaluative literary achievements which makes the historian factually acceptable, but emotionally superfluous.

The humblest citizen in all the land, when clad in the armor of the righteous cause, is stronger than all the hosts of error. I come to speak to you in defence of a cause as holy as the cause of liberty—the cause of humanity.[37]

Bryan's speeches—often, as in this instance, sententious and sentimental—had the same moral, Christian, and socialist fervor as the words of Altgeld and Lindsay. Like Altgeld he championed a part of the community which, if not depressed, had been put on the defensive: agrarian America. He opposed not the principle of the urban-industrial take-over but the lack of provision made for the fair treatment of the original agrarian-rural combine. The key plank in his platform as Democratic candidate for the Presidency in 1896 and 1900 was the unlimited coinage of silver as a panacea for the relatively small share of national prosperity that was going the way of the farmers and the industrial working classes.

The plank was meaningful to the underprivileged, who, in the grass roots tradition of a permanent underlying conspiracy in American history, attributed their wrongs to the machinations of Eastern financiers and monopolists, who had achieved an immoral prosperity under the gold standard. Bryan coupled the plank with a sincere but well calculated appeal to "the people," to "mankind," to "the producing masses of the nation" and to "toilers everywhere." [38] His patent belief in the worth and rights of "the common people" coincided with a need for reassurance among discontented, hard-done-by elements in the community. Small farmers, small businessmen, and the laboring classes, mainly in the West, were going through

> . . . *helpless days*
> *By the dour East oppressed.*
> *Mean paternalism*
> *Making their mistakes for them,*
> *Crucifying half the West.*[39]

Bryan promised to redress the unfair balance of the country. He also succeeded—and this made a strong appeal to Lindsay—in conjuring into existence an American state of mind, a nebulous but real community of feeling among formerly dissociated people who had begun to doubt if they were full members of the American Democracy, so second-rate was the treatment meted out to them. In Bryan they saw a potential President who believed in them, loved them, and told them America was theirs as much as anyone's. From him they learned that they were Herrenvolk and Fuhrer, that they had a Reich which was a democracy, that their voices were to be of equal weight in the silver days to come.

> *He brought in tides of wonder, of unprecedented splendor,*
> *Wild roses from the plains, that made hearts tender,*
> *All the funny circus silks*
> *Of politics unfurled,*
> *Bartlett pears of romance that were honey at the cores,*
> *And torchlights down the street, to the end of the world.*[40]

No definitive historical decision has been handed down on Bryan's political acumen and intellectual ability. His Fundamentalist prosecution of John Scopes, who made himself a test case for the right to teach the theory of evolution in Tennessee's schools, condemned him for most serious thinkers; after all, his interpretation of Genesis was so literal that he calculated the hour, day, and year of creation. But this image of Bryan as conservative to the point of stupidity was contradicted by the Progressive reform policies he advocated in his journal *The Commoner*. Perhaps Bryan was a late developer; certainly, in 1896, the apparent lack of an informed and practical structure behind his rhetoric made his power to convince coterminous with his presence. His speeches were even more unspecific and emotional than was usual in American presidential campaigns. Nevertheless, the Cross of Gold Speech, and Bryan's presence, had a comforting and inspiring impact on millions of Americans (Bryan was the first great whistle-stop tour campaigner). Lindsay saw and heard him in Springfield in 1896, and reproduced his impact.

> *And Bryan took the platform.*
> *And he was introduced.*
> *And he lifted his hand*
> *And cast a new spell.*

Progressive silence fell
In Springfield,
In Illinois,
Around the world.

At the climax of his pre-Progressive speech

. . . these glacial boulders across the prairie rolled:
"The people have a right to make their own mistakes. . . .
You shall not crucify mankind
Upon a cross of gold." [41]

For some of his supporters Bryan's campaign may have meant Western wheat and silver against Eastern cities and gold, self-sufficiency and independence against mass organization and the uniformity it imposed, the old order against the new. For Bryan the campaign may have involved the differently slanted question of securing national parity as a team basis for a prosperous, modern America, of peddling free silver not as a restorative, but as a tonic, a stimulant, a growth medicine which America could take often and indefinitely. But a common feeling that a national turning point had been reached injected tension into the situation. What began as a regular presidential campaign was magnified into the decisive agrarian-industrial battle.

Bryan had early psychological successes.

July, August, suspense.
Wall Street lost to sense.
August, September, October,
More suspense,
And the whole East down like a wind-smashed fence.

Then came "Hanna to the rescue," Mark Hanna, in 1896 campaign manager of the Republican party and its presidential candidate William McKinley, and an unabashed exponent of the mutually profitable liaison between politics and business.

Promising manna,
Rallying the trusts against the bawling flannelmouth;
Invading misers' cellars,
Tin-cans, socks,

Melting down the rocks,
Pouring out the long green to a million workers,
Spondulix by the mountain-load, to stop each new tornado.
And beat the cheapskate, blatherskite,
Populistic, anarchistic,
Deacon—desperado.[42]

It was no accident that Lindsay's description of Hanna's tactics and sources of strength was the most powerful part of "Bryan, Bryan, Bryan, Bryan." The down to earth, slangy vocabulary and organized meter reflected the dominating qualities which brought Hanna victory: organization, acumen, ruthlessness, incisiveness, a conception of ends, and a command of means. He and McKinley wanted power, so they

   . . . *soothed down the city man and soothed down the farmer,*
   The German, the Irish, the Southerner, the Northerner,
   . . . *climbed every greasy pole, and slipped through every crack;*

Hanna swept up "The gold vote, the silver vote, the brass vote, the lead vote/Every vote? . . ."[43]

   Lindsay memorably contrasted Hanna's decisive political expertise with Bryan's apolitical reliance on oratory and the people, his inadequate use of the party machine, and amorphous policy. Implicitly he represented policies which were attractive alternatives to McKinley's government by few for few: planned growth for the nation's economy and industry, the maintenance of morality in politics, and a more equal distribution of the benefits of a flourishing society. Explicitly he communicated only a belief in the old American dream of a natural, unspoiled continent, an old-fashioned image which made him an emotional reality but a practical impossibility, even to malcontents. Lindsay saw the paradox of Bryan's defeat, that "Homer Bryan," the "Boy Orator from the Platte," in spite of his themes of wheat and silver, in spite of seeming to be "prairie avenger, mountain lion," had not infused political actuality into the West. He had merely presented the East with the classic Western conundrum, with "the aspen groves of Colorado valleys," "blue bonnets of old Texas," "alfalfa and the Mariposa lily," "the Pacific and the long Mississippi." [44]

The contributory cause of Bryan's defeat was also the source of his importance to Lindsay. What mattered to him was that Bryan personified the collection of intangibles which was the West. In its myths, its national parks, its oasis-towns, and its new centers of culture, the region was of illimitable importance to the American entity. The failings which had helped Bryan lose the election were the qualities the American entity needed: fervor, dedication, innocence, conscious symbolism, a belief in national equilibrium by regional balance, and an ability to arouse emotional loyalties. Bryan might be a racial purist and a Fundamentalist, and Lindsay neither; Bryan might believe in the reconciliation of Christianity and capitalism, and in the goodness of the American people, and Lindsay subscribe to neither belief; Bryan's mesmeric projection of one America, coupled with his image as the great commoner, commended him to Lindsay, subjectively and objectively.

"What would you say to the young men of our city, if you could speak to them with command this day" asked Mr. Ralph. "I would order them to work" said Mr. Roosevelt, stopping short and striking his hands together with quick emphasis. "I would teach the young men . . . that he who has means owes his to the State. It is ignoble to go on heaping money on money. I would preach the doctrine of work to all and to the men of wealth the doctrine of unremunerative work." [45]

For Lindsay to approve wholly of Roosevelt was impossible. He reviled Indian character, he positively enjoyed war, he was less than reverent toward Washington and Jefferson—views and attitudes which were all detrimental to Lindsay's entity. It was his apparent lack of bias on the political scene of his day, and a seemingly justified claim to be an exponent of the principled practice of government that made him one of Lindsay's contemporary heroes, though his impartiality, conscience, and political principle beyond that of pragmatism are arguable. Was he a great trustbuster? Taft prosecuted more trusts. Was he the apotheosis of muckraking? At first he indicted the movement, and only joined it when it became a bandwagon. But he successfully transmitted his image of himself to the American people, that of an instinctively right man, who, through the application of moral, clean, forthright standards would inevitably choose the best course of action, whose mistakes were honest, whose outbursts well meant, whose principles immovable. Even the *Wall Street Journal* was convinced that "He is a friend of capital. He is a friend of labor. But he is no slave of either." [46] More than any preceding president, he seemed to the public to check the checks and balance the balances: great politics.

With seemingly unfortunate repercussions for the validity of his entity, and almost accidentally, one feels, Lindsay fathomed T.R.'s real nature. He perceived that the man was concerned with his own, not the nation's salvation. Reform was a personal sop. Some of his pet projects—conservation, for example—had incidental humanitarian overtones, but he lacked social conscience, and worked for his own integrity;

> *Megalomaniac, envious, glorious,*
> *Envying only the splendor of worth.*[47]

In the same poem which contained this adverse analysis, "Roosevelt," 1926, Lindsay managed to avoid the repercussions of his insight without losing conscience. For once, in an indirect way, he was perhaps thankful that the twenties were as they were: for in apposition to the criminal negligences and once removed misdeeds of the presidents of the twenties—the existence within Harding's administration of a syndicate for graft and loot, Coolidge's encouragement of the nation's self-indulgent monetary rampage—Roosevelt's jingoistic self-confidence and autocratic government appeared minor vices; "white as the moon and honest as youth" was how Lindsay saw him when compared with men whose

> *. . . sworn word is but barnyard mud.*
> *And their highest pride is to hide in a hole.*
> *They talk of "dollars" and "dollars" and "dollars"*
> *And "dollars" and "dollars" and hate his [T.R.'s] clean soul.*

Lindsay had no praise for Roosevelt's conduct out of office, for his denigration of his successor, Taft, or for his bid for a personal comeback at the Bull Moose convention of 1912, under the pretense of a commitment to Progressivism. But as president, however unjustified he was in his assumption of utter rightness and righteousness, the fact that he had a bedrock of active principle—"truth, God and youth"—was a virtue.

> *His sins were better than their sweetest goodness.*
> *His blows were cleaner than their plainest kindness.*
> *He saw more than they all, in his hours of black blindness.*[48]

Roosevelt was the only candidate for presidential stereotype that Lindsay could choose from his lifetime. Wilson was more ideologically attuned to him but remained too controversial a figure. Had he been a possible choice it is likely that Lindsay would still have plumped for Roosevelt, who was a greater asset to an entity which required an emotional impetus and a permanent emotional fund. He had a cosy "Teddy" image, his name evoked a popular response, he was Everyman's Jefferson: boxer, soldier, historian, family man. His feeling for outdoors, for the strenuous, simple life, for children and for the romance of the West propelled him into Lindsay's Litany as "'Great-heart!' Roosevelt! Father of men!"; "the glittering cinnamon bear" who "fed the children honey and bread," and taught them the Ten Commandments and the sagas of Carson and Boone. Selectively, Roosevelt embodied the paternalism implicit in the warm concept of the American entity. What Lindsay called the "Roosevelt Code"[49] embraced this paternalism, morally founded statements and actions, and a sense of historical pride.

Lindsay succeeded in highlighting people, events, and places he felt to be significant for the American experience, and the vision that lay behind the regional, historical, and hagiological aspects of his entity filtered through. But he underestimated the extent to which, by its very nature, an entity is ever likely to exist or function. He looked for a degree of cohesive nationality that even pocket-sized states rarely exhibit. But in that the United States is something of a far-flung empire, and its ritual and heritage important in holding the empire together, he was justified in emphasizing the initially artificial role of self-conscious tradition.

A travesty of his thoughtful outline of the consciousness of the American nation was the frenzied, coercive, intolerant Americanization which sprang up during the 1914–18 war, when schools, churches, and fraternal organizations drilled immigrants in American institutions, ideas, and language. The movement stemmed not from a sudden concern for the unassimilated, or from an articulate appreciation of what America had to offer, but from a realization that countries of national origin had a strong hold over their American ex-nationals, a hold that it was feared might make for disunity, even subversion, if America was to take a stand with one group of European countries against another.

Lindsay made no comment on a movement at such odds with his attempts to foster common denominators while retaining sectional and group diversities. His Americanization was gentle, educative, perceptive; he hoped to achieve Americanization by desire. He had however, his own emotional reaction to the problems of America's racial diversity. In 1909, in an article, "Give a reception to Reps," and a story, "How the Ice-Man Danced," [50] Lindsay wrote two *War Bulletin* tirades against hostility to immigrants among Americans at all stages of entrenchment. He was bitter against old established and recent American citizens who left it to ward heelers and saloon keepers to welcome and console new Americans, and against those who mocked the melting pot ideals of Israel Zangwill. He felt that one cause of this unreceptiveness was the lack of an embracing, absorbing, warm-hearted, responsible-because-self-conscious American entity; and he tried to indicate for Americans at all stages of assimilation that an American matrix other than prosperity did exist, and though inactive, could function. He expounded the physical and spiritual potential and actuality of America; he sketched factors which could contribute to distinguished Americanness. Twenty years after his two tirades about the lack of Americanness, and near the depressed end of his life, the kind of oneness he hoped for was no nearer, and perhaps farther away; but in "Rigmarole, Rigmarole," a poem written in 1929 about the lives of a group of immigrant Russian musicians, he was charcteristically hoping against hope: "They'll all be Americans yet, I'll bet." [51] He was still governed by the over-Americanness which gave rise in the first place to his concern for American identity.

Art Forms and Society

VI

CHAPTER TEN

Lindsay's
Literary Convention

THE PROTAGONIST OF IDEOLOGICAL LITERATURE

LINDSAY'S APPROACH to art forms showed him at his most ambitious and his most controversial, at his best and his worst, as a man who mixed personal artistic humility with didactic views about the shape and the function of the arts in America. The tone of his attitude to the arts stemmed from a discernible cause, for when he wrote about their function his words had the decisiveness of a professional pronouncing on methodology. It was not solely in his capacity as an American citizen that Lindsay took it upon himself to criticize and suggest change; if the national need arose, the artist, as an individual with exceptional talents of perception and expression had a duty to practice remedial art. Lindsay thus had a writer's concern with style and form, but the nature of his concern was idiosyncratic. He believed that a writer's duty was not to himself but to his audience, which should be all class and nationwide. His artistic conscience told him to put matter and mass appeal before self-expression and aesthetics. Form was to follow the function of social utility; and if erudition and abstract imagery seemed to the American public to smack of irrelevance and preciosity, he felt they should be allowed to lapse, until, on the basis of a firmly established culture, they might elevate national sensibilities a stage further.

Lindsay did not envisage an ultimately single-style national literature. People's needs, tastes, and reactions differed; he held it

an especial quality in a good poem, elasticity and suggestiveness
whereby the reader may see his own emotions on a new framework.
. . . People may never read alike at last. . . . So when this man has
not read this poem, as I felt it when I wrote it, but has yet retained
the relation, a proportional value of each word, he has shown the possibilities of the poem rather than a lack of insight into the author's
sympathy for the author's exact sentiment.[1]

But in the initial approaches to a mass audience of "human
beings . . . incapable of understanding until they are moved"
and with little experience of culture contact, his public poetry was
by turns intentionally loud, sentimental, and whimsical. It was
poetry based on the assumptions that the masses "love best neither
the words that explain, nor the fancies that are fine, nor the voice
that is articulate with well chosen speech" and that "the American people hate and abhor poetry." [2] He did not see his deceptive
attitude, which combined catering to public taste with retaining
artistry, as incompatible with his belief in equality of taste: a
belief that although preferences might differ, the faculty of
appreciation belonged to everyone. It might *seem* that he was out
to perform a conjuring trick, but it was not a question of fantasy;
he was acting in good faith that the faculty, though dormant, did
exist.

He tried to convince himself that the subjugation of his literary
instincts to the diffusion of his ideas through popular forms was
"a perfectly natural relation to society, as far as I am concerned."
But although he persevered in pursuing his self-imposed convention, he found it only intermittently satisfying. As early as 1915
he was claiming aggrievedly that "for seventeen years I wrote
poems as quiet as one would wish to see and it is only in the last
three years I have written half a dozen loud ones, which, whatever
their appeal, certainly do not represent the bulk of my work." In
1921 he was writing even more vehemently:

I would give almost anything to escape forever the reciting and chanting Vachel. Except when immediately under the intense excitement
that comes with facing an extraordinarily concentrated group of lis-

teners, I dislike the very name of every poem I have recited except "The Chinese Nightingale." [3]

He still wanted to be a public writer, but emotionally and artistically he found it more and more trying to subdue his instinctive literary impulses to his social conscience. He felt he was being molded into a "Bryan sensation," that he was expected to make picturesque tours of America "like Tagore in his nightgown." The complacency with which schools, colleges, and women's clubs accepted his presence as their right rather than his gift infuriated him. He felt like goods for market; he was "speculated in like pork" [4]—but was he not himself pushing a commodity, his ideology, and making certain assumptions about the market? But in spite of such outbursts Lindsay continued his career of recitation. That alone brought him the size and the mundane sort of audience he wanted.

Moreover, without admitting that he found his literary convention an unsupportable master—which would have meant rethinking his philosophy—he could not opt out. To do so would not only have entailed a betrayal of self, but a betrayal of America. For Lindsay's ideology, while impelled into being by despair in America and a conviction of the need for improvement, was nevertheless based on the belief that the seeds of growth, as of decay, were to be found in America herself. He celebrated America in "American classic illusions: Liberty and Union, Log Cabins, Lincoln Rails . . . Ladies of the South, Texas Rangers, Prairie Schooners." [5] His very belief in the possibility of communicating a general ideology to a large number of people was based on the fact that mass tendencies were rampant in America. Because "we do the same things from New York to San Francisco"; because "a man that does not move us all moves no one"; because of "the mechanical unity of the nation: the railroad, telegraph, newspaper, public school, and political uniformity"; because of "the same set of magazines on every Carnegie library table. Hearst papers from San Francisco to Boston," and "the same six best selling books read by the gum chewing typewriter girls from the Philippines to the offices of Philadelphia" [6] a new literary convention, geared to its audience, pandering to it, yet changing it, was a possibility. The convention's motto might have been the *Village Magazine* dictum, "Bad Public Taste is Mob Law. Good Public Taste is Democracy," [7] a nice example of Lindsay's mixture of apparent concession and real deception.

IMAGISM AND THE HIGHER VAUDEVILLE

The literary art form Lindsay tried to reshape was poetry. He apparently thought so poorly of his prose style that he felt unqualified to talk about prose as a medium; outside poetry, he relied on the merit of his ideas. He was aware that his general popularity and his recognition in literary circles stemmed from his poetry, and it *was* difficult to put him in any other precise literary category. *The Golden Book of Springfield* was barely a novel; *Adventures While Preaching the Gospel of Beauty* and *A Handy Guide for Beggars* were hardly travelogues; *The Art of the Moving Picture* was unconventional sociology. So when he held forth on literature, he spoke, for greatest effect, from the position that the world had allotted him. Sometimes he was talking about poetry alone, but often he was expressing thoughts which were relevant to his overall literary convention.

The dominant contemporary school of thought about poetry differed so signally in its premises from Lindsay's ideas that it was tantamount to a norm from which he deviated. Broadly speaking, the norm was a reaffirmation of an exclusive art, but in a modern idiom. It sprang from the theory of Imagism—"to create new rhythms," "to use the language of common speech," "to present an image" [8]—which did not sound incompatible with the sort of verse Lindsay wrote. However, although Imagism and its developments were by no means doctrinally exclusive—some of their "rules" were so general that they were applicable to poetry at almost any given time—their practical results did not resemble Lindsay's. Ezra Pound evaluated the situation: "We are not in the same movement, or anything like it." [9] For the dominant poetic philosophy of compression, concentration, erudition, and understatement were alien to Lindsay's wordy, repetitive, expansive style. He used, often to excess, any verbal device which would make his meaning plainer to an audience unused to reading into words and phrases. He wanted to simplify, not intensify, poetry. He indulged in the very technics Imagist condemned: apposition, ornamentation, cliche; and his verse often had the metronomic qualities they loathed.

He acknowledged the antithesis between their new poetry and his own.

I admire the work of the Imagist poets. We exchange fraternal greetings. . . . But neither my few heterodox pieces nor my many struggling orthodox pieces conform to their patterns. . . . The imagists emphasize pictorial effects, . . . while in my Higher Vaudeville I often put five rhymes on a line.[10]

Professing a blithe disregard for skills, technics, and effects not calculated to provoke an aesthetic response in the public at large, Lindsay capitalized on what existed of public appreciation for rhythms and moods. He incorporated the melodic lines and rhythms of hymns and well-known songs in his poems: "Sung to the tune of 'Hark Ten Thousand Harps and Voices,'" "To be sung to the tune of 'The Blood of the Lamb' with indicated instruments." He gave his poems broad moods and unmistakable images which he indicated through the insertion of marginal "stage" directions for recitation: "Begin with terror and power, end with joy," "With a literal imitation of camp-meeting racket . . . ," "Like the wind in the chimney." [11] By way of contrast Imagism reflected precisely the dedication Lindsay deplored: to form for form's sake and to the intrinsic worth of beautifully constructed, but comparatively unread and unheard poems. He scornfully indicted the Imagist "aesthetic aristocracy" for "singing on an island to one another while the people perish," and pointed out "this is precisely not the point of view of the Kallyope." [12] *That* was a poem for the people: its words welded into an art form Everyman could understand and enjoy, and its themes derived from American inspirations, not, like Imagism, from French and Japanese ones.

Amy Lowell, a middle-of-the-road Imagist spokesman occasionally seemed to take a left-wing, Lindsayesque stance. "Poetry is not a thing outside of man; it is absolutely inherent. It is one of the distinct needs of humanity, and it is as important to that need as it is to grow wheat or raise cattle." But she was attempting to have the best of both worlds; for she equated humanity with the intellectual upper crust.

I absolutely disagree . . . that the value of poetry consists chiefly in the arousing of people's emotional qualities. . . . It is very bad to suggest to the poet that his ultimate value is in the attitude of the populace toward him . . . I object to all this theory of democratizing poetry, because poetry can only be democratic in a highly intellectual community.[13]

But it was Ezra Pound, poetry's and Imagism's reactionary, exclusive spokesman, who provided the most striking antithesis to Lindsay's views. In July 1918, Pound gleefully noted in and about *The Little Review*: "The response has been oligarchic. The plain man in his gum overshoes, with his touching belief in W. J. Bryan . . . etc., is not with us." In the September issue Lindsay responded with equally telling exaggeration: "I write for the good-hearted People of the Great Pure Republic";[14] and in the introduction to the 1919 edition of *General William Booth* . . . he laid at the door of the Poundian literary convention the state of affairs

whereby poetry has lost its "springiness," has become a thing too much of the eye, a cult of solitude only too often morose, and of solicitude for the things of the soul that is only too often the refuge of preciosity in those folk who have made of poetry a retreat from life and not an explication and justification of the beauty of life.[15]

It could be argued that Lindsay's disregard for traditional refinements of style and the Imagist experiments of the New Poetry was less revolutionary and independent than it seemed. One of his talents was for the production of large, generous, rumbustious verse, which flowed along in spite of its imperfections, and without a great deal of stylistic reworking. A poet of emotion rather than one of intellectual discipline, he had a voracious appetite for recitation, both professionally and in his leisure time at home. His conscientious response to duty, in fact, came easily, fulfilled his dramatic dimension, and involved genuine pleasure.

But talent and enjoyment did not guide his conscience; on the contrary, he almost failed to make the connection. The national literary circuit acclaimed "The Congo's" choruses of "Boomlay, boomlay, boomlay Boom," and "Mumbo-Jumbo will hoo-doo you," but Lindsay wondered if he was writing poetry. After all, he admitted, "one composes it not by listening to the inner voice and following the gleam, but by pounding the table and looking out the window at the electric signs." [16] Even a prize from *Poetry* in 1913 for "General William Booth . . ." did not still his doubts; it took the approval of William Butler Yeats to do that.

Lindsay and Yeats met at a dinner party given by Harriet Monroe for Yeats in Chicago, in March 1914. Lindsay's recitation of "The Congo" was the sensation of the evening and impressed Yeats. In after-dinner conversation with Lindsay he preached the virtues of folk-culture, and told him that all that survived in America of the much-to-be-desired "primitive singing of poetry" and the Greek lyric chant was American Vaudeville and Vachel Lindsay. The imprimatur reconciled Lindsay to his achievement; a man whose artistic conscience was avowedly a social conscience was bound to develop what he came to call "the Higher Vaudeville."

Yeats commended to Lindsay the half-sung, half-spoken delivery of such vaudeville acts as Tambo and Bones dialogues, which had an apparent spontaneity, and a quick-fire, incantatory rhythm.[17] But when Lindsay went to vaudeville, he found the total medium had relevance for his propaganda. American vaudeville, which flourished c. 1875–1930, was at the height of its popularity in 1914–15. In country areas touring vaudeville shows had attracted a cross section of the population, and in the cities white-collar workers, ex-rural Americans, and immigrants with some degree of tenure made up the vaudeville audience. Yet vaudeville did not merely pander to its audiences' predictable taste for fantasy and vulgarity, stunts and novelties, freaks and animals, broad humor and scanty costumes. The average show regularly included moralizing playlets, dramatic monologues, and the occasional artist of caliber like Ethel Barrymore. Vaudeville got away with comedians who made German-, Jewish-, Irish-, and Italian-Americans laugh at themselves, and think, however briefly, about the state of the nation. The vaudeville audience enjoyed Albert Chevalier without fully understanding his Cockney allusions; it enjoyed Yvette Guilbert's singing without knowing French; it could be mesmerized by art.

Lindsay enviously experienced this sizeable, mundane audience with an appetite for entertainment (and for a kind of knowledge) and with a capacity to be moved in spite of itself. He determined to imitate vaudeville's technics and to build up a recitation ritual which would mix the brash, the exquisite, the everyday, the exotic, the funny, the sentimental, and the admonitory. If he could contrive a succession of swift, overwhelming moods, form and content would fuse in self-evident naturalness and rightness. This was the reason Lindsay became a one-man vaudeville show, willing to don fancy dress, to sing and dance, to use refrains and to repeat lines until they became as familiar as vaudeville fall-lines and catch-phrases. He occasionally achieved this within a single poem —"The Santa-Fé Trail" and "The Ghost of the Buffaloes," for example; but more often within a program of contrasting poems: "John L. Sullivan, the Strong Boy of Boston," "Why I Voted the Socialist Ticket," "The Potatoes' Dance," and "The Chinese Nightingale."

To emphasize that his aim was more serious than vaudeville's, and to counteract its slapstick and revue connotations, Lindsay coined the phrases "the Higher Vaudeville" and "the Higher Vaudeville Imagination" to describe the poems he wrote in "a sort of rag-time manner that deceives them [the American masses] into thinking they are at a vaudeville show." In spite of the rag-time manner, "I try to keep it to a real art"; it was a refined vaudeville, which sprang from his sensitive, critical response to American society, and his awareness of "democracy [which] is itself a paradox." Any beauty the Higher Vaudeville might describe or create was as paradoxical; and the medium was a paradoxical success for Lindsay, as he realized. He understood himself "by going to vaudeville, which I have all my life abhorred." The accidental discovery of his mastery of a popular means of communication hoisted him with his own petard. He saw "how a great many massive superstructures can be built on that primitive foundation," and he had no option but to develop his talent; but his foreboding that "my whole danger is in being set down . . . as a tin horn man" was realized.

By that very [Higher Vaudeville] act I persuaded the tired business man to listen at last. But lo, my tiny reputation as a writer seemed wiped out by my new reputation as an entertainer.[18]

Lindsay's contemporaries had little time for the Higher Vaudeville. Robert Frost, for example, whose simple, reflective poetry made him accidentally rather than intentionally something of a poet of the people, mocked Lindsay's sing-song delivery and marginal notes. " 'Say this in a golden tone' he says. You ought not to have to say that in the margin." [19] The theory and the dilemma of the Higher Vaudeville was passed over, though Lindsay had provocatively summed it up in his alternative phrase for the Higher Vaudeville, "The Higher Irony." "The Kallyope Yell," for example, was "part irony, part admiration, listing in metaphor the things that perplex and distract, thereby trying to conquer and assimilate them." [20] One might usefully coin a third term, Higher Chautauqua, to convey what Lindsay was trying to achieve through his literary convention. The Chautauqua movement (1875–1925), which carried on the popular educational traditions of the lyceums with correspondence courses and tours of eminent speakers ranging from Phineas Taylor Barnum to William Rainey Harper, was a uniquely effective way of communicating with the adult population. With the aims of mass morality and education, Chautauqua's realistic and successful technic was to insert entertainments—minstrels, opera singers, circus acts—among its educational items or even to disguise education as entertainment. It was an object lesson, Lindsay thought, in the possibility and methodology of large-scale appeal, and he pointed out the moral of Chautauqua to his fellow poets:

From Boston to Los Angeles, we American versifiers, democratic poets, face the problem of our potential audiences of one million, or one hundred million that we have never conquered, but which the Chautauqua orator, like Bryan, in a tent-speech, telegraphed to the newspapers, may reach any day.

He emphasized his conception of the poet as the man with the power to reach people and communicate a moral message by describing Bryan as "from this standpoint . . . the one living American poet." He called his tour organizer, A. J. Armstrong, a greater poet than himself, not for any poetry that Armstrong may have written, but because without Armstrong's administrative ability there would have been no audiences; and without audiences, Lindsay did not feel justified in calling himself that exponent of the social art of communication, a poet. He, and all other American "poets" did not really deserve the title "till we learn to make a few songs sturdy enough to outlast merciless newspaper scrutiny." [21]

Lindsay was surely the poet who came nearest his own hope that American poets would "attempt the Chautauqua thing by devising some sort of rhymed oration of double structure, an oration, at the same time a lyric poem of the old school." [22] "Bryan, Bryan, Bryan, Bryan," for example, was a combination par excellence of oratory and lyricism put together like a political speech. With its variations of rhythm and volume and its contrasts between "the ways of Tubal Cain" and the aspirations ". . . of prairie schooner children/Born beneath the stars/Beneath falling snows" it ran the gamut of tension and tenderness. In "General William Booth . . ."

> *Big-voiced lasses made their banjos bang,*
> *Tranced, fanatical they shrieked and sang.*

But with Lindsay's skill their discordance (and his tub-thumping) progressed to a perfectly attuned moment when

> *The lame were straightened, withered limbs uncurled*
> *And blind eyes opened on a new, sweet world.*[23]

The ironic outcome of the strong beat, the syncopation, and the overall modernity of the Higher Vaudeville, and of the interest in music that was deduced from Lindsay's sing-song recitations was the praise he received for his "mastery of the jazz idiom," his "tonal beauty of jazz," for "jazz rhythms," and for raising jazz to "a large vocal expressiveness." [24] Such labels were anathema to a Lindsay who found jazz an unwelcome aphrodisiac. It seemed to him that the Higher Vaudeville had been willfully misinterpreted as well as misunderstood. He countered, forcefully,

I use the word Jazz ironically, have always hated Jazz, and always will and considered *The Daniel Jazz* a mere after dinner skit, and was utterly disgusted, really horrified beyond words, to find it used as the title-poem of the English Book when I arrived in England.[25]

But the epithet stuck, and he was reduced to "complete despair of ever performing again without being advertised as jazz." [26]

For some poems he did use a rhythmic-melodic counterpoint ranging from the compulsive notation of "The Congo" to the audience participation chorus in "King Solomon and the Queen of Sheba" and the gentle delivery of "The Chinese Nightingale" —"part of the time I try to sing like a lady, part of the time like a bird." But he resented the musical labels which were subsequently attached to him. "People have wished onto me a theory of vocalization. I have none." Ninety percent of his poetry he described as "inscriptional and written for the inner ear." But "both the public and the critics discovering I was born with a singing voice have insisted that the ten percent of my verse adapted to vocalization is all I have written." [27] Admittedly the Higher Vaudeville emphasized musical effects, but the music it was concerned with was verbal. Poems were "made musical in the same sense that classic dramas are to be made musical by good actors." It always disturbed Lindsay when "people write asking for permission to set my verses to music. It shows such misapprehension of the point of view from which they were written. It is like asking permission to rewrite the poems entirely, while pretending they remain the same." He was vehement on the subject. "No musical notation ever invented can express the same musical scheme as the twenty-six letters of the alphabet. Stringed instruments destroy the value of vowels." [28] His only concession was that music might be played between lines or stanzas.

Lindsay apparently did not realize that this was a substantial concession, an admission that music could approximate the exact mood of a poem sufficiently closely to alternate with lines and verses. There is little record of his musical likes, apart from his relish for hymn tunes, his feeling for Percy Grainger's English folk airs, and his desire for their American counterpart. He had a sense of tune and rhythm, as his chanting recitations show, but his views on music were instinctive rather than informed. In making his concession he probably said something which he would have retracted had he properly understood the implications of his statement. All he probably meant to convey was that as art forms, as expressions of beauty, music and poetry were striving for not incompatible effects.

For him a more viable way of adding another dimension to spoken poetry was by dancing to it. Some of his most criticized poems—"The King of Yellow Butterflies" and "The Potatoes' Dance," for example, in which most lines were repeated three or four times—were what he called Poem Games rather than poems. He did not envisage a general application for Poem Games, however. He rarely performed them on his nationwide tours, though in front of interested schools and universities, particularly the University of Chicago, he would don costume, and (in Chicago with various regular female partners) dance and chant. He organized Poem Games at the Wellesley Kindergarten (1915) and at the Lewis and Clark High School, Spokane, from 1923 to 1928. Within his family circle there were frequent dramatizations, mimes, and dances to poems, not only his own, but to other story poems such as "Kubla Khan." The Poem Game idea was a "rhythmic picnic" to be recommended to informal parties. It was a good way of interesting children in poetry. In part Poem Games were antimusic gestures, attempts to dissociate dancing from music, to "shake off the Isadora Duncan and Russian precedents for a while, and abolish the orchestra and piano, replacing all these with the natural meaning and cadences of English speech." His instructions for teaching children Poem Games allowed, at first, some "thumping, drumming and musical notation and . . . imitations of singing and orchestras." But they had to give way to "elaborate reading . . . reading that comes to the edge of a chant without having the literary meaning clouded by the chant." [29] He stood firm on the inner expressiveness and musicality of poetry.

AUDIENCE

It is hard to imagine a closer approximation than the Higher Vaudeville Imagination to a convention of democratic literature. Yet Lindsay only succeeded in exciting interest and curiosity in himself and his performances, not in the diffusion of culture and his American ideology, which was the motive behind his public perambulatory career. He did attract a new set of hearers, but they were the American bourgeosie, not the American masses; and as H. L. Mencken devastatingly commented:

Only one [American poet] has ever actually sought to take his strophes to the vulgar. That one is Lindsay—and there is not the slightest doubt that the yokels welcomed him, not because they were interested in his poetry, but because it struck them as an amazing and perhaps even a fascinatingly obscene thing for a sane man to go about the country on any such bizarre and undemocratic business.[30]

Lindsay's was an agonizing career for he never realized that he was trying to do something impossible and blamed himself for his failure. For example, he hoped to influence American millions with whom he never came into contact. The audience of three million readers he claimed in 1923 was stating his case optimistically; it was the people who did not regularly read "edifying" literature that he needed to reach. Even if his heyday had coincided with the era of captive radio audiences, his earnestness and morality, his insistence that America was far from being a healthy society, and that the American character left much to be desired, would have made uncomfortable and unpopular listening. And

given that any writer must be prepared to be ideologically inconsistent in order to appeal consistently to a mass audience which
changes its tastes and mores in less than a generation, Lindsay,
principled to a fault, was doomed to failure. The only principle
of a weathervane culture would be the opposite of Lindsay's theory; a belief in the power of an art form to elevate in spite of its
content.

Why did Lindsay fail to weigh the pros and cons which were
crucial to the success or failure of his literary convention? It is
unlikely that he did not think around the subject in more detail
than is apparent from his writings. For, in spite of his belief in a
dormant equality of taste, he was deeply conscious of existing human bêtises and superficialities; he pinned his faith on God, not
man. He must have wondered whether he was trying to bring
about a level of thoughtfulness and culture of which the average
man was incapable, and whether mass art was necessarily debased
art. Perhaps the right question for us to pose is why Lindsay did
not attempt a refutation of the common doubts about democratic
art forms; perhaps the answer is that Lindsay was frequently silent
about events and theories which undermined what he advocated,
and usually for one of two reasons. Either, as when he refrained
from commenting on the twenties, his evasion concealed despair.
Or, as when he formulated his plan for a world union of religions, he minimized difficulties and differences, and rather than
write in a critical and doubtful vein, thought he could best serve
his ends by making constructive and, if possible, commendatory
comments. It is impossible to state categorically why Lindsay kept
quiet about the dubieties of mass culture; but it is noticeable that
although he managed to say very little about the twenties, enough
slipped through to show the outline of his thought, while there is
no sign that he abandoned his belief in equality of taste. Faith in
mass potential (coupled with a lively conviction of current mass
crassness), seems to have been one of his emotional constants.

Sometimes, however, he lost patience with audience responses,
so deeply buried did this potential appear to be; and he turned to
elite audiences to hear his message, and to prose media to express

it. By 1920, the year when *The Golden Book of Springfield,* although an anticlimax and a failure, showed where his interest lay and where his inclination was taking him, he had developed a speculative, selective attitude towards audiences, and began to make demands on them to cooperate with him. He wrote to his tour organizer, A. J. Armstrong:

I dislike an audience that makes a curiosity out of me, and a committee that makes me talk about myself and listens and listens for queer things. The English departments of High School, College and University never, never, never do that, bless them.

He almost felt that his nationwide tours were wasted on dilettante, pleasure-seeking audiences, for whom he was even more of a curiosity when he talked seriously. Perhaps it would be better to get others to lecture on his work; he might follow later, years later —he was really depressed at this point—if the seed finally showed signs of sprouting. Or perhaps he should limit himself to *"a few very well prepared audiences";* for even "my noisiest and most successful public appearances . . . do me no permanent good even as memories." [31] At one time he was driven to suggesting, half seriously, that only those who could pass an examination on one of his books should be admitted to his lectures, a pathetic notion when people were not clamoring to hear his ideas in such numbers as to make competitive entrance to his lectures a reasonable proposition, and when such a proposition—as a temporarily irate and disappointed Lindsay must have quickly realized—would have meant no audience at all.

In calmer vein it was still important to Lindsay that people should have read his books and have prepared for his visit. He sent out a circular letter, "The Kind of a Visit I Like to Make." When he recited to schools

I expect the English teachers to have my books in the school libraries or the public library the month beforehand. These books are the sole basis of my publicity, and I mean nothing whatever to an audience unfamiliar with my work. They find me neither amusing nor edifying

. . . I want every member of my audience to have at least some notion
of these books.[32]

He thought around the problem of communication. At one time
he envisaged one annual audience of about two thousand people,
a concentration of himself and his public which he hoped might
sustain the habitual but brief enthusiasm he aroused. But it was
never put into operation. He remained faithful to the local, intimate medium in which he could dutifully extend himself, and in
which he might with accuracy gauge local trends. He was certainly
prepared to work hard.

I despise giving only one programme. I enjoy giving three to seven
in a day, and my last is generally the best. I covet the privilege of
laying my entire body of recitations before the community and hearing in between . . . what they have to say for themselves; for instance,
local American poems they want written.

But he expected hard work in return. When he lectured on a
specific book: "Dear reader, either bring the book or stay away!"
The noonday lunch clubs he spoke to "can be taught my verses
by running them in the newspaper with paraphrases and local
applications by the editor."[33] Good publicity mattered; if the
editor would write him up seriously, the community would follow
suit, and reassess him.

Lindsay's attitude to his audience was barely recognizable as
that of a creative writer seeking a hearing. He seemed to think
of himself as a teacher, of his writings as textbooks, of his audience
as a class, of literature as adult education; not a subtle attitude,
as Lindsay was not subtle. A more shrewd, but equally dedicated
man would have lured his audience with the sort of poems they
wanted to hear and have slipped in unobtrusively what he could
in the way of social propaganda. But it was irritating for Lindsay
to believe, however mistakenly, that he was offering a vital service
to a public which would not avail itself of the service; and he
continued to try and get "good citizenship leagues" to hear him
on "The Gospel of Beauty," "The Village Improvement Parade,"
and *The Golden Book of Springfield*.

His attitude was not one of conceit, but of a kind of a do-or-die didacticism, arising out of pangs of conscience at not being able to do the work which he probably thought was the justification for his existence. It was also a tacit acknowledgement that the public was proving unreceptive to the direct statement of his ideas, and that he would have to educate intermediaries (newspaper editors, teachers) whose local influence exceeded his own. His failure made him reemphasize (though he had never ignored it) the mechanism of the New Localism for the diffusion of culture and ideas, rather than rely on his own national image. As people took more kindly to social and political administration when these matters had the appearance of being matters of local sovereignty, so they might be more receptive to Lindsay's ideas if they seemed to originate locally. The conditions which Lindsay reluctantly formulated for audiences, the disappointed scaling-down of plans for mass communication, show how seriously he took his work, seriously enough to concentrate on elite audiences, which in part negated his convention, and in part were proving to be its only hope. It is both an explanation of public indifference and an indictment of the shallowness of human reactions that Lindsay's earnestness and his emphasis on the disciplinary and ideological aspects of literature managed, then and today, to detract from his image rather than to increase his stature.

G. K. Chesterton, perceptive about Lindsay's Spanish-Americanness, was acute about Lindsay's literary convention. For him Lindsay played "the brazen trumpet of publicity as well as the golden trumpet of poetry. He was himself a wholly simple, sincere, and therefore humble man; but the people around him did not believe in his humility." [34] One aspect of Lindsay's humility lay in his lack of literary pride and puffery. Of *The Village Magazine* he wrote: "The less you agree with [it] . . . the more the perpetrator will be pleased. Do him the service to analyse your objections, and write them out. Be explicit. . . . He will welcome essays ten pages long. The editor wants your notion of a visible civilization." [35] Even adverse comment showed that interest had been aroused. Likewise he asked audiences for criticism of *The Golden Book of*

Springfield in almost every conceivable particular, in "1. Spelling 2. Punctuation 3. Grammar 4. Rhetoric 5. Clearness 6. Continuity . . . 7. Thought 8. Practical Utility of the Book." He had no conceit about his craftsmanship and was open to suggestions of ideas which might fill out, clarify, or renovate his design for a mature American society. He even thought that "if I am unable to write *The Golden Book of Springfield* as it should be written, maybe I can persuade Squire [J. C. Squire, literary editor of the *London Mercury,* 1919–34, who entertained Lindsay in London in 1920, and visited him in Springfield] or some other to write it well and clearly and in a more directly stimulating fashion." [36] In its other aspect his humility lay in the social rather than artistic, the altruistic rather than the self-indulgent use to which he turned his poetic talent. His attitude was as extreme as art for art's sake, and as open to disputation.

LINDSAY AND WHITMAN

A sentence from Whitman which Lindsay wrote out in one of his notebooks expressed their common conception of the relation between a democratic society and the arts:

Democracy can never prove itself beyond cavil until it founds and luxuriantly grows its own form of art, poems, schools, theology.[37]

Though the parallel between Whitman's and Lindsay's conventions of literature is obvious, it is important because it associates Lindsay with a strong, if solitary strand of American thought, and because it provides some kind of American standard for measuring Lindsay's ideas. Just as Lindsay combined hope and despair about the democratic mass, and hit out at America's intelligentsia, Whitman sarcastically commented: "man, viewed in the lump, displeases, and is a constant puzzle and affront to the merely educated classes." Both men advocated, and used, American material; both, believing that America had to find herself in her artistic capacity before she became a full democracy, and that her artistic salvation lay in art forms which expressed an unaristocratic, pulsating, advancing society, talked in terms of

. . . a programme of culture drawn out, not for a single class alone, or for the parlors or lecture rooms, but with an eye to practical life, the west, the working-men, the facts of farms, and jackplanes and engineers.[38]

In *Leaves of Grass* and *Specimen Days* Whitman celebrated almost every American place, incident, occupation, and characteristic he could squeeze in; in *Democratic Vistas* he made statements about the possible form a democratic literature might take—its style bold, modern, future-looking, its speech based on "some western idiom, repartee or stump speech." [39] From this point, Lindsay and Whitman began to diverge. Whitman's conception of democratic art forms remained on a general level and rarely moved beyond his resolution that the only indigenous arts, the only unique arts America could develop, were arts for the people. But Lindsay, instead of confining himself to generalizations, looked closely at means of mass communication, and tried to suggest methods by which art, still artistic, could become social. As a result he is much more easily debunked than Whitman. For the broad terms in which Whitman wrote can only be countered by equally vague assertions, while Lindsay, attempting to be specific about a contentious and possibly insoluble subject, is quickly deflated. Compare, for example, the way in which Lindsay thought around, theorized about, and experimented with audiences with Whitman's lofty statement that in America poets, to be great, need great audiences.

It was partly following Whitman's grandiose plea for sacerdotal literatuses that Lindsay called for a "Republic of Letters" and an "Art Revolution" in which intellectuals would infiltrate government departments; but it was with unique, though exaggerated justification that he claimed that he had

as much to say to the American people as Hoover or Hughes or Bryan, and in as loud a *voice* . . . [that] there is as much *politics* in them [his writings] as in a speech by Bryan or Hoover or Hughes or the Republican or Democratic candidates.[40]

Though Whitman wanted the leaven of the creative writer's voice in politics, he did not indicate what the voice would say, nor how , it would gain a hearing; he was thinking more of irresistibly great poetry than of subjects and styles working wonders on and for the people. His view of America's future was magnificent but hazy; Lindsay, by comparison, seems to be a practical and plebeian theorist and much more of a folk-poet.

In view of this substantial difference between the two, Lindsay found it hard to give Whitman the accolade of democratic poet. He approved Whitman's subject matter and suggested using it for motion picture scenarios; but he thought Whitman's involuted, tortuous style negated any democratic literary convention and could only appeal to the sophisticated. In 1919, reviewing for *Poetry Yanks,* a book of American Expeditionary Force verse, Lindsay rejoiced in the book's colloquial style, "the easy American dialect of college boys and farm-hands alike." It was "a step toward the future idiom for our informal use; far from the shackles of Riley, and equidistant from the Brobdignagian tyrannies and distensions of Whitman." Lindsay liked the anthology because it had no pretensions (as he apparently thought Whitman had) to be aesthetic and stoical; it had a ring of sincerity which he found lacking in Whitman. Thus

while we are reading it, it delivers us from Whitman, thank God! If you really want *American* poetry, I suggest that you forget Whitman a moment and read *Yanks*.[41]

If Lindsay was correct in assuming that there can be a successful democratic literature, we may well agree with him that Whitman's idiosyncratic style was unlikely to arouse mass enthusiasm. But his criticism was unkind in view of his own difficulty in sustaining a style that was popular with his audience, but decreasingly congenial to himself, and in view of his inability to write more than a small percentage of his total poetical output in that style. Except when inspiration coincided with indoctrination he found it difficult to write to his own order. His artistic conscience almost regretted the kind of popularity his social conscience made him seek. Moreover, he found that poetry was a medium he could impose on only to a limited extent, and that the sociological ideas he wanted to communicate went better, and were more likely to meet with informed readers, in the prose forms with which they were traditionally associated. Some aspects of his ideology—for example, his poems about great Americans and vignette visions of the future—went well into verse. But the negligible proportion of poems devoted solely to social ideas in the work of a man who set out to propagate social ideas is striking and significant. Lindsay's inability to do what he set out to do is proof of what Whitman indicated negatively: with rare exceptions, poetry can edify only indirectly.

In an indirect way Lindsay acknowledged this fact. He came to use his Higher Vaudeville technic to popularize poetry for itself, not merely for its message; "The Chinese Nightingale," for example, was a love song whose lyricism blurred its American overtones. He wrote increasing numbers of lyrical poems, which were very like self-indulgence. This genre constituted most of his three books of poems published in the 1920s. There was, however, enough poetry with social theories in the three books—"So Much the Worse for Boston" (*Going-to-the-Sun,* 1923), "Virginia," "Old Old Old Andrew Jackson" (*Going-to-the-Stars,* 1926), "The Babbitt Jamboree" (*The Candle in the Cabin,* 1926), for him not totally to invalidate his literary convention. But his small output of directly ideological poetry (though insofar as he hoped that there might be some beauty in each of his poems, and that beauty was a moral force, he would, I suppose, claim to be always writing social poetry), his use of prose for his most important work, *The Golden Book of Springfield,* and his plans in 1931 to devote himself to prose and drawing rather than to poetry indicated that in his poetic capacity he had found his convention unsatisfactory.

Even in the prose medium he felt unsure, and understandably, for his prose was far less controlled than his poetry. He could be intentionally sentimental or rhetorical in poetry, but was unavoidably so in prose. Asides, digressions, and exaggerations spilled out over one another, until he came to have a distinctive, but not a distinguished, style. Fortunately, the vigor and interest of his themes surmounted the shortcomings of his style, an ironic reversal of the success of the Higher Vaudeville technic. In neither instance was the medium the message.

It is hard to imagine why Lindsay had so much more confidence in his drawing than in his prose, for, equally, they mixed interesting ideas with clumsy expression. Perhaps his failure with poetry had made him wary of words, whereas he had yet to confront a public with his pictures and symbols, and could still hope in them.

CHAPTER ELEVEN

Picture and Symbol

ART STUDIES

From first to last I have been an Art Student. I have spent the big part of my life in Art Galleries, Art Schools, and Art Libraries.[1]

I have been an art student all my life, in the strictest sense of the word. I have been so exclusively an art student, I am still surprised to be called a writer.[2]

Practically all my life has been spent as an art student and lecturer in art.[3]

THESE STATEMENTS of Lindsay's, all made in the latter part of his life, between the years 1920 and 1925, expressed a lifelong dedication to drawing and studying visual pictures and symbols. In 1907 he was planning a book of art criticism which would make him a professor of art at Columbia, and a few years later he was imagining himself an octogenarian senator, as well-known for his drawings as for his politics. He was, of course, an "official" art student; from 1899 to 1903 he studied at the Chicago Institute of Art. The training the Institute offered was broadly based, not merely aiming to produce "conventionally" creative artists, but to cultivate such practical bents as book illustration and window display. In the words of one historian, the Institute was trying to make "corn, wheat, hogs, beef, railroads, prairies, skyscrapers, art not absolutely contradictory." In this school—and, like Carl Sandburg, in the school of Chicago—Lindsay was set on his way to express the American beauty of "smokestacks-geraniums, hyacinths-biscuits." [4]

In 1903 Lindsay moved on to the New York School of Art, where, under the influence of Henri's untrammeled, disestablished approach to art, he began to produce drawings which reflected this spirit of artistic liberation, and at the same time retained a personal flavor of traditional study: drawings of ungainly individuality permeated with the Pre-Raphaelite influences of Burne-Jones, Beardsley, and Morris. They had overtones of Art Nouveau (particularly evident in "The Village Improvement Parade" series of drawings in *The Village Magazine*), of Japanese art, and of Blake. Lindsay's drawings, like his writings, were eclectic and imitative, but they had a composite originality.

Lindsay was a species of art lecturer as well as an art student. From the spare time art classes for laymen he taught while studying in New York, he went on in later years to intersperse his recitations with talks on art; but he noted sadly:

After a long and careful lecture on the History of Art, someone rises from the Back of the House, saying, "Now that Mr. Lindsay is through airing his hobbies, will he please recite 'The Congo'?" [5]

Art was thus not a hobby for Lindsay; it was a serious matter. He thought that "the skirmish line of civilization and the skirmish line of art" were identical. The issue at stake was "the power of democracy, the art of democracy, the construction of democracy," and he felt that ultimately an American art must be differentiated. Just as the unprecedented political institutions of the Lincoln rail and the McKinley front porch were virtual national necessities, so American art would be forced to develop similar indigenous phenomena. Whatever the aesthetic superiority of European art, Lindsay believed that "one little thing done from the spirit of the [American] soil is worth a thousand great things done abroad." [6] The function of the artist in America was to discover and picture the distinct American quality which Lindsay himself tried to fathom in his American entity.

Lindsay always had the feeling that pictures, not verses, were "kicking to come out of me." He was sure that "I have pictures in me with as long fluid lines as 'The Congo'" [7] (and with equal potential popularity). In 1920 he described his pictures, all pen and ink drawings (with the exception of one oil painting, "The Tree of Laughing Bells") as "a first consideration," [8] perhaps a resurgence of artistic ambition following the crushing reception of his literary chef d'oeuvre in that year. But much earlier in his life, at some point in the 1890s, he had decided that he had a talent for the social art of cartooning.

CARTOONING

At the World's Fair of 1893, Lindsay was most interested in the demonstration of cartoon making and printing in the Puck Building, and by 1899 he had convinced himself that the way to make a generally unpalatable activity (such as sincerely following the precepts of Religion, Beauty, and Equality) a national, American activity, was through arresting, pithy drawings in wide circulation. He wanted to be a "Christian cartoonist." [9]

Lindsay was not using "cartoon" in its primary sense of a preliminary sketch. He used the words cartoon, picture, and illustration synonymously, to denote a drawing with a moral, a drawing which was a symbol. He described his "Village Improvement Parade" as "a series of picture-cartoons with many morals," and he compared the potential religious impact of the cartoon with the paintings of Leonardo da Vinci. "If the Sistine Chapel expressed the church universal of the middle ages, one can by cartoons, by great, long powerful lines express one's love for the church universal today." [10]

With this conception of a cartoon, Lindsay was unlikely to have much success. His mother had encouraged him on the grounds that the large field of Christian art was unoccupied. This was so, but Mrs. Lindsay was sanguine in thinking that "whatever you are capable of doing you would be sure of having a demand for." [11] Lindsay's beautiful, moral drawings could not fit into either of the accepted categories of cartooning of his period. The first of these was the comic strip, which ran the gamut of whimsy, saccharine sweetness, fantasy, violence, man-in-the-street humor, and pungent social comment. (The best known strip running at the time that Lindsay was cartooning was The Katzenjammer Kids; others which were born in Lindsay's lifetime were Toonerville Folks [1908], Mutt and Jeff [1909], Krazy Kat [1913], and The Gumps [1917].) The vitriol, sentiment, and escapism of comic strips had an indirect morality of indignation and pathos, but it stemmed from topical comment on scandal and abuse, and from calculated audience appeal, not from Christian precepts and beauty consciousness. The second category was that of bitter social comment—Boardman Robinson against Joe Cannon and the liquor industry, Art Young against war profiteers, and Thomas Nast, anti-Tammany—too directly savage an approach for the oblique Lindsay.

In theory cartooning squared better with Lindsay's ambition to reach and influence a nationwide audience than his many-faceted career of speaking and writing. Though he exaggerated when he said that the whole world was "controlled in the end by the political cartoonists of London *Punch* and the like," [12] the cartoon was an apt medium for a man with Lindsay's urge to communicate on a mass scale. In practice he was trying to put over the same unpopular ideas, and even in the form of pictures and symbols rather than words they were unlikely to succeed.

Lindsay's attempted career as an artist went almost unnoticed. Literary dictionaries and encyclopedias tell of his trading his rhymes for bread, but they do not mention that he distributed pictures with an equal zeal. For example, he made a series of large poster drawings of each of the men in his "Litany of Heroes," and he took these with him on his tours, pinning them up in lecture halls, farmhouse kitchens, and squatters' cabins, to the accompaniment of a moralizing commentary, for he wanted to communicate as directly with his art as with his poetry. In the scrapbook he took with him on his tramps in 1906, 1908, and 1912, he had pasted not only his own drawings, but reproductions of some of Ruskin's and Whistler's paintings, and pictures of Tolstoy, St. Francis, Buddha, and Christ. Pictures of and by moral men had for Lindsay an intrinsic morality which fulfilled his conception of high art; they were pictures which, for him at least, were self-evident symbols. This highly personal conception of cartooning was unlikely to have validity for anyone else. The equation of the cartoon with a beautiful picture or a picture of moral content is barely plausible. The cartoon thrives on distortion, caricature, and mimicry which are incompatible with unadulterated beauty. Its criticisms are not self-righteous, nor do they spring from a rigid moral code; they are more often the products of cynicism, disgust, or amusement. The cartoon rarely has even the beauty of sentiment which Lindsay could accept as beauty; and even his own "cartoons" lacked such beauty. Artistically they can be considered to evince a delightful awkwardness, perhaps purposeful, perhaps accidental, or perhaps a sheer lack of talent.

In spite of their shortcomings, Lindsay's cartoons cannot be ignored in a survey of his attempts and failures to instill his gospel in American minds. His cartoons never appeared in the national press, but only in his private publications *The Village Magazine* and *The Spring Harbinger*. And although they lack the topicality and the edge to make them national newspaper material, they are not without interest. They reveal another of Lindsay's talents, not for major political cartooning, but for light and pleasing humor. They show the same amusing, slightly nonsensical cast of mind that is apparent in his children's poetry. They underline his interest in relations between the sexes, his ability to make many variations on one theme, and an unexpectedly tongue-in-cheek humor.

They show, too, an unpredictable side of Lindsay: a capacity to poke gentle but telling fun at domestic situations, and at women in particular, unexpected in a man to whom the home and woman were sacred and inviolate. Perhaps these drawings, made in 1909–10, when Lindsay was a young thirty—just out of art school, unemployed, living at home—and before he embarked on a series of unsuccessful attachments to a number of women, indicate a lightheartedness which gave way before an increasingly serious lifework of national social regeneration, and before the impossibility of remaining quite so youthfully amused about a sex which remained a tantalizing mystery to him. Perhaps—and this may be nearer the truth—these cartoons do not represent a once shrewd, later idealistic attitude to all women; rather, they are comments on exceptions. It would be in keeping with Lindsay's obsession with the general purity and perfection of women to be obsessively concerned about the few less than perfect, and to make them the subject of the bulk of his cartoons. This is merely a suggested explanation of cartoons which defy definitive explanation. If it is correct the humorous content of the cartoons in minimal.

What can be said with certainty is that the following selection of cartoons shows how Lindsay fell short of his ambitions as a cartoonist. The cartoons are not beautiful; they are not Christian; they are neither constructive nor moralizing. In fact, the men and women bicker, but they look reasonably happy. At first sight the caption to cartoon A suggests a straightforward moral, but Professor Brook and his son appear fascinated with the "stupid and vain" beauty. Cartoon B has merely an unconsequential, Thurberesque charm. The rest of the cartoons are comments on relations between the sexes: C—a henpecked husband; D—a spoilt wife; E—a man making advances to a woman; F—the way to a man's heart; G—a woman making advances to a man; H—more Thurberesque humor. The cartoons do have a general domestic validity, but their application is hardly universal in the elevated sense in which Lindsay hoped it would be. They have an independent charm, but in the context of Lindsay's ambitions, they also have pathos, not only because they are lightweight cartoons, but because they are not remotely like what Lindsay had in mind when he hoped to be a cartoonist.

Lindsay's last year of obscurity, 1912, marked the end of his attempt to be a cartoonist. "Up to 1912 I had been first, last and always a cartooning adventurer and a cartooning preacher." [13] He could not pass up his success as a writer and reciter when handed an audience of considerable proportions; and he reconciled his literary activities with still strong artistic leanings by evolving a theory of hieroglyphic art, which was to embrace the two.

"BEAUTY IS BUT SKIN-DEEP,"
SAID PROFESSOR BROOK TO HIS
SON —
"APT TO BE STUPID AND VAIN:
HERE, FOR INSTANCE, IS ONE."

NIKROLAS VACHEL LINDSAY 1910.

B

"I KNOW YOU,"
SAID VAGUE
MRS. BROWN
"YOUR WAYS ARE THE TALK OF
THE TOWN."
"WHY, WHAT HAVE I DONE,
MY DEAR HONEY-BUN?"
"NEVER MIND," SAID VAGUE MRS. BROWN.

WHY SHOULD WIFEY
FIGHT AND SWEAR?
SHE HAS NAUGHT, SHE SAYS,
TO WEAR.

NICHOLAS VACHEL LINDSAY. 1910

D

"I WAS NEVER A SUFFRAGETTE
DEAR HENRY YOU MAKE ME A PET.
I AM HANDSOMELY DRESSED.
I AM FED AND CARESSED.
I HAVEN'T A CARE OR REGRET."

NICHOLAS VACHEL LINDSAY 1910

E

A CHILD OF SUSCEPTIBLE YEARS
WAS CARESSED UPON ONE OF HER EARS
BY THE FINGER AND THUMB
OF A **MAN**.
SHE WAS DUMB;
THEN FELL ON HIS BOSOM WITH TEARS.

F

A SANDWICH DESIGNER NAMED KATE
WAS COOK FOR A TAILOR-MADE SKATE,
AS HE SAMPLED HER ART
DAN CUPID'S SOFT DART
PIERCED HIS HEART   —
AND HE TOOK HER FOR MATE.

G

A MAIDEN ASPIRING AND WISE
LOOKED STRAIGHT INTO MARMADUKE'S
EYES,
AND SAID "THERE IS NOTHING MORE
GOOD
FOR US THAN A WALK IN THE WOOD,
WE STAND IN NO PERIL OF CHILL.
WE ARE WEARING WARM UNDERWEAR STILL."

H

"DO YOU LOVE ME?" ASKED
ERNESTINE GREEN.
"BE SURE SIR, TO SAY WHAT YOU MEAN.
"YOUR SMILE IS THE DAWN
YOU ARE BUILT LIKE A FAWN!"
SAID THE HUSBAND OF ERNESTINE
GREEN.

HIEROGLYPHICS

In his theory of hieroglyphics, first put forward in *The Art of the Moving Picture,* 1915, Lindsay moved further away from a notion of pictures, and nearer to a notion of symbols. Such a move had been foreshadowed in his conception of the implicit morality of beauty, and his addiction to Swedenborg's Science of Correspondences. He viewed hieroglyphics as an extension of the symbolic side of his previous artistic activity: "I consider all my cartooning in some sense hieroglyphic." [14]

Lindsay made a detailed study of hieroglyphics. He inundated his friends with two basic grammars of Egyptian hieroglyphics, Margaret Murray's *Elementary Egyptian Grammar* and Gunther Roeder's *Short Egyptian Grammar.* He filled his home with books on Egyptology; decorated his library with reproductions of friezes from *The Book of the Dead,* and bored both friends and public with his reiterated enthusiasm for things Egyptian. Henry Morton Robinson tells the story of Lindsay lecturing on hieroglyphics to a group of writers and teachers at Columbia. At nine o'clock he started to explain his "Map of the Universe," which, in the sense that it was a symbolic picture, was hieroglyphic; at ten-thirty the room was half empty. When, the lecture over, he struck up "The Congo," the room filled again. "Swedenborg, Confucius and Thoth they could get elsewhere; what they wanted from Lindsay was the good old Mumbo-Jumbo, Sizz-Fizz, and Boomlay BOOM." [15]

His audience's impatience was understandable; for although Lindsay was convinced that he had made revolutionary advances in hieroglyphics, there is no proof that he had any more than an amateur's competent acquaintance with the subject. He illustrated his books with large, accurate reproductions of hieroglyphics; he designed his own hieroglyphic signature, which did not spell a word, but which was simply an amalgam of such favorite hieroglyphics as the two feathers of truth, Thoth, the god of writing, a drawing tablet, a pen, and an ink bottle. In 1948, Professor W. F. Albright, an orientologist at Johns Hopkins University, analyzed Lindsay's hieroglyphic skill, and concluded that although Lindsay could understand and reproduce individual hieroglyphics, he had not mastered the hieroglyphic language.

Albright's analysis, though correct, missed the inspirational point of hieroglyphics for Lindsay, who was not concerned with mastering Egyptian. He described his aims to Robert Hillyer in 1922. Hillyer remembered that Lindsay wanted

to draw an inspiration for pictorial representations from abstract thoughts, thus approximating the creative method of hieroglyphic writing without duplicating the exact results. . . . In other words, beginning with the same mystical symbols which fired the imagination of the ancients, he desired to build up a picture writing of his own. His interest would thus seem to have been romantic and aesthetic rather than scholarly.[16]

Lindsay's interest in hieroglyphics grew out of an admiration for Egyptian society, a society pervaded by religion, by a vivid conception of a hierarchy of gods with active powers in different spheres of life, and by attempts to secure admittance to the next world. In the once functional symbolism of Egyptian hieroglyphics a concept like death was represented by a jackal (Anubis) and truth by a feather. American hieroglyphics was to be a similar value language. But, as Lindsay implied to Hillyer, he gave his Egyptian-inspired picture language an un-Egyptian use. It was not a replacement for the Cyrillic alphabet nor an everyday writing. It was to be a public means of communication in the sense of other pictorial arts. As such, instead of being limited to original works of art, it was to be based on the wide dissemination of pictures reproduced through the technics of the zinc etching block, whose hard, incisive lines were comparable to stonecut hieroglyphics.

Lindsay was astonishingly confident about the evolution of this new art form. "Unless I am much mistaken, I shall sooner or later evolve a special type of United States Hieroglyphics, based on a contemplation of the borderline between letters and art, and the bridges that cross it."[17] One can only attribute his unusual optimism to the enthusiasm aroused in him by the thought that he had hit upon, what was for him, an original contribution to the development of American culture—a contribution which omitted, for example, the intermediaries and secondary sources that he called upon for the planning and architecture of Springfield 2018. For an American hieroglyphics was part of Lindsay's attempt to fulfill his early and lifelong ambition to establish "a simple American Art." At first he had thought of an indigenous school of painting, and had urged himself to "find the absolutely native American painters, study, study, study them." [18] But hieroglyphics, though derivative, offered an art form uncommon in the West, which would set America apart from Europe. And a set of American symbols was also a partial solution for America's problems. Lindsay considered that American growth had been so rapid, and had produced so many undigested phenomena, that the American mind was "an overgrown forest of unorganized pictures" [19] (surely a fair assessment of one of the problems of twentieth century man). Both mind and eye had a surfeited, incoherent impression of the world, and a new language, integrating the visual and the mental processes, could clarify a muddled America for muddled Americans.

Lindsay's analysis[20] of the mechanism of the hieroglyphic picture was complicated. He saw in it a triple meaning. First, visual reality; the hieroglyphic for D, for instance, looked like a hand. Second, it had an associated meaning, based on the association of ideas—the hand of God, for example. In its third sense, the hieroglyphic was an abstraction; D, hand, could indicate death (the pouring of poison), or a Eureka charm (opening all doors). What Lindsay ignored in his theory was that the second and third meanings of a hieroglyphic were subjective, and likely to differ. He wanted to believe in an American type which could come to subscribe automatically to a conscious and national symbolism, which would come to associate a torch with the Statue of Liberty, then with liberty, and the censer with purification, then with civic reform. His conception of hieroglyphics was of an art which knew exactly what it was saying, and which said it unmistakably, and of an art which would contribute to the development of national patterns of thought and conduct.

"All my theories are of the relation of pictures to poems, and I could talk circles round the imagists on that subject . . . ," [21] Lindsay wrote, recognizing such comparable attempts to compress and express an immediately identifiable idea as Ezra Pound's ideograms and Amy Lowell's vignette poems *Fir Flower Tablets,* both inspired by Chinese calligraphic representations. But although Lindsay used the word hieroglyphic freely and almost synonymously with any form of symbol or statement—he called his poems "hieroglyphics" and Buddha "the great hieroglyphic" [22]—his actual theory of the new art medium of hieroglyphics remained a theory of a visual, pictorial character.

Lindsay's excitement about hieroglyphics as a code to the American ethos made him verge on the didactic. But this was in theory only. In practice he fell short of compiling a laborious index to America. His description of hieroglyphic art leads one to expect rows of symbols, neat, dull depictions of recognizable objects: the last thing, in fact, to stimulate the nation. But his hieroglyphics, not obviously hieroglyphics, were romantic pictures, drawn in his characteristically ornate style, which was based on the Spencerian system of penmanship and took the unwindings and vibrating tensions of a watch spring as its decorative unit. As pictures they did not represent a new art form; nevertheless, the idea behind Lindsay's hieroglyphic failures (an idea largely hidden by them)— the development of a visual art with a national and social application—was comparatively novel. As with his "Republic of Letters" characterization of somewhat more intellectual government in America, he overstated his case, and clouded a point which was less pretentious and controversial than would appear from his high flown talk of a "United States Hieroglyphics." But he did seem to think that sets of pictures with obvious meanings, hieroglyphics, could be common currency—new style Currier and Ives in every home—and in this sense form part of the national language. The function of such hieroglyphic pictures was to be unprecedently social and popular, but artistic technics, except in the sense of mass production, were to remain unchanged.

With these goals in mind it is possible to accept for the following selection of drawings the description "hieroglyphic" which Lindsay gave to them. However, the drawings still recall Lindsay's ambitious plan to cross the borderline between letters and art. Although this plan never materialized, as a result his poems were illustrated and his pictures inscribed (a consequence, too, of his determination that his point should not be missed). He intended that "one need not have the Hieroglyphic grammars . . . to go into the understanding of such drawings. . . . One need not have to have read Swedenborg." [23] But the fact that none of Lindsay's hieroglyphics were without captions or text indicated too that he was unable to create what he meant by a hieroglyphic, a picture with a self-explanatory moral.

"The Soul of a Butterfly," "The Soul of a Spider," and "Lincoln's Tomb in Springfield" appeared first in 1910; "The Rose and the Lotus," in 1915; and "Celestial Trees," 1925. The first two are examples of Lindsay's failure to draw a picture with an implicit meaning; they are simply a butterfly and a spider unless it is explained that they are Beauty and Mammon. The third has a strange perspective which makes it hard to recognize as censers swinging over Lincoln's tomb in Springfield. The picture only becomes fully comprehensible through the poem that accompanies it, "The Soul of the City Receives the Gift of the Holy Spirit," that is, incense, or political purification, or civic reform, or social regeneration. It is not a successful hieroglyphic, but an illustration which acquires its significance only in conjunction with the text.

"The Rose and the Lotus" is perhaps Lindsay's closest approximation to designing a hieroglyphic in the Egyptian sense. It is a fusion of the rose and the lotus, complementing the poem "The Wedding of the Rose and the Lotus," written to celebrate the opening of the Panama Canal in 1915. In the full scale drawing it is possible to identify a rose and a lotus; in this solitary case we might understand that Lindsay intended the associated meaning to be harmony between East and West and the abstraction behind the picture, world peace.

The last of these hieroglyphics is taken from *Going-to-the-Sun,* 1923, one of three books of Lindsay's illustrated verse which ap-

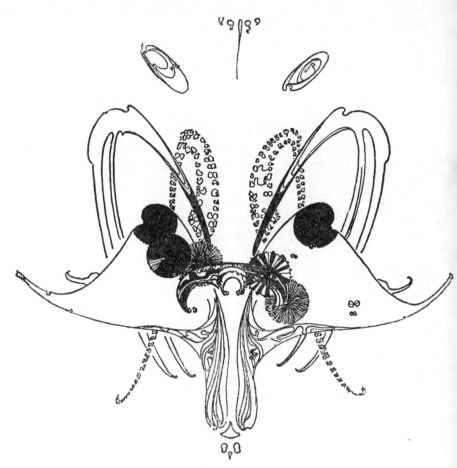

THE SOUL OF A BUTTERFLY

The thing that breaks Hell's prison bars,
  And heals the sea of shame,
Is a fragile butterfly's great soul
  And Beauty is its name.

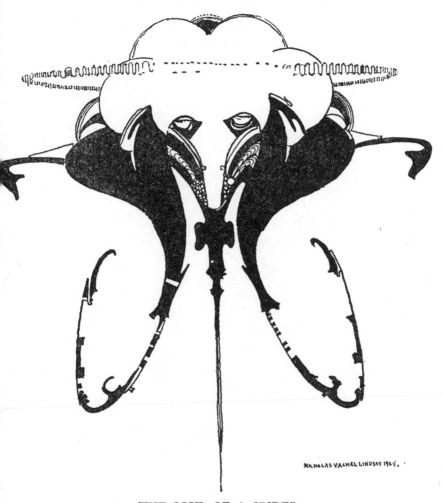

NICHOLAS VACHEL LINDSAY 1904.

THE SOUL OF A SPIDER

The thing that eats the rotting stars
　　On the black sea-beach of shame
Is a giant spider's deathless soul,
　　And Mammon is its name.

Lincoln's Tomb in Springfield

The Rose and the Lotus

peared in the twenties. It is an apology of an American hieroglyphic, with its Egyptian-style sun, pyramids, lotus-type leaves,
and Lindsay's hieroglyphic signature. This illustration of the poem
"Celestial Trees" (though Lindsay claimed the poem described
the picture, not vice versa), emphasizes the continuity of Egyptian
influence and artistic endeavor in Lindsay's life (he was planning
a book on American art, and a book of American sketches—we
know no details—when he died). The contents of this hieroglyphic

(From *Going-to-the-Sun* by Vachel Lindsay © 1923, D. Appleton and Co.)

Celestial Trees

may also provoke surprise that if Lindsay could incorporate such overt and simple symbols of Egyptian society in a picture, he did not devise a picture around Washington's profile, a rail splitter, or the Stars and Stripes. It is unlikely that this was what he was planning for American sketches; for such pictures would visually suggest an unequivocal approval of America, which Lindsay could not in conscience give. He lacked the skill to put into pictures the mixture of caution and hope, pride and reservation which he successfully conveyed in his words about the American entity. One wonders if American sketches would ever have materialized.

The apparent far-fetchedness of Lindsay's theory of hieroglyphics—his claim to have approximated a combination of pictures and words in a new art form, his description of illustrations as independent hieroglyphics, symbolic pictures—is not without aptness for his philosophy. It underlines the intensity, even to incongruity, of his devotion to indigenous American growth in all spheres; though his hieroglyphics falsely suggests precision and a new alphabet, and boils down to imaginative, moral artists making symbolic pictures for deprived, inquiring audiences. Lindsay fell as far short of the ambitions of his hieroglyphics as of his cartoons, but his own failure should not detract from—indeed it makes more poignant—his sincere attempt, both as praiseworthy and as unlikely to succeed as his literary convention, to find a means to diffuse his American ideology through the potentially commanding medium of a mass art.

MOVING PICTURES

Another sort of picture and another sort of mass art which Lindsay considered for its social uses in America was the motion picture. The first edition of *The Art of the Moving Picture* was published in 1915. It aroused little notice then, and has been virtually ignored since, though Lindsay's comments on motion pictures as an interacting artistic and educative medium and on the nature of the medium of cinema were perceptive and farsighted and remain relevant.

A good amount of literature on motion pictures began to appear about 1926, four years after the second edition of Lindsay's book in 1922. The literature fell into two categories. One was negative and censorious, deploring the low moral standard of motion pictures, and the inert leisure activity of movie-going. The other was exemplified in Terry Ramsaye's *A Million and One Nights* and Iris Barry's *Let's Go to the Pictures,* both published in 1926. They were narrative histories of the motion picture industry, lengthy descriptions of films, stars, and producers. Both writers acknowledged the existence of Lindsay's book, Barry in her bibliography and in plagiarizing Lindsay for her comments on films as painting and architecture, Ramsaye in his dismissive prologue.

A slight, tentative beginning of screen discussion and appraisal was made by Vachel Lindsay in his *Art of the Moving Picture,* published about 1916. It was largely a rhapsody from the viewpoint of a poet sitting in Springfield, Illinois, theatre, capable for its day and pleasant, but neither professional nor possessing penetration.[24]

But penetration was the quality that *The Art of The Moving Picture* had in abundance. It recognized, even in the jerky, silent films, artistic potential. The cinema, Lindsay argued, came nearer than any other to portraying the human soul in action. Because of its mobility it was adding a fourth dimension to the existing media of architecture, painting and sculpture, and at its best "THE MOTION PICTURE IS A GREAT ART." [25]

It is impossible to discuss Lindsay's comments on contemporary motion pictures. They are not in circulation and descriptions of them are varied and patchy. Broadly speaking, however, there was little visual art—though plenty of visual entertainment—in the films showing in Lindsay's lifetime. Prior to 1915, cinema had drawn largely on slapstick, sentiment, the Bible, Shakespeare, and history. In 1913 Chaplin starred for the first time (though Lindsay thought that while Chaplin had artistic, even aesthetic qualities, his films as a whole fell short of art). In 1915 "Birth of a Nation" appeared; Lindsay enthused about it technically (it was the first film to experiment with the mobile camera) and he thought W. D. Griffith helped prove Thomas Dixon's point that Simon Legree was not fictitious. Post-war years were dominated by the emergence and dominance of Cecil B. De Mille and sex. Not until 1925 came two films, Eisenstein's "Strike" and "Potemkin," which began to bear out Lindsay's contention that cinema was an art.

The first talkie, "The Jazz Singer," 1927, was paradoxically a setback for the cinema as art: obstrusiveness and lack of coordination outweighed novelty. Lindsay anticipated that sound would initially hamper the visual cinema; that while realism would increase, the incentive to act would diminish. He was hostile to the increase in prices (and subsequently less representative audiences) which he felt would accompany the installation of complicated phonographic equipment. But his theories needed little modification for sound: perhaps a little less emphasis on the deliberate gesture, and the complete repudiation of his notion of talking intelligently to one's companion during films (he virtually made this repudiation in the 1922 edition, having conducted some embarrassing experiments).

The importance of unique visual effects, and, above all, of motion remained. For motion, Lindsay argued, gave the new medium its intrinsic artistic potential and its uniquely American appeal. Cinema had the aesthetic and emotional qualities found in other art forms, with the added advantage, for the restless, unmeditative Americans, that they were in motion. At their best films could be described as painting-in-motion, furniture-in-motion, and sculpture-in-motion. Giant figures, with lights playing on them, were like lime-white plaster casts, gamins like sharply carved wooden figures, cowboys like bronze in the pantherish elasticity of their tendons and ligaments, a tableau of a masked man, a fainting girl, and a hero like an unglazed clay group. Lindsay almost seemed to be anticipating color films; he certainly had a fine and sensitive perception of the tones, planes, textures, and effects possible in the cinema.

He also saw the motion picture as architecture-in-motion; and in the light of his affinity with Frank Lloyd Wright it is curious to find a writer in the *Little Review,* noting that "Wright objects to Lindsay saying his art can be that of moving pictures, its very literalness, its actualness being the very negation of the soul and construction of art." [26] This statement seems an unlikely one in view of Wright's frequent claims for architecture of the characteristics of other art forms. If the statement in the *Little Review* is accurately attributed, one can only conclude that like so many others in various spheres of art, Wright was unable to see past the unaesthetic jerks and crackly textures of early films which make them seem ludicrous art. Lindsay was, in fact, making the Wrightian point that when people, furnishings, decor, and exterior structure were seen as a unit, as they could be on the screen, the harmony and the social function of good architecture would be crystal clear. Perhaps his views were misrepresented to Wright; few reviewers seem to have done them justice.

Lindsay's classification of films and film potential was based on the differences between cinema and stage. (Most people thought that the only claim the cinema might have to art lay in an imitation of the stage.) He was not interested in seeing great plays revived on the screen for mass audiences, but in using the unique qualities of the screen, its immediacy, its technics of close-up, panorama, flash-back, and superimposition to achieve an impact unattainable in any other medium. The "photoplay of action" [27] could harmlessly gratify an already rampant speed mania; the "intimate photoplay" [28] made the audience uniquely privileged, semi-involved viewers of the lives and thoughts of people apparently off guard; and films of "Splendor" [29]—epics—could deal impressively with historical, patriotic, and religious themes; they could bring America's past and the international present to every American. The nation could be indoctrinated and enjoy it. Lindsay likened the nationwide cinema audience, which existed in the early days of cinema, to "an astonishing assembly of cave-men crawling out of their shelters to exhibit for the first time in history a common interest on a tremendous scale in an art form." He was scathing, but hopeful. Before the advent of the motion picture the American masses were "rotting for the lack of folk-imagination. The Man with the Hoe had no spark in his brain. But now a light is blazing. We can build the American soul broad-based from the foundations." [30]

He was making his customary connection between democracy, morality, and culture.

Although Lindsay was speaking with professional authority about a new art form, he genuinely identified with the average movie-goer's fascination with film stars. He had soft spots for John Bunny and Mae Marsh, about whom he wrote poems; but he also approved of the star system because it complemented the national pantheon of historical heroes and contemporary political leaders by pointing up individuals who could be foci for nationally shared emotions. Artists as creators of emotional and cultural American oneness—what could be more pleasing to him? He appraised Mary Pickford in a neo-social sense as "Queen of My People"; and he repeatedly celebrated her national visual impact in a way comparable to such pop art statement paintings as Andy Warhol's "Marilyn Monroe." In many senses he was a precursor and practitioner of present day pop art. He affirmed that movies which catered to popular taste were valid reflections of "the human soul in action," and constituted neo-artistic perceptions; and as an artist, by acts of will, representation, and reproduction, he made these perceptions total art. His belief in the communication potential of silent films as a nationally recognized alphabet of images bears comparison with the pop art theory of the interchangeability of words and pictures. "Edison is the new Gutenberg. He has invented the new printing," [31] Lindsay wrote; and his own hieroglyphics was another would-be public art, an easily identified currency of national symbols. The same can also be said of his verbal collage[32] of popcorn and yellow cabs, Arrow-collar heroes and the Star Spangled Banner, which preoccupied him as realistically and as sentimentally as it does many pop artists.

But Lindsay diverged from the main stream of pop art; while pop artists tend to draw the line at comment, his aim was propaganda. He was as much concerned in creating as in accepting popular culture, and he was interested in new media for the specific purposes of uplifting and educating the masses. He imagined, for instance, that American democracy might be improved by

Whitmanesque scenarios, based on moods akin to that of the poem "By Blue Ontario's Shore." The possibility of showing the entire American population its own face in the Mirror Screen has at last come. Whitman brought the idea of democracy to our sophisticated literati, but did not persuade the democracy itself to read his democratic poems. Sooner or later the kinetoscope will do what he [and Lindsay might have added himself] could not, bring the nobler side of the equality idea to the people who are so crassly equal.[33]

Perennial American theories could find fitting expression. The Passage to India would make a good theme; so would a film about Julia Ward Howe and the "Battle Hymn of the Republic." But, as ever, Lindsay did not confine himself to American boundaries. Ultimately the cinema would have a supra-American function. Films in the spirit of such titles as "Letting the Crowds be Good" and "Letting the Crowds be Beautiful" would not only spread his gospel in America but "would help to make world-voters of us all." The motion picture could mean that the end to isolation and the union of humanity was a little nearer.

The World State is indeed far away. But as we peer into the Mirror Screen some of us dare look forward to the time when the pouring streets of men will become sacred in each other's eyes, in pictures and in fact.[34]

A conviction that the motion picture could go as far as the newspaper into the social fabric led Lindsay to an ambitious program for its development. The fact that neither its audience nor its sponsors were an intellectual elite was for many people an obstacle to putting an artistic construction on the cinema, but was one of the reasons for Lindsay's keen interest in it. Films were often denigrated on the grounds that their popular appeal presupposed a lack of culture in the medium, but Lindsay took the opposite view. In the arts

such work as we have is pretty largely a cult by the wealthy. This is the more a cause for misgiving because in a democracy, the arts, like the political parties, are not founded till they have touched the county

chairman, the ward leader, the individual voter. The [film] museums
in a democracy should go as far as the public libraries.³⁵

Nationally and locally, through the central production of ethical
and artistic films, through motion picture lending libraries, and
through motion picture creativity in the communities of the New
Localism, the level of American education and aesthetic appreciation could be raised. Each town would have its "photographic news
press" and its trailers for local activities. Films should be used as
much as books in schools and colleges, not only as teaching aids,
but for the circularization of state papers and other not readily
accessible materials. Congressmen could send films of their activities to their constituents. Universities could show theses to the
whole faculty on the cinema screen. (He was thinking of large,
captive audiences, not of the scholarly utility of microfilm).

Lindsay did not succeed in popularizing his ideas about the
motion picture as a starting point for painless education in morality, culture, Americanness, and world citizenship even at a theoretical level. But he did have the distinction of being the *New
Republic's* first film critic. Disappointingly his reviews were mere
narratives of the films' stories with a little moralizing thrown in.
He failed to take advantage of the opportunity to put over his
propaganda regularly; he mentioned his motion picture theories
almost casually. Perhaps he expected everyone to have read his
book; or perhaps since he found it hard to be succinct and to
come directly to the point, he could not adapt himself to a medium
of a few hundred words. His reviews were probably prologues to
reviews; by the time he had sketched the story, and was ready to
move on to his own ideas, he had already used up his allotted space.

The Art of the Moving Picture was in use for a time in a
scenario-writing course at Columbia University; and once, in 1923,
Lindsay was invited to lecture to a section of the film world in
Hollywood. It delighted him on that occasion that Mary Pickford
gave a reception in his honor: the apparent accolade from his and
Everyman's queen. But the film world was welcoming the publicity he gave them rather than taking his theories seriously. For
although Lindsay did not talk about censorship, he was unmistak-

ably close to the position made explicit by Pius XI in his encyclical
Vigilanti Cura, 1936, which pointed out that the film's power for
good could just as easily be a power for evil.

In the socio-literary world, only the articulate feminist Charlotte
Perkins Gilman seems to have approached motion pictures in the
same spirit as Lindsay. Their affinity was not surprising; a certain
community of thought was evident from her book titles, bristling
with social conscience: *The Home, its Work and its Influence,*
1901, for example. Like Lindsay, Charlotte Gilman advocated
motion picture libraries, and foresaw an international function
for the motion picture as "the long-sought 'universal language,'
for it spreads communication world-wide and as swift as eye can
follow." Perhaps she was thinking of Lindsay, and his books on
Springfield and motion pictures when she imagined that "vision-
aries, wishing for better towns, could have films made showing
the worst we have, and the better ones we are going to have." [36]

Of all Lindsay's suggestions about the different media for
popular morality and culture—popular in the diffused, not the
debased sense of the word—his advocacy of the motion picture
seems the most sensible and exciting. The role he envisaged for
motion pictures—educative in both knowledge and beauty, com-
municative in current affairs—was an anticipation of the role that
is being increasingly played by television, the descendent of the
motion picture which is available not only as a public but as a
private facility. Lindsay's emphasis on motion picture lending
libraries, the filing of archival material, and on weekly local films,
stemmed from his wish to see a mass medium which functioned
regularly and was available to each American, as television now is.

Lindsay made the same demands of audio-visual mass media
as he did of other art forms: that they should be oriented to a
specific set of ideas, and churn out chosen messages in a number
of disguises. As in his assessment of other art forms, he underestimated the effect of audience demand for pure entertainment,
for the trivial, the sensational, the risque. He had minimized the
fact that the motion picture (and, after his time, television) was a

dangerously commercial proposition; that it involved playing to the audience, and the deliberate creation of light, easy to satisfy, mass tastes. In his eagerness to emphasize the artistic potential of the motion picture he had joined the film makers in opposing their critics: "THE MOTION PICTURE IS A GREAT ART, NOT A PROCESS OF COMMERCIAL MANUFACTURE." [37] He implicitly recognized the pitfalls, but it served his purpose and furbished his hopes to forget them.

Nevertheless, much of what Lindsay wanted for the motion picture in America has come about in television. It is a teaching aid in school and university; local television networks give good coverage to local affairs, and national networks to national affairs. Moreover, what he had hoped would come about through motion pictures has been realized by television: Americans cannot help knowing something about other countries, although with an American bias. Television's artistic qualities are, of course, by nature of the smallness of the screen, not identical with those of motion pictures, but they share the same proximate and mesmeric qualities which seemed to Lindsay their special social merits.

The pictures that appeared on the cinema screen were symbols for Lindsay. They meant that America might come to see herself and improve herself, to draw together and to look outward, and that such a process of social transformation could happen in conjunction with art and beauty. I imagine that even if Lindsay saw the mixture of the trite and the serious on American television, he would not retract his premise that the very existence of a compulsive means of communication is a head start for a would-be democracy. (For democracy, that is, as Lindsay conceived it, compounded of individuals leading not too dissimilar lives and abiding by common philosophical outlines.) Certainly the amount of instructive material put out by American television is considerably more than the amount of film Hollywood and private companies allotted to educational films in his lifetime. Lindsay would, in fact, find democratic art today straggling along the path he thought it should take. Television is a potential art form in potentially moral and cultural homes, a mixture of dross and quality that is at the same time the partial negation of Lindsay's belief in the possibility of social art, the type of mass medium he was searching for, and one which, to an extent, he anticipated.

Conclusion

L INDSAY'S THEORY of art forms and society was yet another manifestation of his solicitude for America, and of the unity of approach which he brought to a diversity of subject. Some words he wrote for the introduction to *Collected Poems,* in 1923, sum up the range of his solicitude, and they serve equally well to point up the conclusion of this book.

This America will take long to ripen. It will be longer to our goal than from Adam to Mary of Bethlehem. If we are millennialists, we must be patient millennialists. Yet let us begin to-day as though the Millennium were to-morrow, and start our "Village Improvement Parade" down Main Street, and turn the corner east toward the rising sun to a land of clear pictures and young hearts.[1]

Here is the Lindsay of realistic analyses and rational expectations, who nevertheless retained a certain innocence and a certain emotional faith: fitting attributes for one who matched his scheme for good old values in brave new surroundings.

But one part of the essential Lindsay is missing from this quotation, the Lindsay who could write, inimitably—

In a nation of one hundred fine, mob-hearted, lynching, relenting,
*   repenting millions,*
There are plenty of sweeping, swinging, stinging, gorgeous things to
*   shout about,*
And knock your old blue devils out.[2]

And again, Lindsay was at one with his words: the man who with mind and voice affirmed so much that was American; not the least by formulating and holding fast his convictions of promise and threat, dream and nightmare in an America where the organic process and the collective mind opposed him. Vachel Lindsay was himself one of the American phenomena worth shouting about.

Selected Bibliography

LINDSAY'S MILIEU has already been documented in the notes to each chapter, but there remain several areas to be covered in a list of sources: primary materials; "standard" commentaries and secondary sources, which, although inadequate, do provide a picture of the old and contemporary images of Lindsay; a short guide to his aims and the reactions he provoked as seen through a selection of letters and comments he sent to periodicals, and their treatment of him; and finally, works worth consulting for their brief but perceptive comments on Lindsay.

PRIMARY SOURCES
Lindsay, Nicholas Vachel

War Bulletin No. I. Springfield, Ill., July 19, 1909.

War Bulletin No. II. Springfield, Ill., Aug. 4, 1909.

War Bulletin No. III. Springfield, Ill., Aug. 30, 1909.

The Tramp's Excuse and Other Poems [*War Bulletin No. IV*]. Springfield, Ill., 1909.

War Bulletin No. V. Springfield, Ill., Thanksgiving 1909.

The Spring Harbinger. Pamphlet. Springfield, Ill., 1909 or 1910.

The Village Magazine. Springfield, Ill.: The Jeffersons Printing Co., 1910; revised editions 1920, 1925.

Rhymes to be Traded for Bread. Springfield, Ill., 1912.

General William Booth Enters into Heaven and Other Poems. New York: Mitchell Kennerley, 1913; New York: The Macmillan Co., 1916; English edition, London: Chatto & Windus, 1919.

The Congo and Other Poems. New York: Mitchell Kennerley, 1914.

Adventures While Preaching the Gospel of Beauty. New York: Mitchell Kennerley, 1914; New York: The Macmillan Co., 1921.

The Art of the Moving Picture. New York: The Macmillan Co., 1915; reissued 1916; revised edition 1922.

A Handy Guide for Beggars. New York: The Macmillan Co., 1916.

A Letter about My Four Programmes for Committees in Correspondence. Pamphlet. Springfield, Ill. [1916?].

The Chinese Nightingale and Other Poems. New York: The Macmillan Co., 1917.

The Kind of a Visit I Like to Make. Broadside, Springfield, Ill., 1919.

The Golden Whales of California. New York: The Macmillan Co., 1920.

The Golden Book of Springfield. New York: The Macmillan Co., 1920.

The Daniel Jazz and Other Poems. London: G. Bell & Sons, 1920.

A Letter for Your Wicked Private Ear Only. Pamphlet. Springfield, Ill., 1920.

Collected Poems. New York: The Macmillan Co., 1923; illustrated edition, New York: The Macmillan Co., 1925. Many reissues.

The Candle in the Cabin. New York: D. Appleton & Co., 1923.

Going-to-the-Sun. New York: D. Appleton & Co., 1923.

Going-to-the-Stars. New York: D. Appleton & Co., 1926.

Johnny Appleseed and Other Poems. New York: The Macmillan Co., 1928.

Rigmarole, Rigmarole. New York: Random House Poetry Quartos, 1929.

The Litany of Washington Street. New York: The Macmillan Co., 1929.

Every Soul is a Circus. New York: The Macmillan Co., 1929.

Selected Poems of Vachel Lindsay. Ed. Hazelton Spencer. New York: The Macmillan Co., 1931.

Selected Poems of Vachel Lindsay. Ed. Mark Harris. New York: The Macmillan Co., 1963.

The best description of Lindsay's broadsides, nearly all of which appear, scaled-down and scattered, in the works listed, is by Cecil K. Byrd in *Indiana University Bookman,* V, December 1960, though his checklist is confined to the Lilly Library's (substantial) holdings.

Other important primary sources were:

Armstrong, A. J., ed. "Letters of Nicholas Vachel Lindsay to A. J. Armstrong." *Baylor Bulletin,* 43 (1940), iii.

The George Mathew Adams Vachel Lindsay Collection, Dartmouth College Library; especially letters between Lindsay and John Drinkwater and Lindsay and Floyd Dell.

The Lilly Library's Lindsayana, Indiana University; especially the Frederic Melcher and Upton Sinclair mss., and Lindsay's yearbook,

The Spider Web, X, Junior Class Annual, Hiram College. Chicago, A. L. Swift & Co., 1900. Copy heavily annotated by Lindsay.

The Vachel Lindsay Collection, Clifton Waller Barrett Library, University of Virginia at Charlottesville. A substantial deposit of Lindsayana, containing drafts and proofs of published and unpublished works, juvenilia, scrapbooks, letters, personal possessions.

The Harriet Monroe Collection and the Harriet Moody Collection, University of Chicago, which contain many letters to and from Vachel and Elizabeth Lindsay.

COMMENTARIES

Graham, Stephen. *Tramping with a Poet in the Rockies.* London: Macmillan & Co. Ltd, 1922.

Harris, Mark. *City of Discontent.* Indianapolis: Bobbs-Merrill, 1952.

Heffernan, Miriam Margaret. "The Ideas and Methods of Vachel Lindsay." Ph.D. dissertation, New York State University, 1948.

Masters, Edgar Lee. *Vachel Lindsay, a Poet in America.* New York: Charles Scribner's Sons, 1935.

Ruggles, Eleanor. *The West-going Heart. A Life of Vachel Lindsay.* New York: W. W. Norton & Co., Inc., 1959.

Trombly, Albert Edward. *Vachel Lindsay, Adventurer.* Columbia, Mo.: Lucas Brothers, 1929.

Yatron, Michael. *America's Literary Revolt.* New York: The Philosophical Library, 1959.

LINDSAY SEEN THROUGH THE MEDIUM OF PERIODICALS

Bookman
> LXXIV, 6, March 1932: Conrad Aiken, "A Letter from Vachel Lindsay."
>
> LXXV, 1, April 1932: Henry Morton Robinson, "The Ordeal of Vachel Lindsay."

The Little Review
> I, March, May, and November 1914 (November: Eunice Tietjens, "Vachel Lindsay's Books.")
>
> II, April 1916. A selection of reactions to Lindsay on the movies.
>
> IV, January 1918. Reader-Critic parody of Lindsay.

The New Republic
> I, December 5, 1914. Reviews of Lindsay's first three commercially published books.

V, December 25, 1915. Review of *The Art of the Moving Picture*.

X, November 18, and December 9, 1916. Francis Hackett and Harriet Monroe disagree about Lindsay.

X, March 10, and April 28, 1917. Two typical Lindsay movie reviews.

XXI, Febuary 1920. George Washington Cable assesses Lindsay.

XXIII, January 23, 1920. Lindsay, "Lincoln and the Political Prisoners," a letter pleading post-war tolerance for dissenters from the American war effort.

Poetry

IV, April–September 1914. "Mr. Lindsay on Primitive Singing."

XI, October–March 1917–18. "A note from Mr. Lindsay."

XVII, October–March 1920–21. "Notes and views from Mr. Lindsay."

XVIV, April–September 1924. Harriet Monroe, "Vachel Lindsay."

XXIX, October–March 1926–27. Harriet Monroe, "The Limnal Lindsay."

XL, April–September 1932. Harriet Monroe, "The Poet in the Orchard of Art."

SOURCES OF PERCEPTIVE COMMENTS

Chesterton, Gilbert Keith. *All I Survey*. London: Methuen & Co. Ltd., 1933.

Duffey, Bernard. *The Chicago Renaissance*. East Lansing: The Michigan State College Press, 1954.

Dunbar, Olivia. *A House in Chicago*. Chicago: The University of Chicago Press, 1947.

Frost, Robert. *The Letters of Robert Frost to Louis Untermeyer*, ed. Louis Untermeyer. London: Jonathan Cape, 1964.

Lindsay, Elizabeth Conner. *Inventory of the Lindsayana Collection in Springfield, Illinois, December 23, 1949*.

Lowell, Amy. *A Critical Fable*. Boston: Houghton Mifflin & Co., 1922.

Mencken, Henry Louis. *Vachel Lindsay: The True Voice of Middle America*. Pamphlet. Washington, D.C., 1947.

Monroe, Harriet. *A Poet's Life*. New York: The Macmillan Co., 1938.

Phelps, William Lyon. *The Advance of English Poetry in the Twentieth Century*. New York: Dodd, Mead & Co., 1919.

Phelps, William Lyon. *Autobiography, with Letters*. New York: Oxford University Press, 1939.

Rittenhouse, Jessie. *My House of Life*. Boston: Houghton Mifflin, 1934.

Notes

INTRODUCTION

1. *Indiana University Bookman*, V (1960), p. 41. Letter to Frederic Melcher, June 10, 1927.

2. Lindsay, *Rhymes to be Traded for Bread* (Springfield, Ill., 1912).

3. Lindsay, *Collected Poems* (New York: The Macmillan Co., 1962), p. 335.

4. "Letters of Nicholas Vachel Lindsay to A. J. Armstrong," ed. A. J. Armstrong, *Baylor Bulletin*, 43, iii (Waco, Tex., 1940), p. 41.

5. *Collected Poems*, pp. 352–53.

6. Ibid., pp. 437–41.

7. Ibid., pp. 15–16; Eleanor Ruggles, *The West-going Heart* (New York: W. W. Norton & Co., Inc., 1959), pp. 37, 258.

8. Armstrong, p. 91; see also pp. 91–97, a letter devoted to Mrs. Lindsay.

9. Jessie B. Rittenhouse, *My House of Life* (Boston: Houghton Mifflin, 1934), p. 295.

10. Olive Lindsay Wakefield, "Alexander Campbell," *The Shane Quarterly*, V (Apr.–Jul. 1944), pp. 101–102; Lindsay, *Collected Poems*, p. 355.

11. *Rhymes to be Traded for Bread*, p. 16.

12. Edgar Lee Masters, *Vachel Lindsay* (New York: Charles Scribner's Sons, 1935), p. 361. The measure of his intermittently acute persecution complex can be gauged from "Twenty Years Ago," Lindsay, *Every Soul is a Circus* (New York: The Macmillan Co., 1929), pp. 109–15.

13. "Vachel Lindsay's Books," *The Little Review*, I (Nov. 1914), p. 57.

14. *The Letters of Ezra Pound*, ed. D. D. Paige (London: Faber & Faber, 1959), pp. 127, 54.

15. Ruggles, p. 389. Reprinted with the permission of the publishers, W. W. Norton & Co., and the Estate of Vachel Lindsay.

16. *Every Soul Is a Circus,* p. 109.

17. Abel Sanders, "Reader-Critic," *The Little Review,* IV (Jan. 1918), p. 55; parodying "Daniel," *Collected Poems,* pp. 159–61.

18. *A Letter for Your Wicked Private Ear Only,* pamphlet (Springfield, Ill., 1920), pp. 5–6; Armstrong, p. 25.

19. Masters, p. 285. Sample critical judgments may be seen in the works cited in Chap. 1, note 4.

20. Masters, p. 354. The seven posthumous books were submitted to the Macmillan Co., New York, in 1932 and were rejected.

21. *Collected Poems,* pp. 5–6.

22. Masters, p. 77.

23. Lindsay, *The Village Magazine* (Springfield, Ill: The Jeffersons Printing Co., 1920), p. 87. This quotation and much of the prose in *The Village Magazine* were printed in capitals throughout, not from typeface, but from Lindsay's own crabbed capitals: difficult to read, but probably intended to personalize, simplify, and enlarge the appeal of his ideas (perhaps too it was an economy measure; the first edition was printed in 1910, before he began to earn). Even in printer's capitals the effect is hard on the eye.

24. Armstrong, p. 27.

25. *A Letter for Your Wicked Private Ear Only,* p. 24.

1. ORIENTATION

1. Lindsay, *Collected Poems* (New York: The Macmillan Co., 1962), p. 71.

2. Edgar Lee Masters, *Vachel Lindsay* (New York: Charles Scribner's Sons, 1935), pp. 203–204.

3. Lindsay, *Adventures While Preaching the Gospel of Beauty* (New York: Mitchell Kennerley, 1914), p. 184.

4. Fred B. Millett, *Contemporary American Authors* (New York: Harcourt, Brace & Co., 1940), p. 138; Louis Untermeyer, *Modern American Poetry* (London: Jonathan Cape, 1921), p. 217; T. K. Whipple, *Spokesmen* (Berkeley: University of California Press, 1963), p. 194. See also Conrad Aiken, *A Reviewer's A.B.C.* (London: George Allen & Unwin, 1961); Bruce Weirick, *From Whitman to Sandburg* (New York: The Macmillan Co., 1924.)

5. *Collected Poems,* pp. 327–28.

6. Ibid., p. xl.

7. Henry Demarest Lloyd, *Man the Social Creator* (New York: Doubleday, Page & Co., 1906), p. 208.

8. *Adventures While Preaching the Gospel of Beauty,* pp. 46–47.

9. Eleanor Ruggles, *The West-going Heart* (New York: W. W. Norton & Co. Inc., 1959), p. 262.

10. *Collected Poems,* p. 201.

11. Ibid., p. 154.

12. Ibid., pp. 273, 331.

13. Ruggles, p. 398.

14. *Collected Poems,* p. lx.

15. Van Wyck Brooks, *America's Coming-of-Age* (New York: B. W. Huebsch, 1915), p. 153.

16. Malcolm Cowley, *Exile's Return* (London: The Bodley Head, 1951), p. 217.

17. George Ade, *Forty Modern Fables* (New York: R. H. Russell, 1901), p. 11.

18. Lindsay, *The Village Magazine* (Springfield, Ill.: The Jeffersons Printing Co., 1910) [p. 67].

19. *Collected Poems,* p. 74.

20. Ibid., p. xxvi.

21. *The Village Magazine,* 1920, p. 68.

22. Ibid; *Adventures While Preaching the Gospel of Beauty,* p. 178.

23. *The Village Magazine,* 1910 [p. 67].

24. *The Village Magazine,* 1920, pp. 68–71.

25. Masters, p. 67.

26. Arthur Schlesinger, *The Rise of the City* (New York: The Macmillan Co., 1910), p. 436.

27. *Collected Poems,* pp. 340–41.

28. Joseph Hudnut, *Architecture and the Spirit of Man* (Cambridge: Harvard University Press, 1949), p. 352.

29. *Collected Poems,* pp. 62–63, 346. With characteristic ambivalence "Springfield Magical" was also "The City of my Discontent," p. 62.

30. Lewis Mumford, *The Story of Utopias* (London: George Harrap & Co., 1923), pp. 292–93.

31. Frank Lloyd Wright, *An Autobiography* (London: Faber & Faber, 1945), p. 280.

32. Carl Sandburg, *Complete Poems* (New York: Harcourt, Brace & Co., 1950), p. 79.

33. *Adventures While Preaching the Gospel of Beauty,* p. 173.

34. Lindsay, *A Handy Guide for Beggars* (New York: The Macmillan Co., 1916), p. 167.

35. *Adventures While Preaching the Gospel of Beauty*, p. 172.

36. *Collected Poems*, p. 53.

37. "John Burroughs at Troutbeck," *Troutbeck Leaflets No. 10* (Amenia, N.Y.: Troutbeck Press, 1926), p. 3.

38. Mary P. Follett, *The New State* (New York: Longman, Green & Co., 1918), pp. xii, 43.

39. John Dewey, *The Public and its Problems* (London: George Allen & Unwin, 1926), pp. 146, 215; *Freedom and Culture* (London: George Allen & Unwin Ltd., 1942), p. 169.

40. *Adventures While Preaching the Gospel of Beauty*, pp. 16, 182–84.

41. Ibid., p. 183; *Collected Poems*, p. xxxviii; Walter Johnson, *William Allen White's America* (New York: Henry Holt & Co., 1949), p. 14.

42. *Collected Poems*, p. 295.

43. *Adventures While Preaching the Gospel of Beauty*, p. 184.

44. *The Village Magazine*, p. 87.

45. Masters, p. 71.

46. *The Village Magazine*, p. 112.

47. Dewey, *The School and Society* (Chicago: University of Chicago Press, 1915), pp. 79–80.

48. *Collected Poems*, p. 277

49. *The Village Magazine*, p. 72.

50. Brand Whitlock, *Forty Years of It* (New York: D. Appleton & Co., 1914), p. 366. See *The Letters and Journal of Brand Whitlock,* ed. Allan Nevins (New York: D. Appleton-Century Co., 1936), p. 145.

51. Lindsay, *War Bulletin No. I* (Springfield, Ill., 1909), p. 2.

52. *Collected Poems*, p. 340.

53. Ibid., p. 192. See also "The Horrid Voice of Science" in *Others for 1919,* ed. Alfred Kreymbourg (New York: N. L. Brown, 1920), p. 100.

54. *Collected Poems*, frontispiece comment.

55. Ibid., p. lii.

56. Ibid., p. lvi.

57. Walter Rauschenbusch, *Christianizing the Social Order* (New York: The Macmillan Co., 1910), pp. 355–56, 420.

58. Lindsay, *The Art of the Moving Picture* (New York: The Macmillan Co., 1922), p. 244.

59. Masters, p. 84; Richard Hofstadter, *Social Darwinism* (Philadelphia: The American Historical Association, 1945), p. 90.

60. *War Bulletin No. III* (Springfield, Ill., 1909), p. 1; Eric Goldman, *Rendezvous with Destiny* (New York: A. A. Knopf, 1952), p. 119.

61. *Collected Poems*, p. 309.

62. Ibid., p. xxxix.

63. Herbert Croly, *The Promise of American Life* (New York: The Macmillan Co., 1912), pp. 401, 453.

64. *Collected Poems*, p. 395.

65. *The Art of the Moving Picture*, p. 263.

2. RELIGION

1. H. L. Mencken, *Prejudices,* 6th series (New York: A. A. Knopf, 1927), p. 108.

2. Lindsay, *Adventures While Preaching the Gospel of Beauty* (New York: Mitchell Kennerley, 1914), p. 15; *The Village Magazine* (Springfield, Ill., The Jeffersons Printing Co., 1920), p. 4.

3. Lindsay, *Collected Poems* (New York: The Macmillan Co., 1962), p. xxviii.

4. Lindsay, *War Bulletin No. III* (Springfield, Ill., 1909), p. 4.

5. Raymond B. Stevens, *The Social and Religious Influence of the Small Denominational College of the Middle West* (n.p., 1928), p. 29.

6. "Letters of Nicholas Vachel Lindsay to A. J. Armstrong," ed. A. J. Armstrong, *Baylor Bulletin*, 43, iii (Waco, Tex., 1940), p. 40.

7. *War Bulletin No. III,* p. 1

8. Lindsay, *The Golden Book of Springfield* (New York: The Macmillan Co., 1920), p. 3. See Robert Frederick West, *Alexander Campbell and Natural Religion* (New Haven: Yale University Press, 1948); Alexander Campbell, *An Address on the Amelioration of the Social State* (Louisville: Prentice and Weissinger, 1839); Robert Richardson, *Memoirs of Alexander Campbell* (Philadelphia: J. B. Lippincott & Co., 1871), the latter read by Lindsay.

9. *Collected Poems*, p. 352.

10. Ibid., pp. xxi–xxiii; *The Golden Book,* p. 7 and passim.

11. *Collected Poems*, p. 290.

12. *A Compendium of the Theological and Spiritual Writings of*

Emanuel Swedenborg (Boston: Crosby, Nichol & Otis Clapp, 1854), p. 59.

13. *The Golden Book*, p. 22.

14. Swedenborg, *The True Christian Religion* (London: J. D. Dent & Co., 1933), p. 836.

15. *Collected Poems*, pp. 163, 285–86.

16. Ibid., pp. xlix–lxii.

17. Algernon Swinburne, *William Blake* (London: John Camden Hotten, 1868), p. 4; read by Lindsay.

18. *Collected Poems*, p. 17.

19. Swedenborg, *Compendium*, p. 120.

20. Alexander Gilchrist, *Life of William Blake* (London: J. D. Dent & Co., 1880), pp. 210, 319; read by Lindsay; Lindsay, *War Bulletin No. III*, p. 3.

21. *The Village Magazine*, 1925, p. 167. See below, Chap. 6, pp. 128–29, for the possible influence of Mormonism on Lindsay. Zion City was a religious experiment he may have observed firsthand; it was a small town in northeastern Illinois, founded in 1901 by John Alexander Dowie for a sect known as the Christian Catholic Church. It survived as an experiment in theocratic government until 1935.

22. *Collected Poems*, pp. 159–60.

23. Edgar Lee Masters, *Vachel Lindsay* (New York: Charles Scribner's Sons, 1935), p. 172.

24. Gilchrist, p. 97.

25. *The Village Magazine*, 1920, p. 119.

26. Masters, pp. 62, 75, 79.

27. *Collected Poems*, pp. 208, 51–52; see also Masters, p. 165.

28. *Collected Poems*, pp. xlii, 212; see also pp. xlii–xliv.

29. Masters, p. 163.

30. *Collected Poems*, p. 124.

31. Ibid., p. 370.

32. Masters, p. 179; see Eleanor Ruggles, *The West-going Heart* (New York: W. W. Norton & Co., Inc., 1959), p. 109.

33. *Collected Poems*, p. lii.

34. Masters, p. 185.

35. Ibid., p. 135; Lindsay, *Collected Poems*, p. 249, also pp. 111–18.

36. Arthur E. Morgan, *The Philosophy of Edward Bellamy* (New York: Columbia University Press, 1944), p. 87; Edward Bellamy, *Selected Writings on Religion and Society,* ed. Joseph Schiffman, The

American Heritages Series no. 11 (Boston: D. C. Heath & Co., 1956), p. xxxvi.

37. *Collected Poems*, p. 318.

38. Quoted in Harriet Monroe, *A Poet's Life* (New York: Macmillan Co., 1939), p. 280.

39. *Collected Poems*, pp. 123, 160–61.

40. Ibid., p. 339.

41. *War Bulletin No. III*, p. 4.

42. See James Dombrowski, *The Early Days of Christian Socialism* (New York: Columbia University Press, 1936).

43. *Collected Poems*, p. 190; a pre-Garvey stance!

44. Ibid.

45. Ibid., pp. 316–17.

46. *Adventures While Preaching the Gospel of Beauty*, p. 40.

47. *Collected Poems*, pp. 347, 42; see also p. xliv.

48. Ibid., p. 27.

49. James Freeman Clarke, *Ten Great Religions* (Boston: Houghton, Mifflin, 1883) II, pp. 128–29.

50. *Collected Poems*, p. 188.

51. Lawrence Faucett, *Six Great Teachers of Morality* (Tokyo: Shinziki Shorin, 1952), pp. 53, 165.

52. *Collected Poems*, pp. 320–26. See below, Chap. 4, pp. 97–99 for an elaboration of Lindsay's view of women.

53. Ibid., p. 212.

3. EQUALITY

1. Edgar Lee Masters, *Vachel Lindsay* (New York: Charles Scribner's Sons, 1935), p. 67.

2. Lindsay, *Collected Poems* (New York: The Macmillan Co., 1962), p. 305.

3. Ibid., p. 260.

4. Ibid., pp. 93–94.

5. Lindsay, *Adventures While Preaching the Gospel of Beauty* (New York: Mitchell Kennerley, 1914), pp. 74–75.

6. *Collected Poems*, pp. 300–301.

7. Lindsay, *The Village Magazine* (Springfield, Ill.: The Jeffersons Printing Co., 1920), pp. 86, 87.

8. Lindsay, *Every Soul is a Circus* (New York: The Macmillan Co., 1931), p. 40.

9. Lindsay, *War Bulletin No. III* (Springfield, 1909), pp. 2–3.

10. *Collected Poems,* pp. 119, 122.

11. *Every Soul is a Circus*, pp. 1–14.

12. *Adventures While Preaching the Gospel of Beauty*, pp. 16–17.

13. Masters, p. 38.

14. Stephen Graham, *Tramping with a Poet in the Rockies* (London: Macmillan & Co., 1922), p. 167. Graham's account is verifiable within the general context of Lindsay's writings (see below, Ch. 7, pp. 172–74); but in *Going-to-the-Sun* (New York: D. Appleton & Co., 1923), pp. 2–3, Lindsay, though greatly attached to Graham, queried the total accuracy of Graham's report of what he (Lindsay) had said on their tramping expedition.

15. Lindsay, *The Litany of Washington Street* (New York: The Macmillan Co., 1929), p. 98.

16. Harriet Beecher Stowe, *Uncle Tom's Cabin* (London: Nathaniel Cooke, 1853), p. 188. Also comparable is the "Declaration of Principles" by the Women's Rights Convention at Seneca Falls, N.Y., in 1848, quoted in *The History of Woman Suffrage*, I, ed. Elizabeth Cady Stanton et al (New York: Fowler & Wells, 1881), pp. 70–71.

17. *Collected Poems*, p. 306.

18. Ibid., pp. 301–302.

19. *The Village Magazine*, p. 118.

20. *Collected Poems*, p. 266.

21. Michael Yatron, *America's Literary Revolt* (New York: The Philosophical Library, 1959), p. 100. Lindsay later abandoned his own pacifism (see below, Chap. 9, p. 201) and his support of Debs on this issue cooled (*Collected Poems*, p. xxxv.)

22. For Lindsay on Marx see *The Art of the Moving Picture* (New York: The Macmillan Co., 1922), p. 279, and Yatron, p. 101.

23. Lindsay, *The Chinese Nightingale* (New York: The Macmillan Co., 1917), pp. 53–54, 52.

24. Ibid., p. 19.

25. Ibid., pp. 20–21.

26. *Collected Poems*, p. 420.

27. Ibid., p. 100.

28. Ibid., pp. 367–68.

29. *War Bulletin No. I*, p. 1, *The Village Magazine*, p. 87.

30. Eleanor Ruggles, *The West-going Heart* (New York: W. W. Norton & Co., Inc., 1959), pp. 205–206. His poems for the very young

—children-to-be-read-aloud-to—were delightful: just credible fantasy. See *Collected Poems,* pp. 67–68, 219–21, 232, 241–42, 263–64.

31. Lindsay, *Going-to-the-Stars* (New York: D. Appleton & Co., 1926), p. 22.

32. *Collected Poems,* pp. 425–33.

33. Samuel M. Jones, *Letters of Love and Labor* (Indianapolis: Bobbs-Merill Co., 1900), p. 34.

34. *The Village Magazine,* p. 72.

4. BEAUTY

1. Lindsay, *Collected Poems* (New York: The Macmillan Co., 1962), p. 71.

2. Ibid., pp. 75, 76.

3. Edgar Lee Masters, *Vachel Lindsay* (New York: Charles Scribner's Sons, 1935), p. 15.

4. *Collected Poems,* pp. 71–72.

5. Lindsay, *The Village Magazine* (Springfield, Ill.: The Jeffersons Printing Co., 1920), p. 75; *War Bulletin No. III,* (Springfield, Ill., 1909), p.3.

6. See Richard Hofstadter, *The Age of Reform* (London: Jonathan Cape, 1962), p. 43. The myth was sufficiently strong for Thorstein Veblen to bother to attack it in *The Vested Interest and the Common Man* (London: George Allen & Unwin, 1919), p. 166.

7. *Collected Poems,* pp. 72–74.

8. A. L. Bader, "Vachel Lindsay on 'The Santa-Fé Trail,'" *American Literature,* XIX, 4 (Jan. 1948), 360–62.

9. *Collected Poems,* pp. 153–56.

10. Bader, loc. cit.

11. Eleanor Ruggles, *The West-going Heart* (New York: W. W. Norton & Co., Inc., 1959), pp. 116, 321; Lindsay, *Collected Poems,* pp. 56, 280, 301.

12. *Collected Poems,* p. 302.

13. Lindsay, *The Tramp's Excuse* (Springfield, Ill., 1909) [p. 8].

14. Ruggles, pp. 127, 332–33.

15. Masters, p. 68.

16. *Collected Poems,* pp. 232, 247, 237.

17. Ibid., pp. 42–43.

18. Masters, *The Sangamon* (New York: Farrar and Rinehart, 1942), p. 349. See below, Chap. 9 pp. 200–201.

19. *Collected Poems,* pp. 414, 433–34.

20. Ibid., p. 101.

21. Ruggles, pp. 311–12.

22. "Letters of Nicholas Vachel Lindsay to A. J. Armstrong," ed. A. J. Armstrong, *Baylor Bulletin,* IV, iii (Waco, Tex., 1942), pp. 40–41.

23. *Collected Poems,* pp. 69–70.

24. Jane Addams, *The Spirit of Youth and the City Streets* (New York: The Macmillan Co., 1909), pp. 146–47.

25. Lindsay pressed friends who stayed with him to read *Were You Ever a Child?* and then to accompany him on critical explorations of Springfield's schools. As associate literary editor of the *Chicago Evening Post,* Dell had encouraged Lindsay in the years 1909–12, when he was trying to get his work published.

26. *Collected Poems,* pp. 65–66.

27. Ibid., p. 272.

28. Lindsay, *Going-to-the-Stars* (New York: D. Appleton & Co., 1926), pp. 14–15.

29. *Collected Poems,* p. 66.

30. Ibid., pp. 134, 330–31.

31. *The Village Magazine,* pp. 14–19.

32. *Collected Poems,* pp. 403, 404, 410.

33. Lindsay, *Adventures While Preaching the Gospel of Beauty* (New York: Mitchell Kennerley, 1914), p. 16.

34. *The Village Magazine,* p. 76.

35. *Adventures While Preaching the Gospel of Beauty,* p. 15.

36. Ruggles, p. 126.

37. *The Village Magazine,* p. 77.

38. Ibid.

39. *Collected Poems,* pp. 347, 74.

40. *The Village Magazine,* p. 77.

41. Theodore Roethke, "Supper with Lindsay," *Encounter,* XIV (Oct. 1966), p. 52.

5. *1918*

1. Lindsay, *Collected Poems* (New York: The Macmillan Co., 1962), p. 368.

2. Eleanor Ruggles, *The West-going Heart* (New York: W. W. Norton & Co., Inc., 1959), p. 257. Katherine Bates, who wrote poetry, was Professor of English at Wellesley.

3. Lindsay, *The Golden Book of Springfield* (New York: The Macmillan Co., 1920), p. 44.

4. Shelby M. Harrison, *Social Conditions in an American City,* (New York: Russell Sage Foundation, 1920), p. 30.

5. *Collected Poems,* p. 23.

6. Harrison, p. 1.

7. Ibid., pp. 8, 2, 18.

8. Lindsay, *The Litany of Washington Street* (New York: The Macmillan Co., 1929), p. 74.

9. Lindsay, *A Letter for Your Wicked Private Ear Only,* pamphlet (Springfield, 1920), pp. 3–4.

10. Harrison, p. 16.

11. See above, Chap. 4, p. 101.

12. Clarence Arthur Perry and Lee Hanmer, *Recreation in Springfield, Illinois* (New York: Russell Sage Foundation, 1914), p. 96.

13. For Lindsay's interest in Mackaye see "Letters of Nicholas Vachel Lindsay to A. J. Armstrong," ed. A. J. Armstrong, *Baylor Bulletin,* 43, iii (Waco, Tex., 1940), p. 47 and passim.

14. John Hilder, *Housing in Springfield* (New York: Russell Sage Foundation, 1914), p. 2.

15. Lindsay, *The Art of the Moving Picture* (New York: The Macmillan Co., 1922), pp. 250–51.

16. Lindsay, *The Village Magazine* (Springfield, Ill.: The Jeffersons Printing Co., 1920), p. 67.

17. *The Litany of Washington Street,* p. 112.

18. *The Golden Book,* pp. 214, 173; Frank Lloyd Wright, *An American Architecture,* ed. Edgar Kaufman (New York: Horizon Press, 1955), p. 38.

19. Louis H. Sullivan, *The Autobiography of an Idea* (New York: Peter Smith, 1956), pp. 275, 327.

20. Frank Lloyd Wright, *When Democracy Builds,* revised ed. (Chicago: University of Chicago Press, 1945), p. 67; *The Living City* (New York: Mentor Books, 1958), pp. 123, 188.

21. Wright, *An American Architecture,* p. 38.

22. *The Golden Book,* p. 222. For an interesting visual comparison see Lindsay's "Village Improvement Parade," *The Village Magazine,* pp. 13–19, and Ebenezer Howard's "Three Magnets," *Garden Cities of Tomorrow* (London: Swan Sonnenschein & Co., 1902).

23. *A Letter for Your Wicked Private Ear Only,* p. 24.

24. *The Litany of Washington Street*, p. 81.

25. Ralph Adams Cram, *Towards the Great Peace* (Boston: Marshall Jones Co., 1922), p. 181. Cram *was* thinking of the American country town untouched by the industrial revolution. *The Litany of Washington Street*, pp. 81–82.

26. Sullivan, p. 318.

27. Ibid.

28. *The Litany of Washington Street*, p. 72.

29. Hamlin Garland, *A Son of the Middle Border* (New York: The Macmillan Co., 1919), p. 457; E. L. Masters, *The Sangamon* (New York: Farrar & Rinehart, 1942), p. 172; Henry Adams, *The Education of Henry Adams* (Boston: Houghton Mifflin Co., 1918), pp. 343, 465.

30. *The Art of the Moving Picture*, pp. 245–46. Lindsay's subscription to broad contemporary interpretations of architecture (see above, Chap. 5, p. 114) was clear in his alternative description of a "Permanent World's Fair" as "An Architect's Dream" (*The Art of the Moving Picture*), p. 248.

31. *A Letter for Your Wicked Private Ear Only*, pp. 4, 24.

32. Nevertheless, most critics have described it as a conventional utopia. See Ruggles, p. 281; Albert E. Trombly, *Vachel Lindsay, Adventurer* (Columbia, Mo.: Lucas Bros., 1929), p. 150; Mark Harris, *City of Discontent* (Indianapolis: Bobbs-Merrill Co., 1952), p. 128. *The Golden Book* was only a utopia by H. G. Wells' definition in *A Modern Utopia* (London: Odhams Press Ltd., 1905), p. 316: "We are to restrict ourselves first to the limitations of human possibility as we know them in the men and women of this world today, and then to all the inhumanity, all the insubordination of nature. We are to shape our state in a world of uncertain seasons, sudden catastrophes, antagonistic disease . . . uncertainties of mood and desire."

33. See below, Chap. 6, pp. 142, 146, where Lindsay cited other causes and countries as equally to blame for 2018's international problems; and Chap. 7, pp. 162–68 for a discussion of Lindsay's nonracialism in the context of "The Golden-Faced People."

6. 2018

1. Lindsay, *The Golden Book of Springfield* (New York: The Macmillan Co., 1920), p. I.

2. Ibid., p. 65.

3. Ibid., pp. 20, 33.

4. Lindsay was sympathetic to the Negro, but not to the extent of fabricating support for him. See below, Chap. 7, pp. 162–70.

5. *The Golden Book*, p. 30.

6. Ibid., pp. 10–11.

7. A poignant explanation, as Lindsay, himself something of a prophet without honor, was also an epileptic. But even Fletcher had good points; ibid., pp. 12–13.

8. Quoted in Fawn M. Brodie, *No Man Knows My History* (New York: Eyre and Spottiswoode, 1963), p. 39. Lindsay certainly had in mind the desirability of some uniquely American contribution to theology, which is one way of looking at Mormonism. In *The Golden Book*, p. 3, he described Alexander Campbell as "the American pioneer theologian."

9. *The Golden Book*, pp. 66, 69.

10. Ibid., p. 94.

11. Ibid., p. 77; above, Chap. 5, p. 119.

12. Ibid., p. 173.

13. Frank Lloyd Wright, *An Autobiography* (London: Faber & Faber, 1945), p. 287.

14. *The Golden Book*, pp. 219–20.

15. Ibid., p. 84. Purple was imperial, but the Negro's status was lowly; green, together with yellow, was the Singaporian color (p. 150 and passim), but also the color of Spring, "a good gift to man" (pp. 144–45 and passim). See above, Chap. 5, p. 123.

16. Ibid., pp. 84, 124–28.

17. Ibid., pp. 128–33.

18. Everlasting trees which had sprung up in Springfield to symbolize Kelly's apple tree city, which should have been consistently good. The white buds, blossom, and red fruit were nipped by frost whenever the city fell from grace.

19. See above, Chap. 5, p. 115.

20. See above, Chap. 1, pp. 40–41.

21. *The Golden Book*, pp. 50, 55.

22. Avanel Boone was a mixture of Irish, Lithuanian, American Indian, and Anglo-Saxon.

23. For Lindsay's view of America's Indian dimension, see below, Chap. 7, pp. 155–57.

24. *The Golden Book*, p. 131.

25. Ibid., pp. 67, 85, 169, 188.

26. Ibid., pp. 182, 151–52. The Springfield survey had recommended that all charities unite.

27. Ibid., p. 179.

28. Ibid., p. 110.

29. Ibid., p. 100.

30. Ibid., p. 105.

31. Ibid., p. 250.

32. Ibid., p. 145.

33. Ibid., p. 86. Cf. p. 301, where an appeal to middle-class respectability showed Avanel's shortcomings.

34. Ibid., p. 95. The only review which came near to understanding Lindsay's allegory was by Padraic Colum in *New Republic*, XXV (Jan. 19, 1921), pp. 234–35.

35. *The Golden Book*, pp. 268–69. This proved fair comment, but Lindsay was obviously expecting Marxism to gain more of a foothold in America than it has.

36. Ibid., p. 96.

37. Ibid., p. 193., a reference to the Monroe Doctrine fixation which helped to prevent America becoming a signatory to the Treaty of Versailles.

38. Ibid., pp. 232, 238–39.

39. Ibid., p. 297.

40. Ibid., pp. 314–15; and other trips to "Map of the Universe" territory, pp. 87–89, 224–25, 309–28; overt reminders of his inscription on the Map, "one beginning of *The Golden Book* . . ."; though for the most part it was assimilated rather than reproduced.

41. "Letters of Nicholas Vachel Lindsay to A. J. Armstrong," ed. A. J. Armstrong, *Baylor Bulletin*, 43, iii (Waco, Tex., 1940), p. 30; Harriet Monroe, *A Poet's Life* (New York: The Macmillan Co., 1938), p. 385.

42. Lindsay, *A Letter for Your Wicked Private Ear Only*, pamphlet (Springfield, Ill., 1920), pp. 5–6.

43. Letter to John Drinkwater contained in a copy of *The Golden Book* . . . in the George Mathew Adams Vachel Lindsay Collection, Dartmouth College.

44. Armstrong, pp. 30, 25.

7. THE AMERICAN PAST

1. Lindsay, *The Litany of Washington Street* (New York: The Macmillan Co., 1929), pp. 1, 2, 100.

2. Apparent from letters from Lindsay to Stephen Graham, seen by the author; see also "The Indian Girl—My Grandmother," *The Candle in the Cabin* (New York: D. Appleton & Co., 1923), p. 87.

3. Lindsay, *Collected Poems* (New York: The Macmillan Co., 1962), pp. 106–107.

4. Ibid., p. 437.

5. *The Candle in the Cabin*, p. 33.

6. *Collected Poems*, p. 79.

7. Stephen Graham, *Tramping with a Poet in the Rockies* (London: Macmillan & Co., Ltd., 1922), p. 214. Graham made the doubtful point that Lindsay could never envisage a Negro president. (See above, Chap. 3, note 14.)

8. *Collected Poems*, p. 89. See "Johnny Appleseed," *Harper's New Monthly Magazine* XLIII (June–Nov. 1871), an article referred to by Lindsay.

9. *Collected Poems*, pp. 82, 83, 84.

10. Walt Whitman, *Leaves of Grass* (New York: New American Library, 1960), p. 322; Lindsay, *Collected Poems*, p. 47.

11. *Collected Poems*, p. 84; Lindsay, *Adventures While Preaching the Gospel of Beauty* (New York: Mitchell Kennerley, 1914), p. 62.

12. Lindsay, *Going-to-the-Stars* (New York: D. Appleton & Co., 1926), p. 37.

13. Frederick Jackson Turner, *Frontier and Section*, ed. R. A. Billington (Englewood Cliffs, N.J.: Prentice-Hall Inc., 1961), p. 160.

14. *Collected Poems*, p. 88.

15. Ibid., pp. 9, 22–23.

16. Ibid., p. 192.

17. *The Litany of Washington Street*, p. 90.

18. *Collected Poems*, pp. 53–54.

19. *The Times*, August 17, 1908, p. 6.

20. Alfred Thayer Mahan, *Naval Strategy* (London: Sampson Low, Marston & Co., 1911), p. 197. Most anti-Asiatic nativist literature succeeded "The Golden-Faced People": Madison Grant, *The Passing of the Great Race* (New York: Charles Scribner's Sons, 1916); Sidney

L. Gulich, *American Democracy and Asiatic Citizenship* (New York: Charles Scribner's Sons, 1918); Lothrop Stoddard, *The Rising Tide of Color against White Supremacy* (New York: Charles Scribner's Sons, 1920). One work that appeared in the same year as Lindsay's story was Homer Lea's *The Valor of Ignorance* (New York: Harper & Bros., 1909), a criticism of American defence policy, and an explanation, with maps and diagrams, of how easily Japan could overrun America.

21. Lindsay, *War Bulletin No. I* (Springfield, Ill.: 1909), p. 2.

22. Ibid., p. 3; Grant, p. 87.

23. *War Bulletin No. I,* p. 3.

24. Ibid.; Lindsay, *The Golden Book of Springfield* (New York: The Macmillan Co., 1920), pp. 37–38.

25. *Collected Poems,* pp. 165–66.

26. Ibid., pp. 178, 179, 180.

27. Lindsay, *The Village Magazine* (Springfield, Ill.: The Jeffersons Printing Co., 1925), pp. 134–35.

28. *The Litany of Washington Street,* p. 26.

29. Ibid., pp. 20, 22. In one place or another Lindsay indianized nearly all his heroes.

30. Ibid., pp. 13–14.

31. Ibid., p. 110; *Collected Poems,* p. 378.

32. Lawrence H. Chamberlain, quoted on back cover of Merrill D. Peterson, *The Jefferson Image in the American Mind* (New York: Oxford University Press, 1962).

33. Thomas P. Abernethy in *Dictionary of American Biography,* 9 (New York: Charles Scribner's Sons, 1932), p. 534.

34. *Going-to-the-Stars,* pp. 23, 16.

35. Ibid., pp. 24, 18, 4.

36. *The Litany of Washington Street,* p. 24.

37. Whitman, p. 387.

8. REGIONALISM

1. Frederick Jackson Turner, *Frontier and Section,* ed. R. A. Billington (Englewood Cliffs, N.J.: Prentice-Hall Inc., 1961), p. 131.

2. Eleanor Ruggles, *The West-going Heart* (New York: W. W. Norton Co., 1959), pp. 189, 305; and note his unfulfilled plans for "a big detailed meditative song—Lindsay's 'American Commonwealth'— about every state." The nearest he came to this was "The Boat with

the Kite String and the Celestial Eyes," *Going-to-the-Sun* (New York: D. Appleton & Co., 1923), p. 42.

3. Ruggles, pp. 276–77; Lindsay, *The Art of the Moving Picture* (New York: The Macmillan Co., 1922), pp. xli–xlii.

4. Ruggles, loc. cit.

5. Lindsay, *Collected Poems* (New York: The Macmillan Co., 1962), pp. 157, 155, 153; Edgar Lee Masters, *Vachel Lindsay* (New York: Charles Scribner's Sons, 1935), pp. 234, 235.

6. Ruggles, p. 277.

7. *Collected Poems,* p. 24.

8. Ruggles, p. 419.

9. Ibid., p. 325; Stephen Graham, *Tramping with a Poet in the Rockies* (London: Macmillan & Co. Ltd., 1922), p. 35.

10. Graham, p. 73.

11. *The Art of the Moving Picture,* p. 186.

12. Ibid., pp. 186, 218, 223.

13. Ibid., p. 223; *Collected Poems,* pp. 313–15, 317.

14. *The Art of the Moving Picture,* p. 220; *Collected Poems,* p. 439. One critic who appreciated Lindsay's "Spanish-Americanness" was G. K. Chesterton, who wrote that Lindsay "was something more than an American, he was (wildly as the term would be misunderstood) a Spanish-American. He was, spiritually speaking, a Californian. He did not get drunk only on the American air; he drank the air of a strange paradise, which is in some way set apart and unlike anything in the New World." *All I Survey* (London: Methuen & Co. Ltd., 1933), p. 33.

15. Thomas Nelson Page, *The Old South* (New York: Charles Scribner's Sons, 1896), p. 5. For Lindsay on Page see *The Art of the Moving Picture,* p. 48. Although Lindsay used the term the Old South for public purposes, it was only the revelation of a South "far indeed from the South that burns negroes alive" that he experienced on his recital tours that made it possible for him to talk approvingly of the old. "Letters of Nicholas Vachel Lindsay to A. J. Armstrong," ed. A. J. Armstrong, *Baylor Bulletin,* 43, iii (Waco, Tex., 1940), p. 5.

16. *Going-to-the-Stars* (New York: D. Appleton & Co., 1926), p. 35.

17. Ibid., p. 37.

18. Ibid.

19. Lindsay, *Every Soul is a Circus* (New York: The Macmillan Co., 1931), p. 39; also p. 41; and see Page, pp. 138, 158, for a similar conception of the Virginian.

20. Quoted in Merrill Peterson, *The Jefferson Image in the American Mind* (New York: Oxford University Press, 1962), pp. 394–95; Lindsay, *The Litany of Washington Street* (New York: The Macmillan Co., 1929), p. 105.

21. Peterson, p. 398.

22. *The Litany of Washington Street,* pp. 105–106.

23. *The Spider Web,* X, Junior Class Annual, Hiram College (Chicago: A. L. Swift & Co., 1900); Lindsay, *Going-to-the-Sun,* p. 56.

24. Ruggles, pp. 237, 301; *Collected Poems,* pp. 410, 411.

25. Lindsay, *Adventures While Preaching the Gospel of Beauty* (New York: Mitchell Kennerley, 1914), pp. 175, 176.

26. Armstrong, p. 30.

27. Ruggles, pp. 207, 226.

28. *The Litany of Washington Street,* pp. 39, 41.

29. *Collected Poems,* p. 353.

30. Masters, p. 73.

31. *Collected Poems,* pp. 10, 24.

32. Quoted in Frederick J. Hoffman, *The Twenties* (New York: The Viking Press, 1955), p. 327.

33. Ruggles, pp. 299–300.

34. H. L. Mencken, *Notes on Democracy* (London: Jonathan Cape, 1927), p. 32.

35. Walter Lippmann, *Men of Destiny* (New York: The Macmillan Co., 1927), p. 70.

9. THE AMERICAN PRESENT

1. Lindsay, *The Candle in the Cabin* (New York: D. Appleton & Co., 1926), p. 101; Eleanor Ruggles, *The West-going Heart* (New York: W. W. Norton & Co., Inc., 1959), pp. 84–85; letter to Harriet Moody, December, 1914.

2. Ruggles, p. 306; F. Scott Fitzgerald, *The Crack-Up* (New York: New Directions, 1945), p. 16.

3. Andrew Sinclair, *Prohibition: The Era of Excess* (London: Faber & Faber, 1962), p. 202. See Lindsay's illustrated broadside "Drink for Sale" and the poem "On Reading Omar Khayyam," which read like classic anti-saloon league propaganda. Lindsay, *Collected Poems* (New York: The Macmillan Co., 1962), pp. 337–38; *The Village Magazine* (Springfield, Ill.: The Jeffersons Printing Co., 1920), pp. 80–81.

4. Lindsay, *Going-to-the-Stars* (New York: D. Appleton & Co., 1926), pp. 48, 50.

5. Sinclair, p. 45.

6. See above, Chap. 4, p. 98.

7. Ruggles, p. 389. He and Armstrong had a temporary quarrel.

8. Letter to the author from Miss Alice Harwood, who attended Mills College with Elizabeth Conner, and remained a lifelong friend.

9. *Collected Poems,* p. xxxi.

10. Ibid., p. 336.

11. Sinclair, p. 320; R. S. Lynd, *Middletown* (New York: Harcourt, Brace & Co., 1929), p. 266.

12. *Going-to-the-Stars,* p. 49; *Collected Poems,* pp. 302–305.

13. Michael Yatron, *America's Literary Revolt* (New York: Philosophical Library, 1959), p. 100.

14. Lindsay, *The Golden Book of Springfield* (New York: The Macmillan Co., 1920), p. 275.

15. *Collected Poems,* pp. 359–66.

16. Ibid., pp. 381–82.

17. Ibid., p. 382.

18. Ibid., p. 384.

19. *Collected Poems of Wilfrid Owen,* ed. C. Day Lewis (London: Chatto & Windus, 1963), pp. 22, 82, 84.

20. *The Faber Book of Modern American Verse,* ed. W. H. Auden (London: Faber & Faber, 1956), p. 115.

21. *Collected Poems,* p. 193.

22. "Woodrow Wilson," *Selected Poems of Robinson Jeffers* (New York: Random House, 1938), pp. 171–72.

23. *Collected Poems,* p. 193.

24. Lindsay, *The Chinese Nightingale and Other Poems* (New York: The Macmillan Co., 1917), pp. 48–50.

25. Ruggles, p. 260.

26. *Collected Poems,* p. 193.

27. Denis Brogan, *The American Character* (New York: A. A. Knopf, 1944), p. 128.

28. Waldo R. Browne, *Altgeld of Illinois* (New York: B. W. Huebsch, Inc., 1924), p. 71. Lindsay read this biography.

29. Ibid., p. 179.

30. Ibid., p. 291.

31. *Collected Poems,* pp. 95–96.

32. Altgeld, *The Cost of Something for Nothing* (Chicago: Hammersmark Publishing Co., 1904), p. 37.

33. *Collected Poems*, p. 96.

34. Browne, p. 337.

35. *Collected Poems*, p. 96.

36. Ibid., p. 96.

37. William Jennings Bryan, *The First Battle* (Chicago: W. B. Conkey & Co., 1896), p. 199.

38. Ibid., pp. 200, 203, 206.

39. *Collected Poems*, pp. 98–99.

40. Ibid., p. 97.

41. Ibid., p. 102.

42. Ibid., pp. 102–3.

43. Ibid., p. 104.

44. Ibid., pp. 99, 103.

45. Jacob Riis, *Theodore Roosevelt* (London: Hodder and Stoughton; 1904), p. 14. Lindsay read this biography.

46. Ibid., p. 390.

47. *Collected Poems*, p. 396.

48. Ibid., p. 395.

49. Ibid., pp. 397–98. "Great-heart" is an epithet probably derived from Kipling's poem of that name about Theodore Roosevelt, 1919; Lindsay's "Roosevelt" was written in 1924.

50. Lindsay, *War Bulletin No. V* (Springfield, Ill., 1909), pp. 1, 2.

51. "Rigmarole, Rigmarole," *Poetry Quartos* (New York: Random House, 1929) [p. 4].

10. ART FORMS AND SOCIETY

1. Edgar Lee Masters, *Vachel Lindsay* (New York: Charles Scribner's Sons, 1935), p. 62

2. Ibid., p. 66; Stephen Graham, *Tramping with a Poet in the Rockies* (London: Macmillan & Co. Ltd., 1922), p. 173; Jessie B. Rittenhouse, *My House of Life* (Boston: Houghton Mifflin, 1935), p. 303.

3. Masters, p. 128; Rittenhouse, p. 312; *Poetry,* XVIII (Oct.–Mar. 1920–21), p. 363.

4. "Letters of Nicholas Vachel Lindsay to A. J. Armstrong," ed. A. J. Armstrong, *Baylor Bulletin,* 43, iii (Waco, Tex., 1940), pp. 7, 15.

5. Masters, p. 118.

6. Ibid., pp. 176–77.

7. Lindsay, *The Village Magazine* (Springfield, Ill.: The Jeffersons Printing Co., 1920), p. 14.

8. Imagist credo quoted in Samuel Foster Damon, *Amy Lowell* (Boston: Houghton Mifflin, 1935), p. 302.

9. *The Letters of Ezra Pound,* ed. D. D. Paige (London: Faber & Faber, 1959), p. 99.

10. Lindsay, *A Letter about My Four Programmes for Committees in Correspondence,* pamphlet (Springfield, Ill.: 1916?), p. 6.

11. Lindsay, *Collected Poems* (New York: The Macmillan Co., 1962), pp. 123, 180, 182, 183.

12. *A Letter about My Four . . . ,* p. 6; Rittenhouse, p. 312.

13. Damon, pp. 416, 500.

14. *The Little Review,* IV (July 1918), pp. 54–55; (September 1918), p. 6.

15. Lindsay, *General William Booth . . . and Other Poems* (London: Chatto & Windus, 1919), p. xi.

16. Rittenhouse, p. 302; Eleanor Ruggles, *The West-going Heart* (New York: W. W. Norton & Co. Inc., 1959), p. 211.

17. For Lindsay on the "Higher Vaudeville" see *Poetry,* IV (Apr.–Sept. 1914), pp. 161–62. For the stimulus of Yeats on Lindsay see the introduction to *General William Booth . . .* ed. cit., pp. xi–xiii; for Lindsay's theory of recitation see the introduction to *Every Soul Is a Circus* (New York: The Macmillan Co., 1931); for a stimulating appraisal of vaudeville see Albert R. McLean Jr., *American Vaudeville as Ritual* (Lexington: University of Kentucky Press, 1965).

18. Ruggles, p. 211; Rittenhouse, p. 303; *A Letter about My Four . . . ,* pp. 4, 6.

19. *Interviews with Robert Frost,* ed. Edward Connery Lathem (London: Jonathan Cape, 1967), p. 200.

20. *A Letter about My Four . . . ,* p. 4.

21. Ibid., p. 6.

22. Ibid.

23. *Collected Poems,* pp. 98, 124.

24. Vernon Loggins, *I Hear America* (New York: Thomas Y. Crowell Co., 1937), p. 104; Bruce Weirick, *From Whitman to Sandburg* (New York: The Macmillan Co., 1924), p. 205; *The American*

Book of Poetry, ed. Edwin Markham (London: Harrap & Co., 1940), p. 567.

25. *Bookman,* LXXIV, 6 (Mar. 1932), p. 598.

26. Armstrong, p. 118.

27. *A Letter about My Four . . . ,* p. 6; *Bookman,* op. cit., p. 600.

28. *Collected Poems,* pp. 3–4.

29. Lindsay, *The Chinese Nightingale and Other Poems* (New York: The Macmillan Co., 1917), p. 97; see also pp. 93–97, and William Lyon Phelps, *The Advance of English Poetry in the Twentieth Century* (New York: Dodd Mead & Co., 1919), p. 217. See also *Every Soul Is a Circus,* pp. xvii–xxix for a description of the way he taught children Poem Games; and for how he seemed to have become more tolerant of Isadora Duncan by 1931 than he had been in 1917.

30. H. L. Mencken, *Prejudices, First Series* (New York: A. A. Knopf, 1919), p. 94.

31. Armstrong, pp. 8, 11, 15–16. His epilepsy was reasserting itself at this time, and he was run-down after excessive traveling and reciting. Signs of a confusion amounting to contradiction are evident in the introduction to *Collected Poems,* first published in 1923; he frequently cited his success with young people (that year he taught a poetry class at Gulf Park Junior College) and his large and diverse audiences, but also made such statements as "I can *easily renounce the crowds forever if they seem to imperil the ultimate purpose of my crusade."* (*Collected Poems,* 1962, p. xlvi).

32. Lindsay, *The Kind of a Visit I Like to Make,* broadside (Springfield, 1919).

33. Ibid.; *Collected Poems,* p. xxx.

34. G. K. Chesterton, *All I Survey* (London: Methuen & Co., Ltd., 1933), p. 32.

35. *The Village Magazine,* 1910, p. 70.

36. Armstrong, pp. 30, 41.

37. Masters, p. 166. Quotations from "Walt Whitman, Statesman-Poet" linked the chapters of *The Litany of Washington Street.*

38. Walt Whitman, *Democratic Vistas and Other Works* (London: The Walter Scott Publishing Co. Ltd., 1888), pp. 20, 43.

39. Ibid., pp. 64–65.

40. Armstrong, p. 69.

41. *Poetry,* XIII (Oct. 1918–Mar. 1919), pp. 329–30.

11. PICTURE AND SYMBOL

1. Lindsay, *Collected Poems* (New York: The Macmillan Co., 1962), p. xxxi.

2. Ibid., p. 1.

3. *Bookman,* LXXIV, 6 (Mar. 1932), p. 599.

4. R. L. Duffus, *The American Renaissance* (New York: A. A. Knopf, 1928), p. 140; Carl Sandburg, *Complete Poems* (New York: Harcourt, Brace & Co., 1950), p. 465.

5. *Bookman,* LXXIV, 6 (Mar. 1932), p. 600.

6. Edgar Lee Masters, *Vachel Lindsay* (New York: Charles Scribner's Sons, 1935), pp. 82, 115, 224, Eleanor Ruggles, *The West-going Heart* (New York: W. W. Norton & Co. Inc., 1959), p. 83.

7. "Letters of Nicholas Vachel Lindsay to A. J. Armstrong," *Baylor Bulletin,* 43, iii (Waco, Tex., 1940), p. 27.

8. *Bookman,* LXXIV, 6 (Mar. 1932), p. 599.

9. Masters, p. 133; also pp. 89–93.

10. Lindsay, *Adventures While Preaching the Gospel of Beauty* (New York: Mitchell Kennerley, 1914), p. 14; Masters, p. 114.

11. Masters, p. 90.

12. *Collected Poems,* p. xxiii.

13. Ibid.

14. *Collected Poems,* p. xxiv.

15. *Bookman,* LXXV, 1 (Apr. 1932), p. 7.

16. Miriam Margaret Heffernan, "The Ideas and Methods of Vachel Lindsay" (diss., New York State University, 1948), p. 40. Letter from Hillyer to Heffernan, Mar. 4, 1948. See William Lyon Phelps, *The Advance of English Poetry in the Twentieth Century* (New York: Dodd, Mead & Co., 1919), p. 217.

17. *Collected Poems,* pp. 17–18; see *Going-to-the-Sun* (New York: D. Appleton & Co., 1923), pp. 4–6.

18. Masters, p. 115.

19. *Collected Poems,* p. xxii.

20. Lindsay, *The Art of the Moving Picture* (New York: The Macmillan Co., 1922), pp. 172–82.

21. *Bookman,* LXXIV, 6 (Mar. 1932), p. 559.

22. *Collected Poems,* p. xxviii.

23. Ibid., p. xxix.

24. Terry Ramsaye, *A Million and One Nights* (London: Simon & Schuster, 1926), p. viii.

25. *The Art of the Moving Picture*, p. 17.

26. *The Little Review,* II (Apr. 1916), p. 20.

27. *The Art of the Moving Picture,* Chap. II.

28. Ibid., Chap. III.

29. Ibid., Chap. IV–VII.

30. Ibid., pp. 207, 263.

31. Ibid., pp. 1, 224, passim; *New Republic,* XI (1917), p. 280.

32. Readers can piece together their own collages from Lindsay's poems; mine was taken from "The Santa-Fé Trail," "Billboards and Galleons," and "Dr. Mohawk."

33. *The Art of the Moving Picture*, p. 65.

34. Ibid., p. 50.

35. Ibid., pp. 185, 225.

36. *The American Academy of Political and Social Sciences, Annals,* CXXVIII (Philadelphia, 1926), p. 144, an interesting symposium volume on motion pictures.

37. *The Art of the Moving Picture*, p. 17.

CONCLUSION

1. Lindsay, *Collected Poems* (New York: The Macmillan Co., 1962), p. xlviii.

2. Ibid., pp. 96–97.

Indexes

SUBJECT INDEX

305

INDEX TO LINDSAY'S WORKS